LeAnne Howe at the Intersections of Southern and Native American Literature

SOUTHERN LITERARY STUDIES

Scott Romine, Series Editor

LeAnne Howe at the Intersections of Southern and Native American Literature

KIRSTIN L. SQUINT

LOUISIANA STATE UNIVERSITY PRESS BATON ROUGE

Published by Louisiana State University Press

Manufactured in the United States of America
First printing

Designer: Barbara Neely Bourgoyne
Typeface: Vulpa
Printer and binder: Sheridan Books

Library of Congress Cataloging-in-Publication Data
Names: Squint, Kirstin L., 1973– author.
Title: LeAnne Howe at the intersections of Southern and Native American literature / Kirstin L. Squint.
Description: Baton Rouge : Louisiana State University Press, [2018] | Series: Southern literary studies | Includes bibliographical references and index.
Identifiers: LCCN 2017037461| ISBN 978-0-8071-6871-4 (cloth : alk. paper) | ISBN 978-0-8071-6872-1 (pdf) | ISBN 978-0-8071-6873-8 (epub)
Subjects: LCSH: Howe, LeAnne—Criticism and interpretation. | Howe, LeAnne—Interviews.
Classification: LCC PS3608.O95 Z88 2018 | DDC 814/.6—dc23
LC record available at https://lccn.loc.gov/2017037461

The paper in this book meets the guidelines for permanence and durability of the Committee on Production Guidelines for Book Longevity of the Council on Library Resources. ♾

For Andy and Jake

CONTENTS

ACKNOWLEDGMENTS

I am deeply indebted to LeAnne Howe for her willingness to sit down with me for two formal interviews (2008 and 2013) to provide context and ways of thinking about her writing. She also worked tirelessly with me to revise both interviews until we created satisfactory final products. Yet, these formal interviews only scratch the surface of the ways in which she has shared her ideas and work with me. She provided manuscript copies of both *Big PowWow* and *The Mascot Opera* for use in my analyses. Perhaps, most significantly, she responded to a litany of questions about her life and work via e-mail and informal conversations, the answers for which could be provided by no other source. This book would be very different without her graciousness and openness.

Academic books are products of extensive research, writing, and conversations with colleagues in the field. I am incredibly thankful for a supportive group of colleagues in both southern and American Indian literary studies. I had a tremendous experience working with Noel Polk, Robert West, and Ted Atkinson, editors at *Mississippi Quarterly: A Journal of Southern Studies,* where an early version of chapter 1, "Choctaw Homescapes on the Gulf Coast," was published. I also appreciate the hard work of Eric Gary Anderson, Taylor Hagood, and Daniel Cross Turner, editors of *Undead Souths: The Gothic and Beyond in Southern Literature and Culture,* in which a shorter version of chapter 2, "Gender and the Sacred: Healers, Prophets, and Ceremonies," was published. I am thankful for Jace Weaver's willingness to talk to me about American Indian studies and the South on various occasions and particularly in an e-mail interview I cite in the concluding chapter. Other fine scholars who have at some point offered me advice, suggestions, or support for this project include John Wharton Lowe, Adelaide Russo, Jon Smith, Leigh Anne Duck, Jay Watson, Lisa Hinrichsen, Michael Bibler, Martyn Bone, Courtney George, Ellen Arnold, Rebecca Tillett, Joseph Bauerkemper,

Laura Adams Weaver, Channette Romero, Patrice Hollrah, Jane Hafen, Nancy Peterson, and Kenneth Roemer. Erica Abrams Locklear, a valued friend and colleague since we studied together at Louisiana State University, has been an endless source of support and advice.

There is one group of scholars that I would like to recognize separately—those who have made significant contributions to the growing field of Native Southern studies. I am indebted to the work of Annette Trefzer, Keith Cartwright, Melanie Benson Taylor, Rain Prud'homme-Cranford, Gina Caison, and Eric Gary Anderson. Gina and Eric, in particular, are always ready to discuss new ideas and offer opportunities for collaboration, and I have come to rely on their insights and friendship. I can't thank Eric enough for reading and commenting on drafts of every chapter of this book.

My colleagues at High Point University also deserve recognition for their support of my research. Jenn Brandt, director of the Women's and Gender Studies Program, provided partial funding for LeAnne Howe's 2014 reading and classroom visit, as did Bill Carpenter on behalf of the Cultural Programming Committee and the Department of English. I deeply appreciate the time Jenn took to give me thoughtful feedback on portions of the manuscript. The staff of Smith Library have provided resources and assistance throughout the years of this project, and I am always grateful for their professionalism. All of my department chairs—Matt Schneider, Bill Carpenter, and Bryan Vescio—have approved funding for professional development opportunities that supported my work on this book, and I am thankful for a spring 2017 sabbatical during which I could complete the project.

Lastly, it has been a pleasure to work with the editorial staff at LSU Press. Margaret Lovecraft encouraged and guided me early on, and James Long not only walked me through the publication process meticulously but also gave me helpful advice about my revisions. Southern Literary Series editor Scott Romine provided me with much-needed insights about my project within the context of southern literary studies. I especially want to thank my two peer reviewers, whose comments urged me to think more deeply about the theoretical bases for the project and who suggested additional resources and ideas to consider. Dean Rader's expertise on LeAnne Howe's work and his willingness to engage my perspective were particularly important during the final revision stage.

LeAnne Howe at the Intersections of Southern and Native American Literature

INTRODUCTION

Choctalking and Code Talking in the South(s)

> Native stories are power. They create people. They author tribes.
> —LEANNE HOWE, "The Story of America: A Tribalography"

> Choctaw verbs have a much broader application, which shades the meaning in ways that English verbs cannot.
> —LEANNE HOWE, *Miko Kings: An Indian Baseball Story*

CHOCTALKING

Renowned Spokane/Coeur d'Alene author Sherman Alexie has described Choctaw writer LeAnne Howe as a "genius poet-professor" and said this of her work: "For years, I've hoped that we Native writers will build a 21st century rocket and blast off into brand new space. LeAnne Howe (along with Adam, Eve, the Three Stooges, the Lone Ranger and Tonto, Crazy Horse and Custer, and the entire cast of Gilligan's Island, along with Emily Dickinson, Walt Whitman, and five or six smiling Indian elders) has done exactly that" ("Back Cover"). Howe is one of the most diverse and complex writers in American literature today. She writes novels, short stories, poems, plays, documentaries, literary criticism, and memoirs, and it is often the case that multiple genres exist within one of her texts.[1] Her works are funny, tragic, historically informed, and wildly imaginative. In the same way that one cannot easily classify her literary production, one cannot easily classify LeAnne Howe, the writer. She is a college professor now, but she has also worked as a waitress, a journalist, and a government bond trader. She is an enrolled citizen of Oklahoma's Choctaw Nation, deeply invested in the well-being of her family and her communities. She is also a world traveler, giving readings and lectures in Europe, Asia, and the Middle East and was a Fulbright professor in Amman, Jordan, during the 2010–11 academic year.

As Alexie suggests, LeAnne Howe is considered to be a twenty-first-century author, given that her first book-length work was published in 2001. Yet, her literary production began in the mid-1980s when she was a member of an American Indian arts scene in and around Dallas–Fort Worth, Texas. This was part of the literary period dubbed the "Native American Renaissance" by scholar Kenneth Lincoln, an era stretching from 1968 to 1995 (Cox and Justice 3). Many renowned Indigenous authors of this era, including Paula Gunn Allen, Leslie Marmon Silko, N. Scott Momaday, and Simon Ortiz, wrote about their relationship to homelands in the Southwest, while James Welch and Louise Erdrich depicted the lives of tribal peoples on the United States–Canada border. Though a few writers, including Louis Owens and Geary Hobson, wrote compellingly about southeastern Indians, none attempted to dive deeply into colonial-era southeastern Native life and then juxtapose it to contemporary life as LeAnne Howe did in her tour-de-force novel *Shell Shaker* (2001).[2]

I decided to embark on a single-author study of LeAnne Howe's work after completing a dissertation at Louisiana State University on representations of American Indian spirituality as resistance to European and US settler colonialism. One of my dissertation chapters dealt with ceremonies, and it was during my research that I read *Shell Shaker.* When I began writing that chapter in 2006, there was very little scholarship on Howe's work, even though she had also published a coauthored play, *Indian Radio Days: An Evolving Bingo Experience,* which had been performed throughout the Midwest in the 1990s; a collection of stories and poems, *Evidence of Red* (2005); individual works in journals and edited collections, and she had written and narrated a PBS documentary, *Indian Country Diaries: Spiral of Fire,* that aired in 2006. In fact, her first play had been performed nearly twenty years before.[3] As a non-Native scholar whose interest in American Indian literature partly stemmed from my own experience teaching in a high school on the Navajo Nation in the 1990s, much of the Native literature I had read was by southwestern writers. I was stunned by the historical and narrative complexity of *Shell Shaker* and deeply moved by its depiction of southeastern Natives.

Though I was born in Texas, I grew up in Kentucky, where my family is rooted, and like many non-Natives of the region, I perceived Native peoples as "vanished," despite the occasional references to Cherokee relations within my community.[4] I was in the final stages of completing my dissertation during the spring of 2008 and concerned about the dearth of scholarship on Howe's work, so I decided to take a chance and see if she would grant me an interview. Howe graciously agreed to speak with me at the Society for the Study of Southern Literature conference in Williamsburg, Virginia, where she was an invited reader.[5] Muskogee Creek critic and novelist Craig Womack and poet Allison Hedge Coke (of Huron and Cherokee descent) also spoke at the conference, and the experience began to make me think about a discipline that has become increasingly known as the "Native South." Though I presented my own research, it is not a stretch to say that the main reason I went to Williamsburg that year was to interview LeAnne Howe. What I left the conference with, however, was a new way of thinking about American Indian and southern literatures and a desire to spend more time writing about Howe's work.

In the years since I began my dissertation, Howe published another novel, *Miko Kings: An American Indian Baseball Story* (2007), a memoir/travelogue, *Choctalking on Other Realities: New and Selected Stories* (2013), and many scholarly articles. The body of criticism on her work is growing, including articles and interviews, as well as discussion in a number of recent monographs.[6] Dean Rader's *Engaged Resistance: American Indian Art, Literature, and Film from Alcatraz to the NMAI* (2011) provides the most comprehensive study of Howe's work to date, including analysis of all of her book-length publications at that time. Howe's theory of tribalography has also taken hold as a significant critical model within American Indian studies, being both employed and analyzed to the extent that the summer 2014 issue of *Studies in American Indian Literatures,* edited by Joseph Bauerkemper, is entirely devoted to the subject. This is a positive trend, one that I hope keeps growing. In *Activism in the American Novel: Religion and Resistance in Fiction by Women of Color,* Chanette Romero argues that the lack of scholarly attention to *Shell Shaker* "is the result of [its] move away from identity politics toward a more complex understanding of the historic and contemporary power of interracial alliances" (55). I agree, but I would also extend this idea to Howe's body of work, arguing that the intricate view of the past she presents, as well as the alliances depicted, need unpacking for readers unfamiliar with Choctaw culture and history, as well as with American Indian culture and history more broadly.

The title of my introduction plays on a neologism introduced by LeAnne Howe in "Choctalking on Other Realities," a story in her collection *Evidence of Red,* first published in 2005; the story metamorphosed into a one-woman performance of the same name at the University of Illinois in 2009; the short story then became the title of her 2013 memoir/travelogue. The proliferation and recycling of Choctalking suggest the import of the idea and the story within the author's oeuvre.[7] I borrowed Howe's word for my own title because I think it suggests a central position from which she approaches critical and creative production. Choctalking can be easily parsed as "Talking Choctaw," which is not the same as speaking Choctaw. How, then, does one "talk Choctaw" in English? Citing Ngugi wa Thiong'o on the relationship between language and culture, Cherokee scholar Jace Weaver concludes, "Language as the bearer of culture and worldview is undisputed" (*That the People Might Live* 12). Ngugi's decision to foreswear English, writing only in Kikuyu and Swahili, is an act of resistance to the legacy of colonialism and one of cultural recovery. Given the violent erasures of Indigenous languages through Indian boarding schools and the lack of publishing opportunities for works in Indigenous languages, very few Native writers write in Native languages (13–14). Though David Murray argues that Native Americans writing in English are "involved in an ambiguous area of cultural identity" (92), Womack takes issue with the idea of English as a colonizer's language,[8] suggesting that a perception of English only as an oppressor's tool is a victimized stance:

> What about when Indians have enthusiastically taken up English and reading? Before there were ever federal Canadian residential and U.S. boarding schools, for example, forcing Indian students to learn English, there were several thousand New England Indians reading and writing by the time Sam Occom penned his autobiography in 1770. I am willing to venture that not all of them were forced to speak English, that they were not all victims of literacy. ("Theorizing" 404)[9]

Womack wants his reader to consider the very definition of English and its relationship to European hegemony by citing the syncretic nature of the language, in particular its influence by—not on—Indigenous languages of the Americas: "Literally, there are thousands of Indian words in English. Maybe Indians colonized English instead of the other way around" (404).

Womack's argument evokes Chinua Achebe's claims in his well-known essay "English and the African Writer" that "[the African writer] should aim at fashioning out an English that is at once universal and able to carry his peculiar experience . . . [but] it will have to be a new English, still in full communion with its ancestral home but altered to suit its new African surroundings" (29–30). One way to think about "Choctalking" is that it is a "new" Choctaw-infused English. The Choctaw language is ubiquitous throughout Howe's works, such as the *huksuba* (chaos) that results when colonial and Indigenous worldviews collide in "The Chaos of Angels," the color *okchamali* (both blue and green) that signifies life in *Miko Kings,* or the Choctaw phrases that bookend *Shell Shaker.* These and many other examples from her writings make it clear that Howe's approach to the English language is one inflected with Choctaw language and epistemologies.

"Choctalking," or "Talking Choctaw," then, is about cultural coding, the way in which one can speak or express through a Choctaw worldview. In Howe's "Choctalking" neologism, the "Choc" precedes the "talk," emphasizing her tribal affiliation. My conviction that tribal specificity should be a central component when analyzing Native American literature is informed by the writings of literary nationalists such as Weaver, Womack, Robert Warrior,[10] and LeAnne Howe herself. In his seminal *Red on Red: Native American Literary Separatism,* Womack argues for more tribal peoples analyzing tribal literatures, and much excellent work has been done along this vein in the years since *Red on Red*'s publication, including the important *Reasoning Together: The Native Critics Collective.*[11] As a non-Native scholar of American Indian literature, I do not come from a culture that would inform my work in the same way as American Indian scholars do; however, I think that it is imperative to attempt to analyze a text from within its cultural, political, and historical milieu. For LeAnne Howe, that context is often specifically Choctaw, but it can be intertribal, and it can be trans-Indigenous.

I am also placing Howe's work at the intersection of southern and American Indian literary studies, engaging in a cross-disciplinary endeavor that requires conversation with work being done in both fields and positioning the author as a representative of a Native, interstate, and global South. Native and global Souths are well-known lenses in the field of southern studies; I am introducing the term "Interstate" South as a paradigm both for the in-between national identity of Indigenous southeastern peoples and for the circulations of these cultures into, within, and outward from the South. Attempting such a cross-disciplinary effort can be tricky, and I appreciate the comments of historian Robbie Etheridge, one of the founders of the journal *Native South,* who has argued that "we . . . need to quit patrolling the disciplinary boundaries so much and give each other leeway for making mistakes . . . since obviously once one crosses the disciplinary boundary one is bound to make some mistakes" (Howe and Etheridge). Though I attempt to thoroughly discuss LeAnne Howe's oeuvre and her approach to storytelling, there will be oversights, especially given my comparative approach. One of my goals is to make LeAnne Howe's complex, insightful, comedic, and poignant literary productions more accessible to audiences unfamiliar with the wellsprings from which she draws inspiration. Yet, I am also taking up a call to action by Native Southern literary critic Eric Gary Anderson in his 2007 *Southern Spaces* piece, "On Native Southern Ground: Indigenous Presences and Countercolonial Strategies in Southern Narratives of Captivity, Removal, and Repossession":

> I would like American and Southern Studies to reimagine their own provocative presences and absences within Native Studies, to rethink—really rethink—the tenets and governing assumptions of these disciplinary "regions," and to be mindful of their own non-Nativeness, the ways in which they remain settlers, assuming a southern sense of home but at the same time remaining, even today, far from home on living Native ground.

I keep Anderson's cautionary language in mind, as well as James Cox's sober argument in *Muting White Noise: Native American and European American Novel Traditions* that the "most serious scholarly transgression [in the study of Native American literature] involves writing about Native literature without privileging, or even acknowledging, the work of Native scholars and other Native creative writers" (3). Both authors cite works by Osage scholar Robert Warrior on American Indian intellectualism as instrumental to their arguments.[12] Similarly, my study of how LeAnne

Howe's "Choctalking" stories, novels, poems, and plays can be read within the genre of southern literature will proceed from the framework of American Indian literary nationalism.

Weaver has argued that American Indian literary nationalism comprises two main agendas: classifying American Indian literatures as a distinct field, rather than a subfield, and criticizing those literatures as such, while also ensuring the work's relevance to Native American communities and their continued struggles for sovereignty ("Splitting the Earth" 15). LeAnne Howe has been clear about her stance as a literary nationalist on several occasions, such as in her essay in *Reasoning Together: The Native Critics Collective* when she claims she is "writing the red history of [the Choctaws] and illuminating the dynamic nature of Choctaw time" (337). Her best-known contribution to Native American critical theory is her conception of "tribalography." Tribalography is an Indigenous methodology, an aesthetic approach, and a political position concerned with how American Indians tell stories:

> Native stories, no matter what form they take (novel, poem, drama, memoir, film, history), seem to pull all the elements together of a storyteller's tribe, meaning the people, the land, and multiple characters and all their manifestations and revelations, and connect these in past, present, and future milieus (present and future milieus mean non-Indians). I have tried to show that tribalography comes from the Native propensity for bringing things together, for making consensus, and for symbiotically connecting one thing to another. ("The Story of America" 42)

Tribalography has proven to be a malleable tool, as employed by scholars such as Bauerkemper, Doerfler, and others. Howe's initial example of tribalography linked Haudenosaunee and US history, relating the creation of the US Constitution to the unification of the six tribes of the Haudenosaunee confederacy (37). This linkage, in addition to other stories that Indigenous peoples shared with colonizing Europeans, such as how to plants their crops, leads Howe to the conclusion that "our stories made the immigrants Americans" (29), defining the word "American" in a clearly Indigenous way. Ultimately, Howe believes that American Indian storytelling is "foundational" ("Choctawan" 216) to American culture and identity and is akin to Craig Womack's searing claim in *Red on Red:*

> I say that tribal literatures are not some branch waiting to be grafted onto the main trunk. Tribal literatures are the *tree,* the oldest literatures in the Americas, the most American of American literatures. We *are* the canon. Native people have been on this continent at least thirty thousand years, and the stories tell us we have been here longer than that, that we were set down by the Creator on this continent, that we originated here. For much of this time period, we have had literatures. Without Native American literature, *there is no American canon.* . . . I am saying with all the bias I can muster that *our* American canon, the Native literary canon of the Americas, predates *their* American canon. I see them as two separate canons. (6–7)

Howe's vision of tribalography stresses unification, unlike Womack's separatist stance in *Red on Red*; however, similar to Womack, Howe asserts that narrative form in American literature is taking its cue from Native American literature, "not the other way around" ("Choctawan" 216). Howe demonstrates more specific concerns with a Choctaw national literature in her essay "Ohoyo Chishba Osh," exploring the story of how corn came to the Choctaws and its function as "national [narrative]" (O'Brien, ed., *Pre-removal Choctaw History* 27). Howe describes how Ohoyo Chishba Osh, or "Woman Who Stretches Way Back," brought seeds that "made it possible for the Choctaws to grow into one of the largest Indian confederacies in the Southeast" (32).

In "Ohoyo Chishba Osh" LeAnne Howe undertakes to demonstrate a Choctaw literary tradition that extends back to the earliest oral stories, yet her work can also be viewed as part of a lineage that is traceable through nineteenth- and twentieth-century Choctaw writers and intellectuals including Israel Folsom, David McCurtain, Ben D. Locke, and James L. McDonald. There are direct connections between Howe's work and that of Muriel Hazel Wright, an acclaimed historian and popular writer who served as editor of the *Chronicles of Oklahoma,* a scholarly journal published by the Oklahoma Historical Society, for eighteen years (Littlefield and Parins, "Muriel Hazel Wright" 213). In particular, Wright's piece "Legend of Nanih Wayah" can be read as a literary antecedent to the eighteenth-century scenes in *Shell Shaker.* Both Wright and Howe have a gift for humanizing their historical characters, placing people in convincing ancient locales and conveying believable fears, joys, triumphs, and losses. In the case of "Legend of Nanih Wayah," a young man who is called the Dreamer of the Chahta comes into conflict with a hunter who is the son of Talking Warrior. This young hunter chastises the Dreamer for killing a panther that he claims should have been his own prize and calls him "bone picker" as an epithet. The Dreamer is disheartened and ruminates on his sense of marginalization from his peers. He consults the Prophet Chief who tells him the story of how bone gatherers became important figures to the Choctaw because of their "sacred duty of caring for the dead" (Wright 218). The Dreamer is a descendent of the bone gatherers who were chosen "because they were intelligent, trustworthy and had open countenances" (218). Wright's theme of Choctaw internal conflict over the role of bone gatherers presages Howe's own circulation of that theme in both her earliest cowritten play, *Big PowWow,* and in *Shell Shaker.* The Prophet Chief in Wright's story explains to the Dreamer that "bone picker" was the name that the *Nahullos* (white people) called the *Na Foni Aiowah* (bone gatherers), suggesting that the young hunter had internalized a negative colonial stereotype of the Choctaw. This type of internalized colonialism is demonstrated in Howe's later characters Blossom (*Big PowWow*) and Delores (*Shell Shaker*).

Phillip Carroll Morgan's essay on nineteenth-century Choctaw literary criticism in *Reasoning Together* provides another bridge connecting LeAnne Howe to a Choctaw literary and intellectual tradition. Morgan's archival digging in the Western History Collection at the University of Oklahoma yielded a pre-Removal Choctaw text by James L. McDonald called "The Spectre and the Hunter, a Legend of the Choctaws." Morgan calls the piece the "Spectre Essay" because the original title suggests a mere transcription and translation of oral tradition, but as Morgan delineates, it is much more than that. In addition to the translated oral narrative, McDonald comments on and contextualizes the text. Morgan argues that the "essay represents the earliest example yet found of Choctaw literary criticism and that [McDonald's] 'performance' of oral traditional forms in the new literacy presuppose what have become some of the defining features of late-twentieth and early-twentieth century Native American literary criticism" (126). Morgan describes McDonald's approach as "formalist" (130) in that its critique focuses on the form of the oral narrative more so than the content. He notes that such an approach is common in contemporary American Indian criticism because "the forms and structures of the oral stories duplicate themselves to varying degrees in the written texts" (130). Yet, Morgan is cautious to distinguish such work from traditional formalism: "Considering the paradigms of the culture studies era we find ourselves operating within in twenty-first century English departments, a critical revolution or two removed from the formalisms of the early- and mid-twentieth century, one might describe some of the propensities of current Native scholars as a neo-formalism, or more specifically, Native formalism" (130).

Such an example of Native, or in this case, Choctaw formalism, can be found in LeAnne Howe's "Ohoyo Chishba Osh," in which she details the story of how corn came to the Choctaws. The story was transcribed by Horatio Bardwell Cushman in 1899, a white man Howe describes as "an invited tribal guest" because of his lifelong relationship with the Choctaw homelands and his support of the Choctaw Nation (27–28). Though Howe's analysis of the piece does investigate content, such as the significance of the setting, she also focuses heavily on the formalistic element of call and response, ultimately adding her own response to the piece, a play called *Unknown Women,* an oral literary form, embedded within her own critical analysis. Similarly, Howe begins her contribution to *Reasoning Together* with a contemporary story about a character named Embarrassed Grief whom she connects to *Ohoyo Chishba Osh,* with the claim that they both "came from far away only to leave behind a strange gift that would benefit the people" (330). Howe makes the point that her theory of tribalography is based in engaging in a "conversation with the past and the present to create a future" (338), much like McDonald's own work. Morgan describes the "lively body of preremoval correspondence between [McDonald] and his young Choctaw intellectual peers—Peter Pitchlynn, Henry Vose, David Folsom, and others" (127), noting that McDonald wrote the "Spectre Essay" at the request of Peter Pitchlynn (134) within a couple of months of the signing of the Treaty of Dancing Rabbit Creek, which resulted in the Choctaws' relocation to Indian Territory (137). Morgan argues that the timing suggests Pitchlynn's own concern "that if the Choctaws failed to develop their own school curricula, much would be lost in terms of Native epistemology, belief, and practice" (137). Thus, the relationship of the "Spectre Essay" to past, present, and future suggests its tribalographic nature.

As Weaver has noted, literary nationalism entails a commitment to Native communities, and this can certainly be demonstrated in LeAnne Howe's writing. Events involving Choctaw tribal government corruption, as depicted in *Shell Shaker,* are partly derived from Howe's own involvement with an advocacy group, Choctaws for Democracy, in the 1990s (Howe, "The Native South" 137). She has stated that she hopes *Shell Shaker* will "help other Choctaws remember their own stories so that they might bring more of the past back into existence" ("Choctawan" 218). Much of her work concerns the impact of European and US settler colonialism on Native communities, such as depictions of Indian Removal (*Shell Shaker* and *Indian Radio Days: An Evolving Bingo Experience*), the General Allotment Act of 1887 (*Miko Kings: An Indian Baseball Story*), and cultural stereotypes (*Indian Radio Days* and *The Mascot Opera, a Minuet*). The documentary she coproduced with Jim Fortier, *Playing Pastime: American Indians, Softball, and the Politics of Survival,* investigates the importance of fast-pitch softball as a means of community-building for Oklahoma tribes. Howe's work has the same kind of potential "to forge a progressive social space" that Alexander Hollenberg suggests is possible in his discussions of *Red on Red,* because of "its very separation from the conventional non-Native canon" (3). For Howe, that "progressive social space" is a continued struggle for sovereignty that is intricately connected to storytelling, as she argues in *Reasoning Together:* "We are people of specific landscapes, and our specific stories are told about our emergence from a specific place" (333).

CODE TALKING

In the spring of 2004, LeAnne Howe's coauthored article "An Ensemble Performance of Indians in the Act: Native Theatre Past and Present" appeared in *Studies in American Indian Literatures.* The article focused on the question of "insider knowledge" (33), that is, how do oral traditions and tribal histories inform contemporary Native American theater? Howe's section of the article concentrated on Choctaw oral tradition and performance and what she learned from staging the second play she cowrote with Roxy Gordon, *Indian Radio Days.* She describes how, in 1993, during her tenure at the University of Iowa, she organized a number of American Indian student actors from Oklahoma's southeastern tribes to form the WagonBurner Theatre Troupe. They performed throughout the Midwest to both non-Indians and Indians and had widely varying responses, depending on the audience:

> [W]hat we discovered while performing throughout the Midwest was that our non-Indian audiences never reacted to the humor. They didn't seem to know the code, or the cues to be able to react. When we performed before American Indian audiences, the reaction was much different. The audience laughed in most of the places we (playwrights and performers) expected. To compensate we wrote audience cues for non-Indian audiences and made them part of future performances. What we learned boiled down to this: if audiences didn't know tribal histories, or even "pan-Indian history" they can't read the cues. They lack insider knowledge. (58)

Howe's experience staging *Indian Radio Days* suggests that, in order to successfully read the codes of her work, audiences must know at least something of Native American history broadly and Choctaw history, specifically.

One critical element of those histories is code talking, a motif that can be found throughout Howe's oeuvre. *Indian Radio Days* contains the most literal depiction of the term embodied in a Choctaw code talker during World War I. In a play comprising anecdotes drawn from American Indian history, this sketch illustrates the difficult position of Native soldiers in World War I, at a time when they weren't even US citizens. The soldier, Simon Anolitubby, declares his patriotism to the narrator and explains his important position coding and decoding military messages. Ironically, his commander's name is Captain John Smith, who promises "medals" (125) to the code talkers. This allusion to early English colonialism and the alliances and betrayals that result foreshadows Anolitubby's later revelation that code talkers never received medals "'cause we are Indians. The Navajo or the Hopi boys didn't receive medals for code talking either" (125). This scene illustrates some of the issues Howe refers to when describing non-Native audience reactions to *Indian Radio Days.* To begin, the reference to a mendacious Captain John Smith contradicts the familiar American myth of a white savior allied with the most famous romanticized American Indian woman, Matoaka (Pocahontas). Also, war veterans are so glorified in the United States that the idea of any veterans not receiving recognition for their valor might shock non-Native audiences.

In fact, Native American Code Talkers were not authorized to receive medals until the passage of the 2008 Code Talkers Recognition Act, after many of the Code Talkers had passed away ("S. 2681"). If non-Natives are aware of American Indian Code Talkers, they are most often familiar with the Navajo Code Talkers who were the largest recruited group of code talkers in World War II (Meadows 271), and who were recognized in 1982 when Ronald Reagan proclaimed August 14 as National Navaho Code Talkers Day (Reagan). And yet, Native American code talking began in World War I when Captain Lawrence of the Thirty-sixth Infantry Division overheard Solomon Louis and Mitchell Bobb speaking Choctaw to one another. Learning that he had several Choctaw speakers in his battalion, Lawrence told Bobb to convey a message in Choctaw to the battalion headquarters. After the success of that first message, "a Choctaw [was] assigned to each of the eight field company headquarters" (Meadows 272). By the end of World War I, six different Indigenous American languages had been used for military coding (271). Thus, the very idea of code talking and the crucial role it played in both World Wars is intricately tied to the Choctaw language.

Both linguistically and culturally, Choctalking is a kind of code talking. Like the Choctaw language, Choctalking is a way of speaking (or writing) that conveys a Choctaw worldview. This argument rests on anthropologist Clifford Geertz's theory that "human behavior is seen as . . . symbolic action" (10). For Geertz, such an approach to culture is "semiotic," providing a way to "[gain] access to the conceptual world" of a given culture in order to "converse" with it (24). Coded communications appear in Howe's other works that speak to this more cultural usage. In *Shell Shaker*, the character Divine Sarah (also known as Sarah Bernhardt and Big Mother Porcupine) is described as speaking "old-code Choctaw" (65).[13] This older iteration of Choctaw suggests Sarah's incalculable age while also underscoring the motif of linguistic and cultural coding. Delores Love elaborates on the relationship between Choctaw culture and language when she says, "You have to understand a lot of codes to be Choctaw" and "We're all Code Talkers" (145). Her comments contextualize an unspoken bond between her and Isaac Billy made apparent in the scene, a bond which exists without the necessity of language. This variation on code talking, the unspoken language of lovers, also surfaces when Adair and Battiste, whose love is blooming, slip away from the rest of the family. Adair's sister, Tema, tells Delores, "You must have been lost in thought when she and Gore ducked out, otherwise you would have noticed the code talking going on" (152). *Shell Shaker* suggests that this particularly Choctaw iteration of love cannot be expressed in English, such as when Isaac and Delores had engaged in *pishechi,* or "baby feeding," a sensual form of eating as foreplay that she noted "[no] white man had ever done" with her (168).

Code talking is also a significant theme in Howe's collection *Evidence of Red,* the final section of which is called "Choctaw Code Talking." The poems and prose in this section nearly all circulate around the theme of love, whether it is the passion of lovers in "Bird Woman Returns," "Horse Dreams," and "Kick Boxing," or the love of family in "Post-Mortem" and "Indians Never Say Goodbye." Yet, even more prevalent is the theme of border crossing. The first piece of the section, "The Lie," depicts an American Indian woman attempting a border crossing into Syria and being refused by a racist bureaucrat.[14] This literal attempt at border crossing is linked to the other works in the "Choctaw Code Talking" section through the challenges, and sometimes, inability, for individuals to communicate, whether that communication is across cultural borders, the emotional blockades of love, or the great divide of death.

The most powerful allusion to code talking in *Evidence of Red* is the prose-poem that immediately precedes the "Choctaw Code Talking" section, a piece called "Still Code Talking." Here, code talking is not about the language of love or even miscommunication; rather it is about the language of diplomacy. The piece includes part of the 1843 speech of Choctaw Chief Cobb to US Captain J. J. McRea, in which the former politely reminds the latter of unfulfilled promises made to the Choctaw: "Our houses have been taken from us. The white man's plough turns up the bones of our fathers. We dare not kindle our fires; and you said we might remain and you would give us land" (89). The poem's speaker offers the following translation of this coded diplomatic language: "*You fucked us and we ain't ever gonna forget it. Not now, not in ten thousand years, not ever*" (89). This contemporary "translation" of the original text exemplifies how code talking is a means of expressing Choctaw literary nationalism.

The relationship between Choctalking and code talking can furthermore be discerned through an analysis of the "Acknowledgments" page of *Evidence of Red,* which is divided into three sections: "The Past," "The Present," and "The Future." Howe's acknowledgment of the past reads as follows: "To the Choctaw Code Talkers of WWI who fought in the Meuse-Argonne campaign in which 171 Germans were captured by Joseph Oklahombi. To the Choctaw Code Talkers of WWII (including my late uncle Schlicht Billy) who used Choctaw to relay messages in campaigns from Africa, Sicily, Italy, and Germany." These acknowledgments make clear the significance of the Choctaw Code Talkers both to American history and to LeAnne Howe personally, and it is obvious that she plays with the idea of code talking both culturally and linguistically in both *Shell Shaker* and *Evidence of Red.* Since the story "Choctalking on Other Realities" first appears in *Evidence of Red,* it would not be a stretch to argue that the term is not just a shorthand way of saying "Talking Choctaw," but can also be read as an elision of the phrase "Choctaw Code Talking."

To understand the relevance of code talking to a discussion of how LeAnne Howe's writings themselves "Choctalk," it is helpful to cycle back to the author's revelation about the difference between Native and non-Native audience responses to *Indian Radio Days.* The question of audience is a problem faced by most American Indian writers. Weaver agrees with James Ruppert's claim in *Mediation in Contemporary Native American Fiction* that Native writers think about audience in multiple ways, classifying it through the types "local, pan-Indian, [and] cosmopolitan" (*That the People Might Live* 36); however, Weaver argues that American Indian writers tend to give preference to Native audiences, citing numerous authors who do so (36–37). Had LeAnne Howe been attempting to "translate" the cultural and historical codes in *Indian Radio Days,* she wouldn't have had such divergent audience responses. It is up to us, as audience members, to decipher these codes in order to gain "a fuller understanding" (36) of how and why LeAnne Howe's works "Choctalk." Decoding Howe's writing will be easier for some readers than others, depending on one's background, knowledge, or both, but doing so will certainly illuminate some of the most fascinating work being done in American Indian and southern literature today.

WHY THE SOUTH(S)?

That Oklahoma-born-and-raised LeAnne Howe can be read as a southern writer is not a revolutionary or even surprising argument to scholars who travel in southern-studies circles, yet it still needs some unpacking. A good point of departure may be to consider some of Howe's evocative descriptions of food in *Shell Shaker,* such as Susan Billy's dinner of pre-Contact Choctaw fare: venison roast, mashed potatoes, fried squash, red beans, sunflower cakes, and nut pudding made from peanuts (*bapho*) (81). Most of these foods are familiar to a southerner's palate, yet the scene in which Delores and Dovie Love have come to the Billy home and are cooking for the traumatized family may be an even more salient example: "Steam rising from the frying chickens covers the walls with droplets of a greasy elixir only Southerners appreciate" (151). Though fried chicken is not exclusive to southern foodways, Howe is clearly identifying Choctaw peoples as southerners. By extension then, can cultural productions, such as writings by Choctaw author LeAnne Howe, also be considered southern? According to Howe, "Absolutely" ("The Native South" 135). That Howe would take such a position is not surprising given the swipe she takes at one of southern literature's most renowned writers in another scene in *Shell Shaker* after Choctaw history professor Auda Billy gives a disastrous lecture: "But if she thinks I'm one of those perverse William Faulkner Indians, a mute character of the Southern literati, she has another think coming" (46). Auda is defending herself against an audience member who is offended by her Choctaw-centered version of American history; similarly, Howe is defending her own writing as a person indigenous to the place that becomes Mississippi against the legacy of the settler colonial writer whose stories have come to define it. As Howe's character makes clear, Faulkner's representations of Indians are troublesome, and much attention has been paid to such representations by scholars including Robert Dale Parker, Patricia Galloway, Jace Weaver, Melanie Benson Taylor, and Phillip Carroll Morgan.[15] By critiquing Faulkner (and the "Southern literati" by extension), Howe attempts to destabilize the center of southern literary studies in much the same way her history professor character destabilizes a hegemonic historical narrative. In our 2013 interview, "The Native South, Performance, and Globalized Trans-Indigeneity," Howe discusses her frustration that southern studies "excluded" southeastern Natives in favor of a perceived black-white cultural binary and how she attempted to address that exclusion in works like *Shell Shaker* and her story from *Evidence of Red,* "The Chaos of Angels": "I'm really railing against that earlier southern literary tradition that wholly and completely left us out of the discourse."

Howe's perception of her position as a southern writer is supported by increasing numbers of publications in a field that has come to be known as the "Native South" within the larger field of southern studies. By the turn of the twenty-first century, critics of southern literature had become highly attuned to the South's changing cultural landscape. In the 2002 collection *South to a New Place: Region, Literature, and Culture,* edited by Suzanne Jones and Sharon Monteith, Barbara Ladd's essay, "Dismantling the Monolith: Southern Places—Past, Present, Future," makes the following point: "Although the traditional narrative of the South tells the story of the displacement of Native Americans, the introduction of slave labor from Africa . . . there are many other stories to be told" (54). Similarly, in her 2003 monograph, *Reconstructing Dixie: Race, Gender, and Nostalgia in the Imagined South,* Tara McPherson argues that "Southern studies needs an infusion from feminism, from American studies, from scholars of race and ethnicity, from other ways of seeing the region and the world" (249). Changes have come, as Ladd and Hobson rightly note in the introduction to the *Oxford Handbook of the Literature of the U.S. South* (2016): "the black/white binary has given way to a southern multiculturalism that recognizes Hispanic and Latino, Asian, and contemporary as well as historical African and Native presences in the South" (2). Today's southern literary critical landscape stands in stark contrast to the mid- to late-twentieth-century view of southern literature that it contained "a tragic sense, a sense of place, and a sense of the past in the present" (1), and that it "was almost always rural, and . . . nearly always seen in relation to 'the North'" (1). Yet a study of American Indian literature of the Southeast cannot be categorized solely under a broad umbrella of contemporary multicultural studies; such a move, however well intentioned, would negate the long history of

Indigenous peoples in the Americas and the system of settler colonialism that continues to affect their cultures. Eric Gary Anderson's essay in this same volume explains that a Native American South "in all its plurality and complexity—differs materially, historically, textually, and indeed radically from the South as it has been understood by nearly all prior literary scholars" (30).

It has only been quite recently that both southern and Native American studies have turned a critical eye toward southeastern Indian writers.[16] In Annette Trefzer's 2007 critical work, *Disturbing Indians: The Archaeology of Southern Fiction,* she describes the South as a "'place' that signifies a lack," exemplified by the Indian mounds that appear in the writings of modernist, non-Native southern writers (3). As a result of this "lack," Indians have been textually constructed as Other; such constructions are predicated upon Native peoples' assumed absence in the post-Removal South, and thus, their supposed inability to speak for themselves. Of course, the myth of Native American vanishment is not exclusive to the South, but its ubiquity is peculiar in a region where "no less than 40 percent of southerners claim Native ancestry" (Taylor 27).[17] The editors of the groundbreaking collection *The People Who Stayed: Southeastern Indian Writing after Removal* (2010)—Geary Hobson, Janet McAdams, and Katie Walkiewicz—argue that Native American "absence" in the South is not simply the result of US settler colonialism; rather, it is more specifically the legacy of Jacksonian Removal: "A very real 'rhetoric of disappearance' is in force with regard to Indian people in the South, and it has been for decades. It is a collective mindset that has, at almost every turn since the 1830s, sought to 'disappear' a people whose homeland was taken from them" (7).

The term "Native South," as a referent to the Indigenous peoples originating from the US region that became known as the South, a one-time nation of its own, is also relatively new. The term became institutionalized with the first publication of the journal *Native South* by University of Nebraska Press in 2008. Per the journal's masthead, its editors define the Native South as "the area occupied by the pre- and post-contact descendants of the original inhabitants of the South, wherever they may be" (Howe and Etheridge). This sweeping classification hasn't been fully embraced by all scholars working in a Native Southern arena. In the first monograph attempting a study of the literary Native

South, *Reconstructing the Native South: American Indian Literature and the Lost Cause,* Melanie Benson Taylor focuses her attention on "the large, diverse body of literature emerging from Native Americans *in* the contemporary U.S. South, issuing from the descendants of tribes and individuals who evaded Removal and have maintained personal and communal affiliation with their southeastern homelands" (3). Taylor's definition of Native Southern literature is in line with the editors of *The People Who Stayed,* who "purposely [omit] the writings of Indian people who are descended from southeastern tribes that were removed to Indian Territory and whose orientation is essentially from 'Oklahoma' rather than the southeastern United States" (19). Taylor describes LeAnne Howe as "only marginally southern," receiving such designation because she "traces her heritage back to both the Mississippi Choctaw and the Eastern Band of Cherokee in North Carolina" (24).

In light of arguments made by Taylor, Hobson, McAdams, and Walkiewicz then my claim that LeAnne Howe's work can be read through a southern lens is somewhat contentious. Certainly, to say that the land on which the present-day South is situated is central to the continued existence of southeastern American Indians, whether they live there or not, is not a new idea. In *That the People Might Live,* Jace Weaver explains the epistemological implications of Removal policies: "When Natives are removed from their traditional lands, they are robbed of more than territory; they are deprived of numinous landscapes that are central to their faith and identity, lands populated by their relations, ancestors, animals, and beings both physical and mythological. A kind of psychic homicide is committed" (38). Howe is attempting to heal herself and her people of this "psychic homicide," claiming that her writings are about "land and all of the manifestations in our lands that have to do with Southeastern-ness" ("The Native South" 142).

Though I rely on Howe's own perception of her cultural position, I am clearly indebted to the work of Eric Gary Anderson, who asserts that "the South before the South remains very much a living presence, a transcultural complex that geographically, as well as rhetorically, operates on Native ground" ("On Native Ground"). Situating southeastern land clearly as Indigenous, not colonized, space, Anderson argues that scholars should think first about indigeneity when considering the complexity of the region. LeAnne Howe has made similar arguments, insisting that cultural touchstones such as regional accents be investigated for their American Indian, rather than European traces (Howe and Etheridge). Anderson's view of the relationship between contemporary Native American literature and the South suggests a kind of dynamism: "Native writers occupy Southern territory both physically and discursively, turning to and talking about the South from Southern homelands and (more frequently) from points outside the South" ("South to a Red Place" 7). His use of the word "occupy" here is telling: whether American Indian writers inhabit the South or reclaim its lands from afar, they are present, and that presence needs to be accounted for. Yet, despite seeming to be a proponent of a "Native Southern literary studies," Anderson also questions the comingling of Native and southern studies, speaking to concerns voiced by Philip Deloria[18] and others about the ways that Native studies could be consumed by the agendas of nationally or regionally oriented professional organizations. Anderson argues that to impose "regionalism onto Native peoples, writers, and texts thus replicates more than it redresses the constrictive and often deadly excesses of colonialism, not least because such regionalist designations, contingent as they are on notions and practices of US nationalism, prolong and encourage a still-depatriated indigenous dependency and/or imprisonment on non-Native ground" (21). I take Anderson's problematization of "Native/Southern" studies very seriously and seek, through my analysis of LeAnne Howe's work, to skate the boundaries of each field in ways that are both responsible to living Native American communities and relevant to studies of southern literature in a globalized, twenty-first-century United States.

As Taylor has noted, one useful model for engaging Native literature within a regionalist frame is Tol Foster's notion of "relational regionalism" ("Of One Blood" 268), which considers that "Native southerners' hybrid and occluded presence both within the region and broader terrain of Native studies makes fitting them into tribal-national models particularly complex and challenging" (Taylor 18). Foster describes how relational regionalism differs from the regionalism of late-nineteenth- and early twentieth-century American literature:

> Relational regionalism accepts the constructedness and contingency of the notion of a region in both time and space. A region can be configured

> differently depending on which element and historical moment is being traced. However, in order to be effective, the new historicist and regionalist impulse must include and articulate the frames of the region's constitutive members without privileging or silencing unsavory components of those frames. (273)

In my own study, I find Foster's idea that tribal specificity and regionalism do not have to be mutually exclusive to be most compelling. In the examples of Creek writers Craig Womack and Joy Harjo, Foster sees "an outward-looking dynamic cosmopolitanism based in notions of relation as the central 'tradition' of Creek cultural life" (271). It is LeAnne Howe's tribally specific cosmopolitanism that leads my analysis beyond the boundaries of what has been historically viewed as the US South.

In "On Native Ground," Anderson specifically addresses *Shell Shaker,* asserting that the novel "works to decenter Indian Removal—without repressing its lasting trauma—by thinking about it in the contexts of Indigenous historical and political engagement in multiple 'Souths.'" The multiplicity of the South in the clearly Indigenous way that Anderson describes is at the heart of my argument about the southern dimension of LeAnne Howe's work. To attempt to reconcile the problems of a colonizing regionalism or disciplinarity, I am introducing the term "Interstate South," complementary to and coexisting with an already institutionalized Native South. I define the Interstate South as a space in which Native Americans travel physically and metaphorically between tribal national and US boundaries. In particular, I am concerned with the way indigeneity has circulated within the region that became known as "the South" and the way that contemporary Indigenous people and culture travel within, into, and out of the South, reinscribing and reinforcing ancient cultural memories, resisting US settler colonialism, and influencing non-Native cultures of the South.

It is not a new idea to say that southern culture has traveled and affected other regions of the country. The Great Migration of African Americans and poor whites during the Depression culturally and demographically influenced northern urban centers such as New York, Chicago, Detroit, and Cincinnati. It is also not a new idea that descendants of southerners have returned to the South—consider the growth of Atlanta, particularly the influx of African Americans in the latter part of the twentieth century. What I mean by Interstate South, however, is quite specific to the travels of southeastern Indigenous peoples. American Indian migratory stories are some of earliest records of those travels. According to Jodi Byrd's retelling of Chickasaw oral tradition, "twin brothers, Chikasah and Chatah," led their people to present-day Mississippi, and a disagreement ensued that led to the group splitting. As a result, the Chickasaws came to occupy northern Mississippi, while the Choctaws made central Mississippi their homeland (*The Transit of Empire* xvi). Such stories are not uncommon considering the numbers of Muskhogean-speaking, Algonquian-speaking, Iroquoian, and Souian peoples that came to populate "the South" in the twenty-two thousand years since the first Paleo-Indians arrived (Hobson, McAdams, and Walkiewicz 2). Hunting, trading, and diplomatic journeys were also central to Indigenous existence. Once the Spanish and French arrived on the Gulf Coast, southeastern Natives were captured and sold as slaves, circulating their cultures throughout the Caribbean (Brown 5). The best-known, horrific, and traumatic Interstate Southern experience is nineteenth-century Indian Removal. Not only were a majority of southeastern peoples removed from their lands for the purposes of white settlement and ethnic cleansing, they were forced to move thousands of miles away from those lands to an unfamiliar territory, leaving behind physical spaces in which they and their ancestors had cultivated familial, cultural, and spiritual relationships.

Indian Removal is the anchoring event for an Interstate South, though perhaps it is best described as a series of events, since the displacements of the Indian Removal Act of 1830 continued for most of the decade. Theda Perdue notes that the federally mandated Removal of the "Five Civilized Tribes" of the Southeast was followed by a series of state-sponsored dispossessions of Native lands held by numerous tribes, including South Carolina's Catawbas, Virginia's Gingaskins and Nottoways, North Carolina's Tuscaroras, and Louisiana's Tunica-Biloxis ("The Legacy of Indian Removal" 6–7). Our national memory is etched by those tribes affected most by the Indian Removal Act, however, because they were numerous, powerful, and forced to travel great distances to their new "homelands." Even though that relocation was not from one state to another, since the state of Oklahoma did not exist at the time, from a contemporary perspective, we imagine that journey as one of interstate crossing. The physical displacement of Native southeasterners was also a displacement of culture. LeAnne Howe has described how the Choctaws picked up handfuls of earth from around their emergence mound, *Nanih Waiya,* in present-day Mississippi, and carried that land with them on the Trail of Tears. Not only was southeastern land transported to Oklahoma, but so were southeastern Indigenous cultures in the form of language, foodways, and spiritual practices. The fact that geographical markers, such as place names, were also transferred to Indian Territory suggests the way that southeastern land was recreated in the new geography ("Choctawan" 223).

Though a contemporary mapping of Indian Removal inevitably evokes an "interstate" envisioning of that journey, it is also true that the word will probably immediately connote the idea of an "interstate highway" or operate as a metonym for the US interstate highway system. Interestingly, if you travel north on Interstate 57, in southeastern Illinois, you will encounter the "Trail of Tears" rest area at milepost 32 ("Rest Area Locations"). The rest area commemorates the Cherokees, who camped in the area during the winter of 1838–39, reminding travelers of an earlier, darker "interstate journey." Similarly, archaeologist Jim Wilson has noted that "[from] thousands of years ago, southeastern tribes built their mound cities near waterways—the ancient highway corridors of the world" (Howe and Wilson 17). He points out that, in the twenty-first century, southeastern Native peoples are still building their cultural complexes, such as the Chickasaw Cultural Center in Ada, Oklahoma, and the American Indian Cultural Center and Museum in Oklahoma, by "corridors of mass automotive travel" such as Interstate 35 and Interstate 40 (17).

I have a more compelling reason to use the word "interstate" for the journeys of Indigenous southeasterners, however. "State" is sometimes used as a synonym for nation, and the legal relationship of Native American tribes to the US government is complex, going back to their appellation as "dependent nations" by Chief Justice Marshall in 1831. To consider the forced movement of Indigenous peoples from a US state to a Native state[19] (then called Indian Territory) has both legal and metaphorical ramifications. Oklahoma is not, of course, a state comprised only of Native Americans, a topic Howe takes on when discussing the problems of allotment and the dissolution of Indian Territory in *Miko*

Kings. However, I think *Shell Shaker*'s journey in which Delores Love, Isaac Billy, and many other Choctaws accompany the body of Redford McAlester from Oklahoma to Mississippi is an illuminating example. They begin on the Choctaw nation in Oklahoma, and they travel via interstate highways to the Mississippi Band of Choctaws' land. Not only have they traversed US states, they have also traversed tribal nations, existing in an inter-state, with a kind of dual citizenship, unique to American Indians.

This claim has evolved from my reading of Kevin Bruyneel's *The Third Space of Sovereignty*, which derives, to a degree, from Homi Bhabha's third-space theory. Bruyneel argues that at the intersection of US settler colonialism and Indigenous resistance to it is "a conflict over boundaries, a conflict that has defined U.S.-indigenous relations since the time of the American Civil War" (xvii). For Bruyneel, "spatial and temporal" boundary crossings are necessary to Indigenous resistance. Byrd succinctly characterizes the effects of third-space theory read as an opportunity for sovereignty: "the third space offers a way for tribal sovereignty to exist concurrently with US state sovereignty and functions as an antistatist, postcolonial supplement that disrupts the logics of colonial rule" (*Transit of Empire* 188). Bruyneel also describes a "third space of citizenship" (107) resulting from the 1924 Indian Citizenship Act which "simultaneously [drew] indigenous people into the American polity through the conferral of citizenship and then, in the next sentence, [placed] many of these same people at least somewhat outside by affirming their rights to citizenship in their own tribes" (120). I have described Indian Removal as an anchoring event, or really a series of events, for an Interstate South because it both demonstrated the American Indian position of national and tribal national in-betweenness and created a platform for continued resistance to settler colonial rule. Thus, a third space of sovereignty is imbedded in my model of an Interstate South.

The circulation of tribal nations and tribal nationalism throughout the region is a notable part of contemporary southern life. Clara Sue Kidwell describes recent bus tours from the Oklahoma Choctaw Nation to the *Nanih Waiya* and Pearl River in Mississippi in the introduction to *Choctaws and Missionaries in Mississippi, 1818–1918*. Similarly, Howe claims, "Practically every Choctaw I know from Oklahoma has returned to visit *Nanih Waiya*, the Mother Mound of the Choctaws in Winston County,

Mississippi" ("Embodied Tribalography: Mound Building" 91), and she depicts such a return through the burial scene of Redford McAlester in *Shell Shaker* (196). Howe also notes that "the Chickasaws built a new mound at the Chickasaw Cultural Center in Sulphur, Oklahoma" (91), exemplifying the circulation of Indigenous Mississippian traditions. A different iteration of an Interstate South, Pan-Indian powwows have been an important part of North Carolina's Native American culture since the 1960s. Though Plains Indian dancing and clothing styles dominate these powwows, the events are also opportunities to showcase Tuscarora, Lumbee, or Saponi cultural aspects: "When powwow culture reached the American Southeast in the 1960s, it was grafted onto existing cultural festivals and celebrations and quickly became a new forum for the expression of ethnic identity" (Ellis 93). Most importantly for North Carolina Native peoples, this interstate movement of Indigenous culture provides an opportunity to assert difference from a non-Native southern community, marked by biracial assumptions (87).

Another example of the Interstate South is the Trail of Tears National Historic Trail, parts of which can be found in Alabama, Arkansas, Georgia, Illinois, Kentucky, Missouri, North Carolina, Oklahoma, and Tennessee. According to the National Park Service's web site, the trail is designed to "Remember and commemorate the survival of the Cherokee people, forcefully removed from their homelands in Georgia, Alabama, and Tennessee, to live in Indian Territory, now Oklahoma." The Trail of Tears National Trail provides an opportunity for Natives and non-Natives to memorialize the Cherokees' trauma and remember their land claims by providing markers and information for travelers in quite a few southern and non-southern locations. This memorial also signifies the way southeastern indigeneity moves outward and away from the South. Despite the value of this national trail, the Park Service has missed an opportunity to also memorialize the journeys undertaken by many thousands of Choctaws, Creeks, Chickasaws, and Seminoles who were also forced westward by the Indian Removal Act.

To argue that LeAnne Howe's writings to some degree represent an Interstate South speaks both to their movement within and outward from traditional Choctaw homelands and to their positioning of Choctaw peoples as tribal and US citizens whether they reside in Mississippi or Oklahoma or Texas or California. This dual identity suggests the in-between condition forced upon southeastern Natives through US settler colonial law that creates a manifold relationship to place. The reunification of Oklahoma and Mississippi Choctaws in *Shell Shaker* comes in the form of the funeral ceremony, led by Delores Love, who has been called back to Mississippi by the land itself, the literal mud of *Nanih Waiya,* which manifests in a bowl of bread dough she mixes for her family. The mud gives her a vision of her people's birth at the *Nanih Waiya,* which she interprets as a message to bury Redford McAlester's body there in order to "placate his troubled spirit" (160). The funeral ceremony comprises women from Louisiana, Texas, Alabama, Mississippi, and Oklahoma, leading to what Delores describes as "a miraculous beginning as she and the other Chahta women of the Southeast join hands and sing" (197), a hopeful ending of return and reunification. Like the *Nanih Waiya* mud in Delores's bread bowl, the Interstate South operates as a nexus of relationships to place, spiraling outward from Choctaw origin stories on southeastern land.

The first three chapters of *LeAnne Howe at the Intersections of Southern and Native American Literature* play around and through these ideas of Native and Interstate Souths, resisting "mainstream, familiar concepts of a bordered South" (Anderson, "South to a Red Place" 7). The first chapter, "Choctaw Homescapes on the Gulf Coast," investigates LeAnne Howe's representations of southern spaces/places, specifically in Louisiana and Mississippi, the ancient and contemporary homelands of Choctaw peoples. The analysis spans both of her novels, *Shell Shaker* and *Miko Kings: An Indian Baseball Story,* her play *Indian Radio Days: An Evolving Bingo Experience,* and her collection *Evidence of Red: Poems and Prose,* considering Choctaw relationships with physical spaces and the epistemological implications of those relationships, particularly within the context of European and US settler colonialism. The concept of "Indigenous groundwork at colonial intersections" (5) introduced by D. Anthony Tyeeme Clark and Malea Powell forms the theoretical framework for the chapter, taking into account both physical spaces and theoretical possibilities for what space may mean in light of a history of removals, treaty making and breaking, reservation creation, and continued struggles for recognition, rights, and land. In addition to Clark and Powell's work, I discuss the ways in which Martyn Bone's postsouthern study of place is both useful and problematic for an analysis of the Native South. The chapter first examines the selected primary sources and their representations of actual physical places in the Southeast such as trade routes, emergence mounds, and ancient stickball fields. Since "Indigenous groundwork" is also about the theoretical meaning of space, the analysis explores struggles against and for hegemony on southeastern land within Indigenous-Indigenous relationships, Indigenous-European relationships, and cross-cultural alliances against oppression. In addition, "Indigenous groundwork" is concerned with the interconnectedness of land to spiritual beliefs and the implications of disconnection from that land; thus, discussion of Indian Removal and Howe's depictions of its impact on the Choctaws historically and in the present plays a valuable role in my argument. Lastly, I connect the American Indian nationalist concerns of "Indigenous groundwork" to work being done in the new field of Native Southern literary studies, establishing links between the two. Though this chapter's focus on southeastern space and place suggests that it falls within my classification of Howe as writer of the Native South, it also introduces the intertwined relationship of a Native and Interstate South.

The second chapter, "Gender and the Sacred: Healers, Prophets, and Ceremonies," offers more examples of the braided relationship between Native and Interstate Souths. This analysis of *Shell Shaker, Miko Kings,* and *Evidence of Red* considers the ways that men and women in a matrilineal Choctaw society operate as *alikchi* (healers) and other spiritual practitioners. Though the research in this chapter relies heavily on the work of Choctaw historian Michelene Pesantubbee, who has attempted to rectify the dearth of scholarly inquiry on the roles of Choctaw women (11), it also aligns my approach with the movement toward gender analysis within the field of southern literary criticism. The chapter begins by examining the relationship between the feminine, the earth, and the corn plant for the Choctaw. I explicate Howe's depictions of *Ohoyo Osh Chisba,* Corn Woman, and *Ohoyo Ikbi,* First Woman, in the creation stories of the Choctaw peoples in *Evidence of Red,* arguing that they are spiritual matriarchs to Howe's strong women healers, Shakbatina and Delores Love of *Shell Shaker* and Ezol Day of *Miko Kings.* The chapter also discusses a male healer in *Miko Kings,* Kerwin, an *Ohoyo Holba* ("like a woman but not"), specific to Choctaw cultural traditions (Howe, "Choctawan" 223). Another significant spiritual role played by men in both novels is *hopaii* (prophet), a figure who can communicate with spirit beings. Because of the spiritual aspects of these characters, they enact a variety of ceremonies to heal themselves, other individuals, and their communities. Ultimately I argue that the numerous ceremonies in both of Howe's novels create larger ceremonial events, the novels themselves; I support this idea with evidence about the way Howe uses language to frame each narrative. In addition, I claim that the Choctaw-specific gender roles discussed in the chapter disrupt a Western tradition of patriarchy and gender binarism and recuperate cultural and spiritual practices overrun by colonialism.

The third chapter, "Interstate Simulations and Postindian Warriors," mostly shifts away from direct representations of Choctaws within southeastern landscapes to engage more deeply in how indigeneity circulates to create an Interstate South. It aims its lens at the ways that "Indianness" is performed in *Shell Shaker; Miko Kings; Evidence of Red; Indian Radio Days; The Mascot Opera, A Minuet; Indian Country Diaries: Spiral of Fire; Choctalking on Other Realities;* and Howe's unpublished play, *Big PowWow,* including the material gains and emotional losses that result from such simulations. These performances resist dominant cultural ideology, both by parodying stereotypes and by portraying a number of characters I read as "postindian warriors" (Vizenor 4). Anishinaabe author Gerald Vizenor's neologism describes those who defy simulations of Indianness in culture and in its artifacts, such as Western movies, sports teams' mascots, and new age spiritualism, by arming themselves with "humor, new stories, and survivance" (5). Vizenor's concern with simulated Indianness parallels Scott Romine's study of simulated southernness, and I draw the two together through an analysis of Howe's representations of Native and Interstate Souths. The chapter begins with a deconstruction of the European Enlightenment creation of the "Noble Savage" as depicted by Howe in a series of satirical poems that also feature characters including Indian Mascot and Pocahontas and continues to track the way Howe ironically resists stereotypical representations of Native peoples by giving them new life across the spectrum of her work. The chapter also investigates Howe's depictions of Indians "playing Indian," in California, Oklahoma, or among the Cherokees of North Carolina, demonstrating that such performances can have detrimental emotional effects on American Indians. My argument concludes with the ways that Howe's characters, and LeAnne Howe herself, as playwright and performer, act as "postindian warriors" through their humorous resistance of the construct of Indianness which has been attached to the Indigenous peoples of the Americas since Christopher Columbus's original misnomer.

Chapter 4, "Choctalking Global (Dis)Connections," addresses representations of global culture by Howe in *Shell Shaker, Indian Radio Days, Evidence of Red, Choctalking on Other Realities,* and the blogs written during her tenure as a Fulbright professor in Jordan during 2010–11. I situate these representations within contemporary theoretical discussions regarding globalization, in particular, James Peacock's arguments about the global South, Chadwick Allen's ideas about trans-indigeneity, and Jace Weaver's conception of a Red Atlantic. The chapter begins with an analysis of global economic connections/disconnections by first interrogating capitalist elements of Indian gaming as depicted through the machinations of the corrupt casino chief in *Shell Shaker* and the possibility of intra–solar system Indian gaming in *Indian Radio Days.* The analysis continues with an examination of the commodification and appropriation of Native American cultures such as the global use (and abuse) of the sacred corn plant in *Evidence of Red.* The chapter then turns to global political and cultural connections/disconnections through its analysis of the short story "Choctalking on Other Realities," expanding upon my early, tribally specific definition of the term "Choctalking" and investigating its cross-cultural dimensions. This argument is extended through my analyses of Howe's travel essays "I Fuck Up in Japan" and "Yaa Jordan, Yaa 'Ayouni." Howe's work also represents life-affirming cultural cross-currents such as the intersection of Choctaw spirituality and Sufism in *Shell Shaker* and the Jordanian birds singing in Arabic that connect her to Choctaw birds in her homelands which she details in her travel blogs. The chapter closes with a return to Howe's claims as an American Indian literary nationalist and puts them in conversation with current theories about cosmopolitanism and trans-indigeneity, in light of the author's (and her characters') global outlook and adventures.

The concluding chapter places my analysis within the larger field of Native Southern literary studies. Though at this point, only one other monograph of this nature has been published, Melanie Benson Taylor's *Reconstructing the Native South: American Indian Literature and the Lost*

Cause (2012), several scholars have been publishing essays and organizing conference panels on this topic, especially in the last ten years. In this chapter I make links between my study of LeAnne Howe, her forthcoming works, and the works being done by others in the field; one example is her theorization of "embodied tribalography" in *Choctalking on Other Realities,* which is integral to the new play she is cowriting with Kuna/Rappahannock actress and playwright Monique Mojica called *Sideshow Freaks and Circus Injuns.* This new work intersects with innovative research being done by Eric Gary Anderson on southeastern earthworks. I also argue for more approaches to Native Southern literary studies, including additional single-author studies of Native Southern writers, comparative analyses of works by Native Southern and southern authors, investigations of nineteenth-century and other archival materials, and discussions of the impact of institutionalizing Indigenous studies in the New South, such as Native American studies programs at major universities in Georgia, Florida, and North Carolina.

My second interview with the Choctaw author, which appears here as the appendix, "The Native South, Performance, and Global Trans-Indigeneity: A Conversation with LeAnne Howe," took place on March 23, 2013, at the Native American Literature Symposium (NALS) in Minneapolis. The interview begins with an exploration of Howe's perception of herself and her work within a southern cultural context, as well as her frustrations with the fields of southern literature and southern studies for what she views as a longstanding disregard for Native Americans' presences in the South. Howe's anger comes from the significance of land to Choctaw cultural and spiritual traditions and the history of ethnic cleansing that accompanied settler colonialism. Howe also connects Oklahoma's culture to the South because it became the space occupied by relocated southeastern Indigenous peoples. The conversation then turns to Howe's coauthored play-in-progress, *Sideshow Freaks and Circus Injuns.* The authors' hope is that the play will revitalize Native performance strategies, and Howe explains how such strategies are connected to ancient southeastern ceremonies. I also ask Howe about her other in-progress work, a novel about a Choctaw missionary who travels to the Middle East in 1913 and stays through the Arab Revolt. Her description of the novel leads to a comparative analysis of tribalism in the United States and in the Middle East, an interest of Howe's for a number of years. The conversation then turns toward formal strategies in Howe's current works, including the use of mixed media, and her own differentiations between story and history. The interview ends with a brief discussion of humor and how the author uses it both in her writing and in her life.

My approach to Howe's body of work defies the expectations of traditional literary criticism because I circle back to the same texts again and again as my lens widens from the local to the global. This methodology mirrors traditional Indigenous American conceptions of time and space in the Southeast and elsewhere. In chapter 2, I discuss Paula Gunn Allen's assertion that American Indians perceive time cyclically and space spherically (59). Howe's character Ezol Day in *Miko Kings* notes the circular nature of ceremonies such as stomp dances and ball games (43). Yet my approach is more of a spiral than a circle, a land-based analysis that moves from the Choctaws' traditional home in the Gulf South to the lands that become their home in Oklahoma to their global presence as represented in the works of LeAnne Howe. This spiraling metaphor can be found at the beginning of her documentary about the Eastern Band of Cherokee Indians, *Indian Country Diaries: Spiral of Fire,* when Howe connects the language of her first essay on tribalography, "The Story of America: A Tribalography," to the Cherokee belief in a sacred fire: "Native stories have power. They create people. They author tribes. They burn through our lives like a sacred spiral of fire." This Cherokee cultural reference is important for Howe because the documentary combines her own desire to learn more about her Cherokee birth father with the tribe's contemporary lifeways. She ends the documentary with the image of a Cherokee double-weave basket in which "one story [is] woven within another story inside another and another." In addition to using a set of spiraling frameworks to investigate Howe's work, I am also attempting to demonstrate the ways Howe's stories are interwoven, creating cyclic patterns as she has moved through time as a writer.

I chose to embark on a single-author study of LeAnne Howe's work because I am fascinated with the connections she makes between cultures, the intellectual rigor that underpins all of her creative and critical works, and her ability to use humor in the most difficult of situations. I also see her writing as a model for Native Southern literary studies: Howe is the daughter of a Choctaw woman and a Cherokee man, who was adopted into a Cherokee family, and who has spent her life's work examining and envisioning the world through her identity as a Choctaw woman and as a southeastern Native. Howe tells a poignant story in *Indian Country Diaries: Spiral of Fire* which seems synechdochal of her own position: she recalls a conversation with her aged Cherokee mother, a painter. One of her last paintings was of a girl on the Trail of Tears looking back to the mountains she was leaving. The image contains both the interstate movement of southeastern Natives and the commitment of those removed to find ways to maintain their ancestral homelands, in this case through art. The girl depicted in the painting is LeAnne Howe. Like her representation in the painting, Howe is dynamic, adapting to the situation at hand; yet, she will not forget her ancestors. No matter what the subject matter, Howe makes clear that she is Choctalking to her reader, a cultural process that was born on southeastern tribal lands and that continues to exist in and circulate throughout and beyond the colonial boundaries imposed on them.

CHAPTER ONE

Choctaw Homescapes on the Gulf Coast

> This is the South. I look for evidence
> of other Creeks, for remnants of voices,
> or for tobacco-brown bones to come wandering
> down Conti Street, Royale, or Decatur.
> —JOY HARJO, "New Orleans"

One way to think about the Native South and its interstate dimension is by engaging in "Indigenous groundwork at colonial intersections," an idea put forth by D. Anthony Tyeeme Clark and Malea Powell in their introduction to the winter 2008 issue of *American Indian Quarterly* (5). The editors propose the concept as a way to invigorate scholarly studies focused on place and space, in particular the relationship of Indigenous peoples to those spaces and places. Their argument is intellectual, political, and ethical:

> *Indigenous groundwork* marks Indigenous epistemologies that inform identities, resistances, and survivals. Understood as resistances to hegemony yet still as struggles *for* hegemony (or, better, hegemonies), Indigenous groundwork names long-standing responsibilities to the well-defined and marked landscapes on this planet that *Original Peoples* call home and those starting places that make us and therefore require our honor and respect. (5)

Clark and Powell's vision of such scholarly work is informed by American Indian literary nationalist arguments about the rights of Native peoples in relation to the land, as well as the responsibilities of writers and critics. In particular, they link groundwork to the concept of *homescapes*, as coined by Craig Womack.[1] Powell and Clark envision Indigenous *homescapes* as a theoretical construct, the intersection of colonizing ideologies and Native epistemologies "that intimately and interdependently are interwoven with and emergent from the territories in which Indigenous people live" (13). Thus, in the United States, Indigenous groundwork takes into account both physical spaces and theoretical possibilities for what space may mean in light of a history of removals, treaty making and breaking, reservation creation, and continued struggles for recognition, rights, and land.

LeAnne Howe has situated sections of works and entire works on the Gulf Coast, in Mississippi and Louisiana, the original and contemporary homelands of the Choctaw. Both states are home to federally recognized Choctaw tribal peoples (the Mississippi Band of Choctaws and the Jena Band of Choctaws)[2] with historic and contemporary ties to Gulf Coast lands. Given their long history in the region, it is not surprising that the topography and geography of both states still hold meaning for those Choctaws who were removed to Indian Territory in the early nineteenth century. Womack's "home-scape" neologism derives from his claim that "some writers do not have enough tribal experience to negotiate these realities [of tribal life] where one both draws from the community and forges his or her own path—these kinds of critical decisions involve a lived relationship with the people and land and government of a particular home-scape" ("Review of *Anti-Indianism*" 136). Some critics might find my application of "homescape" to LeAnne Howe's Gulf Coast representations contentious, considering that she was raised in Oklahoma. However, Howe argues in my interview with her in *MELUS* that Choctaw spaces and places traveled with those who were forcibly removed from the Southeast:

> [W]hat did we do when we came to Oklahoma or to Indian Territory? Just about every place name in Louisiana and Mississippi was transferred and then renamed in our new homelands, now the state of Oklahoma. . . . Tannehill where my family is from around McAlester, Oklahoma, is one example, and there is also a Tannehill, Louisiana. Tupelo, Mississippi, becomes Tupelo in Indian Territory, now Tupelo, Oklahoma. Every place name is renamed by the people. Nanih Waiya in Mississippi is Nanih Waiya, the lake at Tushkahoma, Oklahoma. The Choctaws took handfuls of earth from the land around the Nanih Waiya, our mother mound in Mississippi, as they began their journey on the Trail of Tears. Why is that

> important? When we brought our earth, when we brought our people, the names came with us. The Choctawan names are thousands of years old. The names. So the *falaya,* the long of it, is renamed. And that's to remind us, and remind the people who live in our territories today, who are newcomers, that we are from ancient places; we are people who sprang up out of the Lower Mississippi Valley. (223)

As Howe suggests, both Mississippi and Louisiana are Indigenous homescapes, demonstrating Choctaw "connections and prolonged existences within their unique territory [that] in turn yield a history—a shared memory and an organic peoplehood" (Clark and Powell 6). Given that this conception of a homescape "imaginatively links pasts to presents to futures for *people* emergent from a particular place and [accumulates] a set of reciprocal responsibilities that colonization and state-sanctioned power do not absolve scholars from engaging" (6), LeAnne Howe's representations of Mississippi and Louisiana in her century-crossing, history-drenched novels, stories, and drama seem ideal cultural artifacts through which to engage a process of Indigenous groundwork. This groundwork will illustrate the ways in which Howe's Choctaw stories operate as part of a larger Native Southern body of literature and how indigeneity travels as part of an Interstate South. My application of groundwork in the context of a post-Removal South intersects to some degree with Thadious Davis's conception of a "southscape." Though her project centers southern literary and cultural discourses on African Americans, she is "invested in understanding the political and power dynamics of the South as a spatial object and ideological landscape where matters of race are simultaneously opaque and transparent" (Davis 2).

To investigate American Indian literature set in what became the southeastern United States, it is helpful to consider how southern literary criticism has engaged the preoccupation with place in southern literature noted by Hobson and Ladd (1). In *The Postsouthern Sense of Place in Contemporary Fiction,* Martyn Bone analyzes the intersection of capitalism and twentieth-century southern literature through a "historical-geographical materialist lens" (vii). His approach is an intervention in the etymological development of Lewis P. Simpson's neologism, "postsouthern," which had been evolving in works by scholars including Michael Kreyling and Scott Romine.[3] Bone argues that these previous approaches divorce southern literature from the materiality of place:

in the case of Kreyling, postsouthernism is related to postmodernist parody (45), and in the case of Romine, postsouthernism leads to a "less real" form of literature (Romine, "Where Is Southern Literature?" 25). Bone agrees that a conception of postsouthern parody has value as a critique of previous representations of the South, but in furthering his own argument he "[insists] that we must pay attention to the historical-geographical, material reproduction of place as real estate, and the creation, destruction, and mediation of place under capitalism more generally" (46). "Place as real estate" is central to any argument about settler colonialism and what we have come to call the "Native South." It is the idea of "place as real estate" that led to Andrew Jackson's support of the state of Georgia's bid for sovereignty over Cherokee land (McLoughlin 430). Unfortunately for the Cherokees, gold was discovered near Dahlonega in 1829, making it virtually impossible to keep out white encroachers (431). Once the Indian Removal Act was signed into law in 1830, Georgia immediately divided up Cherokee land and gave it to white settlers via lottery (437). When the Supreme Court ruled in 1832 that the Cherokee Nation did not have to follow the laws of the state of Georgia, the Cherokees seemed to have maintained a degree of sovereignty (444); however, political pressures led seventy-five Cherokees to sign the Treaty of New Echota in 1835, a very small representative group of fifteen thousand tribal members, most of whom were opposed to Removal (450). Theda Perdue traces the land lost by all the southeastern tribes by the Indian Removal Act and various state-sanctioned removals that followed and notes that such moves "permitted the expansion of the cotton kingdom, and subsequent efforts to remove [Indians] or deny their ethnicity served the interests of white supremacy" ("The Legacy of Indian Removal" 36).

Bone argues that historical-geographical materialism is necessary due to "capitalism's tremendous impact upon the material production of place in our time," making it "all the more important to consider texts that *do* try to represent the sociospatial reality of the post-South" (46). I would argue that my own study takes a historical-geographical materialist approach because of Howe's (and many other Native writers') focus on land—its loss, its recovery, its significance to cosmological ritual, its etching within collective memory. Yet, for a field called the "Native South," the very idea of postsouthernism is problematic. How do we talk about indigeneity in the Southeast in the context of southern literature when settler colonialism dictates the central signifier? We might, instead, consider the signifier "the postsouthern pre-South" as a way to talk about place within the context of global capitalism and neoliberalism and their impact on the geography now called the US Southeast. Yet, all of these terms—"the Native South," "the Interstate South," "the pre-South"—do not immediately suggest indigeneity. We can find the traces of original places in the Native place names still remaining in the South like Bogalusa, Natchez, Calloosahatchie, Mobile, Ocracoke, Wanchese, Atchafalaya, Houma, Tallahassee, yet the layers of colonial history have obfuscated Indigenous presences, historically and today.

LeAnne Howe's representations of the Gulf Coast's Choctaw historical, cultural and national presence intervene into this problem of place, forcing readers to reconsider what they know about Louisiana and Mississippi, especially given their individual forms of exceptionalism within the larger context of the South. Louisiana has maintained the strongest connections with French colonial heritage of all the Gulf Coast states, and Mississippi has been particularly marked by its history of white supremacy and affiliated racial violence. Howe's *Shell Shaker, Evidence of Red, Miko Kings: An Indian Baseball Story,* and *Indian Radio Days: An Evolving Bingo Experience* depict Choctaw homescapes in the lower Mississippi Valley that resist these relatively recent cultural connotations, underscoring an ancient history of earthworks and trade routes, emphasizing the important role the Choctaw played in the early years of French colonial Louisiana, highlighting the significance of Choctaw emergence in present-day central Mississippi, and reinscribing Choctaw culture on both states' intellectual, economic, and physical landscapes.

Clark and Powell's vision of groundwork as a means of deconstructing colonial hegemony in Indigenous places/spaces literally starts on the ground, with the relationship of Native peoples' knowledge of the land and the resulting "marks" made by that knowledge, including "earthworks, petroglyphs, and particular agricultural practices" (5). LeAnne Howe references mound-building by Choctaws and earlier Mississippian peoples in her works: the *Nanih Waiya* mound in Mississippi, the Choctaw emergence site according to tribal oral histories, is central to the plot of *Shell Shaker,* and *Miko Kings* notes the existence of "old ballfields along river bottoms and next to mound sites" (127). In addition, Howe remaps spaces in the lower Mississippi Valley through her representations of southeastern Choctaw trade routes. In *Shell Shaker,* Anoleta, daughter of Shakbatina, the powerful shell shaker of the title who sacrifices herself for her daughter and for the tribe, remembers childhood trading trips up and down the *Atchafalaya,* or Long River, exchanging items such as beehives, alligator hides, and bear oil (181). The warrior Koi Chitto, Anoleta's father, wanders for months alone along Big Trace, an ancient Choctaw trade route after Shakbatina's death (97–102). Since Clark and Powell argue that Indigenous groundwork is "[u]nderstood as resistances to hegemony yet still as struggles *for* hegemony," then Howe's representations of the *Nanih Waiya* and ancient ballfields resist dominant narratives about sites of power in these Gulf Coast spaces, and her depiction of trade routes reinscribes a Choctaw economy on Gulf Coast waterways and land routes—many of which maintain Choctaw names though they are occupied by the descendants of European settlers and Africans displaced by the Atlantic slave trade (5).

Shell Shaker's depictions of Choctaw struggles against and for hegemony within the context of Indigenous-European relationships clearly manifest in economic and political contexts. The contemporary characters Auda and Adair, descendents of Shakbatina and Koi Chitto, both reflect on the trade alliance in which the French and Choctaw had entered. Auda is a history professor intrigued by the diplomatic relationship between Bienville and the Choctaws. She notes that, in 1701, the Choctaws were fighting several other Indian nations; the following year Bienville traded muskets for them to use against the English and Chickasaws in return for the Choctaws' political alliance (121). Auda believes Bienville was adopted by one of the warrior societies because he had Choctaw women living in his home and was tattooed. When the novel reverts to the eighteenth century, Bienville is indeed depicted as having been tattooed and describes Shakbatina as his "dearest friend" (133). Adair is also intrigued by this history, imagining the French Quarter home in which Bienville entertained Choctaw guests with whom he traded French commodities for protection against the English and other regional tribes (42). It is true that the French-Choctaw alliance, described by historian James Taylor Carson as a "kinship discourse" (*Searching* 29) began in 1702 when New France's governor, Pierre Le Moyne, Sieur d'Iberville (co-explorer and brother of Bienville) welcomed Choctaw chiefs to Mobile, "[establishing] the patterns of exchange and support that characterized the Franco-Choctaw relationship throughout the first half of the eighteenth century" (29). Though Jean-Baptist Le Moyne, Sieur de Bienville, didn't establish New Orleans until 1718, it seems likely he would have continued his elder brother's diplomatic engagements in the Crescent City.

Howe's depiction of the alliance between the French and the Choctaw is furthermore echoed in French colonial documents of the seventeenth and eighteenth century. Germain Bienvenu's "The Beginnings of Louisiana Literature" discusses the prominent role played by American Indians in works of poetry, prose, and drama written by adventurers and settlers in the French colony. The French colonial writers distinguished between various tribes and their customs, their representations tending to be more complex than later Anglo writers' one-dimensional depictions of savage Indians (31). Bienvenu observes that the predominance of stories about tribal peoples and their relationships with the French colonists underscores the importance of Native Americans to the French colonial enterprise; in fact, the French viewed the relationship as "symbiotic" (46). Such a perception was obviously misguided; as the author argues, "Blinded by their idealism and even aware at times of the hegemony inherent in their agendas, Louisiana writers gloss over the reality that French penetration and subsequent control of the Native Americans ultimately means the complete subjugation of Amerindians' prerogatives to those of European newcomers" (46). Carson's research further illustrates French incomprehension of the Choctaw perspective, claiming that since Choctaw cosmology "valued order and balance . . . they had regarded the French as 'dangerous people,' and that when they looked at the expanding city of New Orleans they saw Balabanjer—the 'town of strangers'" (*Searching* 56).

Despite her fictional representation of the French-Choctaw alliance against the English, Howe's novel does not romanticize the relationship between her ancestors and the colonizing Europeans. Adair, a New Orleanian, loves her home city because it is a space rich with Choctaw history, but is stunned by the absence of her people and any evidence of their presence in that place. As a commodities trader, Adair views her job as a product of her cultural heritage, like a Choctaw trader in the early eighteenth century exchanging French goods with other Native groups in the lower Mississippi Valley, before the tribe was divided by Removal. At one point, Adair wonders if "she's her ancestors [*sic*] toehold in New Orleans, the one to re-establish a Choctaw power base" (42). In this literary move, Howe is both revealing the palimpsest[4] of Choctaw history beneath the colonial history in New Orleans and reinscribing a Choctaw presence into the Crescent City. As Trefzer argues, when "place is as complex and ideologically charged as the 'South,' the layers of cultural stratification concerning Native Americans are often buried under the weight of the region" (29).

Adair's ruminations on reestablishing Choctaw hegemony on the Gulf Coast is not the only evidence of ambivalence toward French colonialism, despite the tribe's historical alliance. On the morning that Adair's sister, Auda, plans to kill Redford McAlester, her pet French angora rabbit (Jean Baptiste) is described as "dancing in his cage" (27). Auda is the twentieth-century manifestation of the eighteenth-century character Anoleta, and Jean Baptiste (the rabbit) is the French explorer's doppelgänger. Despite the overt allusion to the Treaty of Dancing Rabbit Creek, Auda feeds Bienville "lovingly" (27). The treaty reference then suggests a history of betrayal of the Choctaws by their leaders (Redford McAlester, Red Shoe, Red Shoes, and Greenwood LeFlore),[5] and the French colonial leader's role as an ally to the Choctaw. Yet, his reincarnation as a pet does not indicate a relationship of parity. Anoleta reflects on Shakbatina's feelings for Bienville, who "seemed to like [being treated as a pet]. She had always teased him, saying when he first arrived he was like a baby, only able to express himself with cries of wonder, mad leaps, or with objects he took from his bundle" (134). These representations are antithetical to dominant discourses about colonizer-colonized power relations. Howe relates the historical Choctaw point of view regarding the encroaching Europeans: "The foreigners spoke like babies, and in the case of the French, the Choctaws treated them like babies, and tried to give them things" ("Choctawan Aesthetics" 214). The author's literary creations suggest that this paternalistic attitude shifts after the sale of the Louisiana colony to the United States and the removal of southeastern Indigenous peoples to Indian Territory.

An example of this shifting Choctaw attitude toward French colonial power is portrayed in "The Chaos of Angels," a story in *Evidence of Red.* The contemporary Choctaw protagonist of this story describes Bienville as someone her ancestors liked, but "[t]he first time they invited him for dinner he started making problems that have continued until now" (24). After spending some time in New Orleans, the protagonist boards a plane, and Bienville appears in the seat next to her looking like a bullfrog wearing cowboy clothes. Bienville's sudden appearance is not too surprising given that the protagonist had already seen him once in the French Quarter, a saxophone-playing street musician who "resembled a tree frog hugging a lamppost" (24). On one level, the campy getup in which Howe dresses Bienville on the airplane simultaneously evokes a common slur used against French people and the most potent cultural symbol of US domination over Indians. However, when considering the historical trade negotiations between the Choctaw and the French, the imagery is even more suggestive. According to the protagonist, the Choctaws decided to play a joke on Bienville when he asked to trade beads for land, so they traded "a huge flood plain" that belonged to their cousins, the Bayougoulas (26). This was obviously a joke since "six months out of the year it was knee deep in water, snakes, and alligators. Nowhere were there more mosquitoes than on that piece of land. Most days of the year the air was so thick with mosquitoes that you couldn't distinguish one person from another ten paces away" (26). When Bienville later complained about the deal while standing knee-deep in a swamp (thus becoming a frog-like creature of both land and water), the Choctaws decided he must not have been entirely mentally sound; however, the protagonist acknowledges, "it wasn't until much later that we realized the joke was on us" (27). "The Chaos of Angels" does not shift back and forth in time in the same way that *Shell Shaker* does, but history remains in the narrator's cultural memory from the point of emergence—"Chahtas crawled up through the mud of the Nanih Waiya" (31)—to the Trail of Tears—"I can see my relatives now, walking west at sunset" (32). Bienville, however, is not a part of this history; instead, he is a living, breathing street musician or a cowboy frog. In either manifestation, he haunts the protagonist in these Choctaw homescapes, a constant specter of colonialism and its legacy.

LeAnne Howe's short play *Indian Radio Days: An Evolving Bingo Experience,* cowritten with Roxy Gordon, also depicts struggles against colonial hegemonies, including both French and US settler colonialism. Like "The Chaos of Angels," the play juxtaposes humor with historical events, such as the arrival of the French to the Gulf Coast. As the title suggests, the play is in the form of a radio show, and the narrator interviews numerous Native and non-Native figures engaged in key historical moments. When the French arrive near the mouth of the Mississippi, in the early eighteenth century, the narrator describes them as "adversaries" of the Choctaw (115). Despite this, the Choctaw Indian being interviewed is described comically: "The Choctaw is dirty. He is forty years old. He is mostly naked. Bird feathers stick out of his hair. He is carrying some skins. Written on his chest in big block letters is: 'LIFE'S A BEACH'" (115). When the Frenchman conveys fear of his surroundings and company, the Indian offers him some skins for trade, to which the Frenchman responds: "Monsieur Savage. Hum. Let us discuss zee bezineez" (116). Thus, the early trade economy between the Choctaws and the French commences underscored by the grand narrative of the civilized European/savage Indigenous American. Howe and Gordon's text complicates this representation, however, with their portrayal of the laid-back, economically savvy Choctaw man.

Howe and Gordon connect Choctaw struggles against French colonialism to struggles against US settler colonialism in a later scene when the narrator interviews Chief Greenwood LeFlore in Jackson, Mississippi, in 1850. Like the Choctaw who made first contact with the French explorer, LeFlore is also wearing a beach-themed T-shirt under his waistcoat, except his asks, "WHERE'S THE BEACH?" The evolution of the T-shirts' messages suggests that choosing to trade with Europeans and the resulting political repercussions have left the Choctaws without direction, even questioning their own existence. LeFlore's own role was central in terms of a shifting Gulf Coast Choctaw homescape. Carson has described LeFlore as a "Southern Creole"[6] and "a Choctaw nationalist who sought to carve out a new and powerful nation for his people within the cotton kingdom of the Old South" ("Greenwood" 223). LeFlore, as principal chief of the Choctaw Nation in 1830, had been pivotal in negotiating the Treaty of Dancing Rabbit Creek. Though the treaty signed nearly ten million acres of Choctaw land to the federal government, LeFlore had seen to it that each Choctaw household maintained a reserve of land. LeFlore viewed this as a way of maintaining Choctaw land rights, arguing that resisting Andrew Jackson's 1830 Indian Removal Bill would be "futile" (230). Yet, the US government did not uphold the treaty's fourteenth amendment, which would have permitted the Choctaws to keep their Mississippi land, and approximately fifteen thousand of the eighteen thousand Choctaws living in Mississippi were forced to move to Indian Territory (231). In *Indian Radio Days,* LeFlore expresses his dismay at having been betrayed by the US government, and specifically, Andrew Jackson: "You know, I fought for him [Jackson] in the War of 1812. I made speeches to my people about how good this one white man was. But I was wrong. I thought Andy had seen enough dyin' to last him a lifetime, but I was wrong. I think on the walk to Oklahoma, the Trail of Tears, the Choctaws lost four thousand, maybe more" (180). Eventually, the fictional LeFlore dies, presumably from alcoholism, a painful allusion to one of the most notorious stereotypes of American Indians. The historical LeFlore's own life did take a tragic turn after the Treaty of Dancing Rabbit Creek, given that he was declared unfit to rule the Western Division Choctaw council and that he could not go to Indian Country with his people "owing to the death threats that awaited him" (Carson, "Greenwood" 231).

Despite LeFlore's sad ending in the play, *Indian Radio Days* attempts to show the complexity of the man, in particular his struggles with identity: "being Indian is a very complicated matter, and I have not always been accepted. You see, my father was a French-Canadian. My mother was Choctaw: *n'est-ce pas.* I once believed what the father said. Now I am full-blooded Choctaw: *Tchatas sia hoke!* Okay. That is final" (120). One could argue that LeFlore, the son of a Canadian trader, Louis Le Fleur, and a Choctaw woman, Rebecca Cravat, was "full-blooded" given the matrilineal kinship system of the Choctaw. He also maintained his Choctaw cultural identity after Removal, despite having adopted numerous elements of US culture: "He owned slaves, read and wrote, and prayed at camp meetings, but he also presided over a political hierarchy of pipe lighters and captains, provided food, shelter, and educational opportunities for his followers, and promulgated his vision of the Choctaw future at the foot of the mound that had given his people life" (Carson, "Greenwood" 232). Ultimately, though LeFlore's death in *Indian Radio Days* can be read as tragic, he bears witness and reports the "Indian ethnic cleansing" (120) to the narrator, ensuring that his regret over his role in the events leading up to the Trail of Tears is a part of the historical record.

In addition to their representations of colonial-Indigenous power struggles, LeAnne Howe's works are particularly important for Indigenous groundwork given her depictions of Choctaw battles against and for hegemony within the context of Indigenous-Indigenous relationships. Superficial examples of such struggles and resulting enmities and affiliations are depicted in *Shell Shaker* during Koi Chitto's hunting trip. During his journey he makes contact with the Houma, trading allies of the Choctaw, and expresses derision for the Attakapas, practitioners of cannibalism.[7] He also expresses contempt for the *Inkilish okla,* or the English people, because they have traded axes with the Attakapas (97–102). Koi Chitto's disdain for the English suggests the larger rift that occurred between southeastern tribes as the English and French vied for power in the region. A more complex rendering of these power struggles are the machinations of the character Red Shoes, the son of a Chickasaw woman and a Choctaw warrior, and a central figure complicating trade relationships during the colonial era along the Gulf Coast. Shakbatina hates Red Shoes for his greed, demonstrated when he spies on Choctaw towns in exchange for English trade goods, including weapons (11). His insatiable desire for power leads to a Choctaw civil war, as a result of his attempts to play European powers and different tribes against one another.

In *Shell Shaker,* Red Shoes is reincarnated as Redford McAlester, a late-twentieth-century Choctaw chief, who also becomes consumed by his own power-hungry nature. Though he works with Auda to bring many improvements to the Choctaw Nation, he also allies himself with the Mafia to build the Casino of the Sun. Like his historical predecessor, he plays one side against the other, stealing "millions from the Mafia and [giving] it to the Irish Republican Army to kill Englishmen for crimes they committed against the Choctaw two hundred and fifty years ago" (141). Other Choctaw characters describe each man as an *Osano,* or bloodsucker. The first *Osano* to whom the novel refers is the man whom Shakbatina calls Hispano de Soto, an invader whose greed had never before been known among the Gulf Coast tribal peoples and who committed unspeakable acts of violence as a foreign conqueror (2–3). That Red Shoes and Redford McAlester are linguistically linked with de Soto suggests the degree to which the Choctaws feel betrayed and hurt by their actions. Historian Arthur DeRosier describes that initial meeting of Europeans with Choctaws, de Soto's sixteenth-century expedition for gold, as extremely violent. Upon meeting the Choctaws near Mobile, Alabama, in 1540, de Soto demanded their treasures; the Choctaws resisted, resulting in a bloody rout, having been overpowered by the Spaniards' superior weaponry, including horses, lances, and armor (14). This incident led to a great distrust of whites, which became evident when the French entered the Mississippi Valley in 1650 (15).

The character of Red Shoes provides another perspective on Choctaw-European trade relations. Ethnohistorian Patricia Galloway has written about the Choctaw Civil War and the role of the warrior Red Shoe, a figure just as controversial as Howe's fictional personage. Galloway contextualizes Red Shoe's ascendancy as a warrior and a leader:

> The Choctaws chose to ally themselves with the French in the first place because they were hard-pressed by gangs of Chickasaw and Creek slave-catchers, armed and instigated by the English traders who had extended their activities to the Mississippi River as early as 1698. To acquire firearms and to defend themselves, the Choctaws entered eagerly into a French alliance in 1702. Thus, the French gained a powerful buffer to the east and north of their infant colony, and the Choctaws, in return, acquired guns and other trade goods. ("Choctaw Factionalism" 78)

Red Shoe rose to power in the 1730s, eventually becoming recognized as supreme chief by the English; this alliance with the English set off a series of events that led to the Choctaw Civil War, in which various factions supported the different European powers. This Civil War is the first division of the tribe depicted in *Shell Shaker*; the second division came when Andrew Jackson's Indian Removal Act was signed into law in 1830.[8]

In addition to representing Choctaw struggles for hegemony and against other Indigenous and colonial hegemonies, Howe's Gulf Coast homescapes also depict cross-cultural alliances against oppression. These alliances speak to the "power of homescapes and the *relational* therapeutic politics they generate" (Clark and Powell 6). The title of Howe's story "The Chaos of Angels" is an allusion to the Choctaw word *huksuba* which the protagonist describes as the "chaos when Indians and non-Indians bang their heads together in hopes of cross-cultural understanding" (23). The story begins as the protagonist takes a late-night swim in the outdoor pool of a New Orleans hotel, and a woman, later identified as Haitian, stares at her and then appears to perform a vodou ceremony on a balcony above. The Choctaw woman describes her actions as a "tease," claiming that "the crowless rooster" she sets free is proof that the woman is "craving attention" (23). The Choctaw woman performs a ceremony herself, summoning "[a]ncient ones out of the mud of the Mississippi River," and says, "They've come to remind her that the conquering hordes only thought the Choctaw camps were abandoned and the dogs were mute . . ." (23). When the protagonist boards the airplane the next day, the Haitian woman is a flight attendant, forcing her to reconsider the spiritual confrontation of the night before. After her encounter with Bienville, or rather his ghost masquerading as a cowboy frogman, the protagonist has dream memories of the holy moment when the Choctaws first emerged from the *Nanih Waiya* and the pain and grief of her ancestors on the Trail of Tears. When she awakens she is joined by the Haitian woman, who asks her, "Haven't you forgotten that the French took some of your relatives to Haiti where they made a new home there? How could you forget that we are sisters? Maybe the joke is on you after all?" (32).

The previous night's ceremony had been an implicit offering of alliance, misread by the Choctaw woman, who is angry about the absence of her people on their ancestral homelands. The story ends with the protagonist, the Haitian woman, and a matriarchal Choctaw Grandmother figure who links the protagonist with her ancestors' memories, sitting in the first-class section of the airplane, watching *Star Wars,* specifically the scene in which the Death Star is blown up. This moment, in which the Choctaw relatives and the Haitian woman gather to watch the destruction of an evil weapon of imperial power, suggests a coalition of women of color against tyranny. When the protagonist expresses her lack of understanding for all that has happened, Grandmother explains that the Haitian woman played a joke on her the night before in the hotel courtyard, but she had responded with force, not humor. Grandmother had returned to "[finish] the joke" (32) because cross-cultural misunderstandings continue into the afterlife, and she "is learning how to survive the chaos of all these ethnocentric angels" a tactic which she claims "beats banging our heads together" (33). This scene exemplifies both the importance of cross-cultural alliances, as well as the ability to laugh in the face of oppressive hegemonies. Grandmother's lesson is similar to an argument made by Laguna Paula Gunn Allen: "humor is the best and sharpest weapon we've [Native Americans] always had against the ravages of conquest and assimilation" (qtd. in Lincoln 7).

Jodi Byrd has argued that Howe's use of the term *huksuba* in "The Chaos of Angels" can operate paradigmatically as a theoretical construct underscoring cross-cultural alliances: "the *haksuba* [chaos] that Howe's story describes provides a foundational ethos for Indigenous critical theories that emphasize the interconnectedness and grievability embodied within and among relational kinships created by histories of oppressions" (*The Transit of Empire* xxviii).[9] Her reading is couched within a poststructuralist and postcolonialist framework, noting the chaos that ensues when the "colonial, imperial referent" (19) of "Indian" continues to represent and replicates forms of otherness under US imperialism. This application of *haksuba* is reminiscent of Clark and Powell's reading of "homescapes" as a "theoretical construct . . . located at the crossroads of colonization" (13). Byrd's emphasis on the linguistic significance of Howe's use of *haksuba* also emphasizes the intersection of southeastern Indigenous epistemologies (chaos) and the Western colonizing ideologies (angels) that tensely occupy the title of Howe's story.

"The Chaos of Angels," like *Shell Shaker,* represents historical time as permeable: characters from the past slip into the present as ghosts or through ceremonies, finding ways to bring peoples of seemingly diverse, but actually related,[10] groups together for healing purposes. Time travel is also possible in *Miko Kings,* demonstrated both through ceremony and through the formulas of a Choctaw physicist and postmistress, Ezol Day. As in "The Chaos of Angels," this novel explores cross-cultural alliances against hegemonic powers both in the traditional Choctaw homelands and in the space that has been known as Indian Territory, Oklahoma Territory, and today, the state of Oklahoma. Another kind of "*relational* therapeutic politics" (Clark and Powell 6) plays out in the love affair between Hope Little Leader and the Black Indian character Justina Maurepas. Hope and Justina meet when he is a student at Hampton Normal School for Blacks and Indians (present-day Hampton University), and she is his math teacher, whom he lovingly nicknames Dusky Long Gone Girl. Hope's experience at Hampton is traumatic, as are the stories of many children sent to boarding schools, a seemingly consistent series of punishments for speaking in Choctaw, practicing Indigenous beliefs, and attempting to run away. Hope is additionally marginalized as a Choctaw, told that the "school didn't want Indians from the Five Civilized Tribes because they'd once held slaves" (65). Though Justina has left Hampton by the time he is released from a period of solitary confinement, eventually she and Hope meet again later in life when he is playing for the Miko Kings, an all-Indian baseball team (62–66).

Like their relationship, Justina herself represents an intersection of African American and Native American cultures. She is described as "a mixture of Louisiana Indian, African, and French" (71). In the period between meeting Hope at Hampton and their reunification in Oklahoma, she is a math teacher for the children of prostitutes in the Storyville District of New Orleans. During this era, in 1900, it is purported that she dynamited a brothel called the Courteson. This act earned her the nickname Black Juice, and according to Algernon Pinchot, a fictional history professor at Morehouse University who interviews Justina late in life, she is considered to be an early black nationalist figure. Though she refuses to discuss the bombing, Justina explains that there were no societies protecting children from cruelty at that time; Professor Pinchot tells her that she has been attributed with "focusing attention on the child sex market—for the most part Black and Indian children—in the District" (77). Regardless, Justina regrets the death and destruction that came about from her actions, telling Professor Pinchot that she would prefer to discuss her relationship with Hope Little Leader, the father of her child and the only man she "truly loved" (80), despite the barriers of a racially segregated society.

Another Choctaw character in *Miko Kings* whose cross-cultural affiliations represent resistance to oppressive forces is Ezol Day. Ezol learns to read English in the Good Land Indian Orphanage, and one of the works of particular meaning for her is Longfellow's *Evangeline: A Tale of Acadie.* Part of the text is excerpted in *Miko Kings* along with pages from her personal journal. The significance of this text is multilayered, beginning with the fact that Ezol once had a twin named Evangeline whose death left her *isolé,* French for "isolated" or "insulated," hence her own name, Ezol Day. Ezol explains the irony of her name: "This is the elegance of chance. My twin sister and I were nearly a single event. Evangeline died and insulated me against death. Therefore I am called Ezol. Aunt Fancy named me for isolation. I wonder if I marry and change my name, will I change my future?" (161). In fact, Ezol will not marry the man she loves, Blip Bleen; she will instead die in a fire, in the same isolation in which she spent most of her life.

The tragic separation of these lovers by circumstances outside of their control resonates thematically with Longfellow's *Evangeline.* The famous epic details the separation of Evangeline and her lover, Gabriel LaJeunesse, as a result of Le Grand Dérangement of the French Acadians from Nova Scotia in 1755, after the British had taken possession of the former French colony. The Acadians were sent to various places, including the New England colonies, England, France, and eventually Louisiana (Gilmore 79). Though Longfellow's poem does not conclude in Louisiana, the story has mythic meaning in the Pelican State; a famous version of the story claims that Evangeline awaited her lover under a live oak tree in St. Martinville, only to discover he had wed another. In any version, the personal tragedy experienced by the lovers resonates with the descendents of the Acadians because it speaks to the larger pain of being forced from one's homeland and wandering until a new home is found where one can began again.

Miko Kings is replete with separated lovers and tragic endings. In addition to what happens to Ezol and Blip, Hope and Justina's relationship ends tragically when the Ku Klux Klan carries a burning cross to Hope's home because of his relationship with a black woman (171). This is their relationship's (and the novel's) turning point, and it leads to the downfall of the Miko Kings. Hope, a pitcher with supernatural abilities, has been offered money to throw the game against the US Seventh Cavalrymen baseball team from Ft. Sill. Justina, frightened by the Klan and pregnant with their child, wants him to accept the bribe so they can flee Indian Territory for a better life elsewhere. When Justina leaves him, Hope, distraught by her departure, does throw the game (193–98). A loss to the US Seventh Cavalry, the notorious regiment involved in the Battle of Little Big Horn and the Wounded Knee Massacre, symbolizes the larger history of European and US settler colonialism and undermines the promise of an all-Indian baseball league envisioned by team owner Henri Day.

Yet another tragic instance of separated lovers is the story of the narrator, Lena, framing the tale of the Miko Kings. Lena is a Choctaw woman newly returned to Ada, Oklahoma, after years living abroad, most recently in Jordan, as a freelance writer. She, too, is grieving the loss of her lover, Sayyed, a Palestinian photographer killed in a terrorist attack in Amman, Jordan. She remembers a tender moment between them just after she learns that Ezol, her time-traveling ancestor who has been helping her write the story of the all-Indian baseball teams, also died by fire (208). The fire of the burning KKK cross, the fire of the terrorist bomb, and the fire that consumes the Miko Kings' office where Ezol is trapped all speak to the searing pain of loss, not only of one's beloved, but also of one's home, one's land, and one's way of life. Each of these fires is linked to a history of imperialism, its affiliated ideologies of scientific racism and Manifest Destiny, and the painful exiles and dispersals concomitant with it.

This reading of *Miko Kings* exemplifies how Clark and Powell's vision of Indigenous groundwork takes into account more than Indigenous peoples' relationship with land in its physical form. Such groundwork is also concerned with land and its interconnectedness to spiritual beliefs, as well as the implications of disconnection from the land: "We think of physical landscapes and Indigenous geographies as they connect and constitute the world above, below, and on earth as a series of mutually constitutive and interdependent relations. We also think of countless efforts, historical and ongoing, to exile—to delink and disassociate—Original peoples from their responsibilities to their places" (10). The motif of tragic separated lovers in *Miko Kings* underpins the macrocosmic problems of land loss represented in Howe's work and in the history of southeastern Natives. Disassociation and reconnection with Choctaw homescapes are significant themes, particularly in *Miko Kings* and *Shell Shaker*. In the former, the most significant exile in the text is not the Choctaws' nineteenth-century removal from their Mississippi Valley homelands, though its echoes haunt the novel, but instead the continued disenfranchisement of Native Americans from their land by the Dawes Act of 1887, which over the course of fifty years resulted in "the federal government['s privatization of all] of the tribal lands of Indian Territory into individual plots, much of it going to non-Indians" (16).[11] The end of Indian Territory also results in the end of all-Indian baseball teams such as the Miko Kings; the novel represents this loss as synecdochical of the loss of land and cultural traditions born in the new home the Choctaws have made for themselves since Indian Removal. Longfellow's *Evangeline* resonates so deeply for Ezol because she understands the pain experienced by the Acadians who made a life in a fresh land, only to be forced out to begin anew once more. Exile is the pain that links the Acadians and the Choctaws, just as racial discrimination and oppression link African Americans and Native Americans in the novel.

The Trail of Tears is another "disassociation" of Choctaws from their lands. Howe's most powerful depiction of the devastating consequences of the Choctaws' removal from their Mississippi homelands occurs in *Shell Shaker* when Nowatima, Shakbatina's descendent, shares her memories: "Some laid down by the roads to die. They were resigned. As we passed by they gave away their shoes. We were surrounded day and night by our enemies. It was very unsanitary as to our personage. No way to make a toilet. We all had fevers. Millions of flies ate from our flesh. They left many scars on my body" (148). According to McGowan, 15 percent of the Choctaw population died during their removal from Mississippi in 1836. Other southeastern tribes also suffered severe mortality rates, some as high as 50 percent (61). It is both this forced division of the tribe, and the earlier tribal division by civil war, which the ceremonies depicted in *Shell Shaker* seek to heal.

Healing ceremonies are dependent upon physical spaces occupied by Choctaw peoples, historically and in the present day. These spaces are, of course, occupied by other peoples as well, and as a result, have multiple cultural associations. Howe's representations of Louisiana, culturally, geographically, and economically, privilege the interests of Choctaw peoples,[12] ultimately forcing readers to revise their view of the state's French colonial past as a primary cultural touchstone. Similarly, Howe's representations of Mississippi do not rely on the typical black-white binary opposition that so often characterizes representations of the state. Such representations are obviously not without warrant, given its reputation as "the most racially restrictive and oppressive state during the entire segregation period" (Hoelscher 659). This well-earned history hangs heavily over Mississippi, yet readers of Howe's work also know that Mississippi is home to the sacred emergence place of the Choctaw peoples, the mound called *Nanih Waiya. Nanih Waiya* is located near Philadelphia, Mississippi, and its significance as the Choctaw place of genesis is described by Carson in his retelling of the emergence story: "Out of the subterranean womb of the Great Mother crawled the 'beloved people,' and they lay on her belly to dry themselves in the warm rays of their Great Father Aba, the sun. . . . The sun god had chosen the

Choctaws as his people and the land around the mound as their world, and so long as they followed his law, they would remain on the bright path to a righteous life" (*Searching* 8). In *Shell Shaker,* Howe depicts the creative and healing power of the earth through the mud of *Nanih Waiya.*

The healing ceremony is held by Auda and Adair's Aunt Delores, the *Imataha Chitto,* the greatest giver and uniter of her tribe (161). Delores receives her vision as she kneads dough, the dough becoming the fertile mud of this Choctaw "sacred space" (161). She learns that Red McAlester's body must be buried in Mississippi so that the tribe can begin to heal from centuries of psychic and physical division. Delores says, "Somehow I know it will reunite the two Choctaw communities: the ones in Oklahoma with the ones in Mississippi. We've been separated too long. . . . Each of us has only half a heart until we're rejoined" (166). As the novel comes full circle and the healing begins, the spirits of Auda and Redford, Anoleta and Red Shoes, arrive at *Nanih Waiya* where seven shell-shaking Choctaw women, from different states across the Southeast, transform themselves into birds, invoking a similar ceremony by Grandmother of Birds, who resisted Hispano de Soto. Red Shoes, Redford McAlester, is buried in the mound of the *Nanih Waiya,* and Delores and Auda's uncle, Isaac Billy, sacrifice themselves so that his spirit will stay put in the healing mud at the center of Choctaw sacred space. This return to the novel's original ceremony by Grandmother of the Birds is a way of unifying all the Choctaw peoples, as LeAnne Howe explains: "The scenes were really about trying to recover some of the larger Confederacy that existed. That's really what I was trying to do in the hope that this book, this text, read by my own community, will help other Choctaws remember their own stories so that they might bring more of the past back into existence" ("Choctawan" 218). Such reunification resists the colonialist and genocidal policy that removed southeastern tribes from their homelands. These scenes of reunification also emphasize that, in many ways, Removal failed. McGowan explains that, "for all the federal muscle used in trying to force Southeastern peoples off their land, remnant bands of every nation escaped Removal, remaining in their traditional homelands, living in traditional ways. In the twenty-first century, the Cherokees, Choctaws, Muscogees, and Seminoles still have communities and a few reservations in their homelands" (62).

In *Reconstructing the Native South,* Taylor discusses the cultural invisibility of Native Americans in the South, citing Tom Mould who makes the point that "many residents of Mississippi really don't have any idea that 'there is a major American Indian community' still dwelling nearby" (32). There are numerous contemporary Native American writers, including LeAnne Howe, Craig Womack, Janet McAdams, Geary Hobson, Allison Adelle Hedge Coke, Marilou Awiakta, and Karenne Wood, who live in, have lived in, or have cultural ties to the South, and who are producing creative and critical works that are ripe for the kind of analysis proposed by Clark and Powell. Eric Gary Anderson has argued that the writings of Native southeasterners redefine that iteration of southern identity marked by biracialism and Indian absence:

> Native theories and practices of intellectual sovereignty, self-determination, and literary separatism emphasize Native cultural identities, looking to Muskogee Creek, Cherokee, Osage, and other tribal-national southern homelands and, in the process, operating as a form of strategic counter-removal. In these and other ways, this body of indigenous literary work continues to speak indigenous truth to colonial power, giving the lie to any suspicions that anti-Indian colonialism, persistent as it is, has succeeded in silencing, assimilating, speaking for, and otherwise colonizing Indians out of existence in the South, however broadly defined and whomever [*sic*] does the defining. ("On Native Ground")

Anderson's vision for the possibilities of current Native Southern theories and cultural practices aligns with Clark and Powell's belief that Indigenous groundwork provides "compelling analytical frameworks and critical theories with broad and therapeutic applications" (11) which may even build bridges between the academy and communities beyond. LeAnne Howe's description of Choctaws traveling across the South, and uniting at a sacred earthwork in what is now the state of Mississippi, is not only a "form of strategic counter-removal" exemplifying the Interstate South in both its circulatory and resistant iterations, but it is also a therapeutic move toward healing the wounds of nineteenth-century Indian Removal. Continued analysis of place and space in Howe's work, as well as that of other writers of the Native South, is vital for discussions of contemporary southern culture as well as for American Indian literary nationalism. As Clark and Powell argue, "Homescapes provide places to stand to take a stand" (5).

CHAPTER TWO

Gender and the Sacred

Healers, Prophets, and Ceremonies

> He was not crazy; he had never been crazy. He had only seen and heard the world as it always was: no boundaries, only transitions through all distances and time.
>
> —LESLIE MARMON SILKO, *Ceremony*

In much the same way that colonialism and Indian Removal laid siege to the diverse ethnic and cultural groups of the South, both systems also significantly affected alternate models of women's and other gender roles embodied by southeastern Natives. In *Haunted Bodies: Gender and Southern Texts,* Anne Goodwyn Jones and Susan Donaldson argue that "gender . . . may be as important an analytic category for making sense of the South as race itself traditionally has been acknowledged to be" (16). Barbara Ladd has noted that, though patriarchy and paternalism were not solely markers of the antebellum South, "they were made explicit and instrumentalized in a slave economy that subjected southern women (black and white, rich and poor) and African American men to a disciplinary regime in which some were spiritualized and others imagined as animals" (*Resisting History* 13). The gender roles of southeastern Natives defied the race-based patriarchy that emerged in the South, complicating an economy that relied on the oppression of male and female black bodies and the subordination of white women. In *Cherokee Women,* Theda Perdue describes how Selu, or Corn Woman, became a model for Cherokee women as farmers and explains the matrilineal nature of Cherokee society, as well as the roles of Cherokee women in war, trade, and government. James Taylor Carson details the roles of Native women across the Southeast in the production of corn and notes a number of important Choctaw women leaders, including "Ohoyao Minko," a female chief honored in oral tradition ("Dollars Never Fail to Melt Their Hearts" 19) and the seven women who refused to cede any land to the United States at the Treaty of Dancing Rabbit Creek (26). Carson notes that after the treaty negotiations ended "most of the men and women returned to their homes, but a rump council consisting solely of men signed away their homeland" (27).

LeAnne Howe's Gulf Coast homescapes defy connotations of southern lands and their attendant hegemonies and ideologies. Similarly, Howe's representations of gender both resist a Western patriarchal tradition and recuperate significant cultural practices. Considering that "Choctaws took handfuls of earth from the land around the Nanih Waiya, [the] mother mound in Mississippi, as they began their journey on the Trail of Tears" (Howe, "Choctawan" 223), it seems evident that such roles, born in the Choctaw homelands, would also travel to Oklahoma. Thus, gender and its relationship to sacred practices in Howe's works reveal yet another variation of Native and Interstate Souths.

In the poem "Evidence of Red," from Howe's collection of the same name, the importance of the female in the matrilineal, matrilocal Choctaw society is demonstrated in this line describing the moment of emergence: "In minutes we tunneled through / corn woman's navel into tinges / of moist red men and women" (5). Here, Choctaw peoples are depicted as coming into existence through a birth by Corn Woman, Ohoyo Osh Chisba. The poem "Hashi mi Mali," also in the first section of *Evidence of Red* called "Creation," describes Choctaw emergence similarly: "When *Ohoyo Ikbi* [First Woman] pulled / freshly made *Chata Okla* [Choctaw people] / out of her red thighs, / we were very wet, so / one-by-one / she stacked us / on the mound" (7).[1] The mound referred to here is *Nanih Waiya,* also known as *Oholitopa Ishki,* or Beloved Mother (Pesantubbee 23; Swanton 30). In *Choctaw Women in a Chaotic World: The Clash of Cultures in the Colonial Southeast,* Michelene Pesantubbee details the interdependent relationship of the feminine, the earth, and the corn plant for the Choctaw:

> Corn itself not only provided sustenance for the people of this world, but through its roots and stalks tied the three parts of the world together—Above, Below, and This World. Because the corn plant crossed the boundaries of the three worlds it was considered powerful. It was beloved. It was beloved woman. And because women had primary responsibility

> for the corn, they were the mediators between the fertility and power of the corn and the Choctaw people. (119–20)

The oral stories upon which Howe's poems are based speak to the sacred significance of land to the Choctaws. According to Choctaw/Creole/Métis scholar Rain P. Cranford Gomez, "Our land, like our blood, keeps memory. It is in Choctaw *yakni isht ikhana*: land memories, land record keeper" (91). This idea is the basis of her argument that events are "acts on lands (geographically connected)" and as a result are "land based, linked to the peoples who occupy certain spaces" (91), rather than the linear succession that forms a Western view of history. This land-based theoretical view is what informs Indigenous groundwork as well as Nishnaabeg scholar Leanne Betasamosake Simpson's argument that Native oral stories demonstrating engagement with the land comprise a traditional form of pedagogy.[2]

The separation of corn from its sacred position and subsequent commodification are bemoaned by *Ohoyo Chish-Ba Osh* in Howe's play *The Unknown Women,* also in the "Creation" section of *Evidence of Red.*[3] The disconnection of Choctaws from the ideal of corn as sacred began with the collapse of the Green Corn Ceremony, an annual period of diplomacy, as a result of a severe population reduction in the eighteenth century. English and French colonialism had led to disease, slave raids, civil war, and intertribal wars, which made it difficult to hold a ceremony that required the contribution of an entire community and its neighbors. The collapse of the Green Corn Ceremony for the Choctaws meant a lost opportunity to purify the community and to carry out the annual reinforcement of the importance of women to society (Pesantubbee 132–33).

Pesantubbee's central thesis in *Choctaw Women in a Chaotic World* is that the role of "beloved women" declined because of contact with European patriarchal cultures;[4] however, she also contends that the importance of women to Choctaw society can be traced historically through other cultural practices such as funeral rites. LeAnne Howe has taken issue with Pesantubbee's claim, arguing that "today, there isn't an organization . . . or community group at home that isn't run, or managed by women. You want something done, go to the women. I see that as a continuance of something very old. Who is at the head of my family? I am. I'm the oldest girl. This remains true today as it was in the past" ("Choctawan" 220). Howe's novels *Shell Shaker* and *Miko Kings* highlight sites of gendered power mobilized against patriarchal European colonizers and their cultural legacies. These centers illustrate the author's conviction that Choctaw women have maintained their traditional position of cultural strength, as well as her commitment to accurately depict Choctaw gender roles within healing and other ceremonial contexts.

Both *Shell Shaker* and *Miko Kings* are novels replete with women working individually and in groups to heal people and communities from the pain and division resulting from European and US settler colonialism. *Shell Shaker*'s Auda Billy sees herself as a continuation of women leaders in her family, and it was her backing of Red McAlester, along with the other women in the community, including the Choctaw women's society, the *Intek Aliha,* that got him elected chief (21). The power of the *Intek Aliha* is also referenced in the section of the novel set in the eighteenth century, when Anoleta is plotting to kill Red Shoes (181). In *Miko Kings,* Howe describes how the Four Mothers Society, "an organization that boasts twenty-four thousand Choctaws, Creeks, Chickasaws, and Cherokees as members" (116), works to fight the allotment of Indian lands by organizing at stickball games and "burning the Indian agent's outhouses, sand houses, and train depots all over Indian Territory" (107). Rooted in the Cherokee Keetoowah Society, the Four Mothers Society came about when members of the Choctaw, Creek, Chickasaw, and Cherokee tribes organized to fight plans for allotment and find ways to return to traditionalism (Fogelson 169). Though the Four Mothers Society was not strictly a women's organization, its name reflects the reverence of women's political and cultural strength by southeastern Indian nations.

While Howe's novels depict quite a few powerful Choctaw women, two of the most notable are Ezol Day of *Miko Kings* and Shakbatina of *Shell Shaker.* Both women are ancestors who find ways to effect change in the contemporary era, ameliorating the painful histories of individuals and communities torn apart by colonialism, racism, or greed. Even though they are not referred to as such, Ezol and Shakbatina are kinds of *alikchi,* or healers, intervening in the lives of their descendents, guiding them to paths of reconciliation with their pasts. Interestingly, both ancestors use methods of traditional Choctaw *alikchi,* as described by Pesantubbee: "In the case of female patients, a female medicine giver had to be present when women took medicine, and a male medicine giver had to be present when men did" (10). This practice reflects the Choctaw values of balance and interdependence. Pesantubbee explains that everyone in a community needed to participate in its functioning, both men and women and young and old (151). Howe depicts community interdependence through her portrayal of two male *alikchi,* Hope and Kerwin in *Miko Kings,* whose acts also contribute to the novel's healing ceremony. Another female *alikchi* figure in *Shell Shaker,* Delores Love, conducts the funeral rites for Red McAlester, a complex undertaking that requires male and female interdependence in order to bring reconciliation to the Choctaw.

The *alikchi* figure is discussed most in *Miko Kings,* and it is Ezol Day who explains the complexity of Choctaw healing practices to her descendent, Lena. Lena remembers going to see a Choctaw *alikchi* for a healing ceremony when she was ten years old, and she describes what happened when tornado clouds appeared: "Grandmother and I had to hold on to a big cottonwood tree to keep from blowing away. I was terrified, but the *Alikchi* kept on pitching his ax into the ground until the earth opened up a large crater. Then, as the winds died down, he walked counter-clockwise around and around the crater. After awhile the clouds disappeared and the sky was blue again" (42). When Ezol, an autodidactic (meta)physicist, explains that mathematical codes at the heart of rituals make it possible to control the cosmos, Lena is skeptical. Ezol argues that the Western distinction between scientific and sacred knowledge does not apply to Choctaw beliefs and uses another example to drive her point home: "Indians in North and South America built cosmic observatories in the form of mounds and pyramids, very complicated structures that require geometry. A stomp dance and a baseball game[5] mimic natural phenomena, such as tornado winds, that are counter-clockwise. Why can't you believe that the *Alikchi* knew how to interact with the chaos?" (43).

Ezol herself has found a way to "interact with the chaos," by virtue of her physical presence in a room with her cousin's granddaughter nearly a hundred years after her death. Her interest in the topic of exploring the dimensions of time and space manifested as a young woman when she wrote a paper called "Moving Bodies in Choctaw Space," the premise of which was that Choctaws and Euro-Americans experienced time and space differently, given their differing linguistic expressions of time, particularly through verbs and verb tenses (38).[6] She exemplifies her theory through the word *okchamali,* meaning "both blue and green" (38). Her extended argument is that the word also signifies "life," given that it might also suggest "the blue sky and green swamplands" of the emergence place of the Choctaw peoples, attributing a temporal quality to the term (38). She tells Lena, "After I understood that there might be other spacetime terms embedded in our language, I looked for them in plants that contain sacred geometric expressions. I studied the patterns in our stomp dances and baseball games. Words make equations the same way that numbers connect us to other dimensions and to *okchamali*" (39). Lena begins to understand when she remembers her own departure from Jordan, where she lived as a freelance journalist. After her Palestinian lover, Sayyed, is killed in a terrorist bombing, she hears a voice accompanying the call to prayer, repeating the phrase, "*The time has come to return home*" (41). Lena understands that her own repetition of the phrase four times, followed by her return home, gives credence to Ezol's theory about a relationship between speech acts, time, and space.

Ezol's theory of the differing ways Euro-Americans and Native Americans experience time and space is not new. Paula Gunn Allen discussed the subject in 1983 in *The Sacred Hoop: Recovering the Feminine in American Indian Traditions:* "the American Indian [tends] to view space as spherical and time as cyclical, whereas the non-Indian tends to view space as linear and time as sequential. The circular concept requires all 'points' that make up the sphere of being to have a significant identity and function, while the linear model assumes that some 'points' are more significant than others" (59). Given the circular movements around baseball fields and during stomp dances, Allen's ideas are interesting to consider in light of the ceremonies at work in *Miko Kings.*[7] Some of Allen's ideas in *The Sacred Hoop* have since been critiqued as essentialist, as Craig Womack points out: "Allen often reduced diversity among Native people to a gynocratic utopia and made other totalizing statements about a singular Indian consciousness. She pointed to Indian difference from Europeans but did not extend the notion to Indian diversity across and within tribes, at least in any way that might have challenged her problematic gynocracy" ("A Single Decade" 23). One of the more compelling aspects of Ezol's theory of time and space is its focus specifically on Choctaw experience through its very language.[8]

The power of language has been a notable theme in American Indian literature, particularly in the works of Kiowa writer N. Scott Momaday. His novel *House Made of Dawn* reflects Momaday's belief in the creative possibilities of language and its significance in human existence (Momaday, "The Man" 636). The novel's Kiowa peyote priest, Tosamah, spreads this belief to his pan-tribal congregation: "[I]n words and in language, and there only . . . [could a storyteller] have whole and consummate being. . . . And the simple act of listening is crucial to the concept of language, more crucial even than reading and writing, and language in turn is crucial to human society" (83–84). Through Tosamah, Momaday conveys the power of language in its ability to create existence. The author expands upon this point in an interview with Bettye Givens: "Language is so creative in itself, it is intrinsically so powerful that storytellers, people who use language, are in possession of a great power. When the storyteller tells his listener a story, he creates his listener, he creates a story. He creates himself in the process. It's an entirely creative process." Though Womack also describes Momaday's ideas about the power of language as "essentialist," he argues that it is a kind of "good essentialism" and demonstrates what this might mean through Creek-specific uses of language in religious ceremony ("Theorizing" 363–67). The "sacred dimension of language" (367) Womack describes is akin to the ways that both LeAnne Howe and N. Scott Momaday represent the power of language in their writings.[9]

Stories and ceremonies are both created by language, and each of these kinds of creation occurs in *Miko Kings.* Using her understanding of linguistic power, Ezol transcends time, space, and even death to visit her descendent in order for the story of the Miko Kings all-Indian baseball team to be told. The two women write the story together, Ezol giving Lena clues about the events of the past and life in early twentieth-century Indian Territory, while Lena researches Ezol's diary and other artifacts she finds in a satchel in the wall of her grandmother's house, in which she is living and renovating. In fact, the renovation of the house is a central symbol of the "renovation" of the Miko Kings' story, which comes about as a result of Ezol and Lena's joint efforts. The story they write together is itself a healing ceremony, one that is a balm for Ezol's pain, Lena's isolation, and at least some of the suffering caused by the allotment of Indian lands.

Ezol's desire to heal herself and Lena likely comes from the painful events of her own childhood and her own experience with an *alikchi* as a child. Her father was killed by "invading *Nahollas* [white people] . . . for twenty five cents" (147), and she also lost both her mother and her sister to illness, ultimately living in an orphanage from the age of eight to twenty-one. Before she was sent to the orphanage by her Uncle Henry Day, however, her Aunt Fancy took her to an *alikchi* who healed her from attacks by an eye tree which she illustrates in her journal (135). The healer "winnowed the branches and sucked out places of its bark from within that plagued [her]" (137). Both her friend, Justina Maurepas, and Lena think the eye tree may be akin to cataracts, which Justina has experienced; however, Lena explores the idea more closely: "Normally cataracts would have blurred her vision not enhanced it, as the drawing suggests. The eyes almost look like seven angry fish. When I look up 'cataract' in the dictionary I find it means floodgate (of heaven)" (185). This passage hints at Ezol's ability to see and possibly even exist in multiple times and spaces. As Patrice Hollrah notes, the eye tree is a "visual example of tribalography's ability to make connections among different points in space and time" (50).

Ezol sees her own isolation mirrored in Lena, which is part of the reason she travels through time to help her descendent write the story of the Miko Kings. Ezol's isolation from her family is manifested in her very name; she sees this same loneliness in Lena, explaining to her at the novel's end, "I may not be your blood grandmother—but I should have been. And I have always been with you in spirit. That is the true story I came to tell" (221). Ezol had planned to marry Lena's grandfather, Blip Bleen. Instead, Blip was seduced by Cora, Ezol's cousin, whose ulterior motive was to entice Blip to throw the final game of the series against Ft. Sill's Seventh Cavalry on behalf of her gambler boyfriend, Beau Hash. Not only did Cora betray Ezol, but she also appears to have had a hand in her death. Per a 1907 newspaper clipping, the authorities seemed to think that Cora was involved in starting the fire that burned the Miko Kings' office, and where, unbeknownst to her, Ezol was trying to save the book of shares from gamblers who would take over the baseball team (205–6). Ezol's spirit reaches out to her descendent to ameliorate what she sees as a cycle of trauma. Lena had run from her life in Oklahoma because her mother died, her father was often physically absent, and her grandmother spent a lifetime punishing herself for the betrayal and possible homicide of her cousin. Lena doesn't return until the voice urged her back during a call to prayer in Jordan. Romero argues that the beliefs of people of color, as depicted in the works of LeAnne Howe and others, "in an ever-present link among themselves, ancestors, spirit beings, deities, and the animate earth, provide a meaningful connection to the past and future necessary for survival" (58). Such a link between Ezol and Lena creates a temporal and discursive space for them to recover and rewrite the story of the Miko Kings, thus healing themselves and their tribe.

The novelistic ceremony enacted in *Miko Kings* is not just about healing personal histories; it also works to heal the pain of an early twentieth-century Choctaw community torn apart by allotment. The Miko Kings baseball team is both a source of entertainment for the community and a potent symbol of Choctaw power against continued US settler colonialism. Thus, Hope Little Leader, star pitcher, is more than an extraordinary athlete; he is also a kind of *alikchi.* Like Ezol, Hope was exposed to an *alikchi* as a child: his grandfather was a healer, who "could split tornadoes" (50). Blip tells Hope he has a *tikba* (power) that he received "from the original ball players who play nightly among the stars" (54). Ezol explains to Lena that Hope had the same kind of power on the ballfield as an *alikchi,* "working in collaboration with the earth's mathematical systems" (44). This power manifested in his signature pitch, named an "up-down" (163) by the newspapers, which Ezol recognized and recorded in her journal as a way of manipulating time and space, like the *alikchi* she had seen as a child, and like she herself also learns to do: "when Hope looked up into the sky he disappeared completely on the mound. For a split second the sky cracked open and a blinding light flashed on the ball field. McAlester's batter at home plate appeared to have already struck out before Hope released the ball" (160). Hope wastes his power when he decides to throw the final game in the series against the Seventh Cavalrymen and is subsequently punished by his teammates, who chop off his gifted hands.

The healing ceremony which Hope completes occurs at the moment of his death in 1969, and requires the assistance of Kerwin, his Choctaw caregiver at the nursing home, and his vision of an ancient *toli* (stickball) player. There are two important points to note about these other participants in Hope's ceremony. Kerwin is identified as an *Ohoyo Holba,* "like a woman but not" (66), a Choctaw cultural figure which Hope describes as "a respected person . . . [a giver] who had multiple kinds of powers inside them. That's why a man would put on a woman's dress. By wearing the dress he was showing the world that he was in a state of grace, so to speak, a man without limitations" (89). In fact, Kerwin feels tremendously guilty after receiving disciplinary leave for coming to work in a dress and wig, which he had worn in a protest march against the Vietnam War. Because of Kerwin's absence, Hope has been neglected, resulting in a huge, deep bedsore that will probably lead to his death, given his diabetes and crippled hands (83). Kerwin is aware that he is one of the few nurses in the home who cares about welfare-dependent Indians, and his presence shields them from the discriminatory practices of the other caregivers. Kerwin, as an *Ohoyo Holba,* is a kind of healer, but there is more to this cultural figure, as LeAnne Howe explains:

> Ohoyo Holba was . . . many things, including homosexual. Often they weren't just involved with other men but had many levels of relationships. They were also involved with our community in very special ways. They could be healers. They're people that protected our children because they embodied more than one thing. And what is part of Choctawan aesthetics is that we revere things that are unusual. Different. So when you look at the spirit that's connected in Ohoyo Holba, and when they put on that dress in olden times, they are saying "the embodiment of many." . . . Kerwin is a ball player; he is a healer; he is attempting to try to find his own way in a contemporary society that doesn't recognize the spaces he lives in. ("Choctawan" 223)[10]

It is significant that Kerwin is a ball player and that he is "a man without limitations," given that the novel also describes baseball as a game "without limits" (199) and Hope's ceremony will manifest in the form of a baseball game. The *toli* player is another vital element of Hope's ceremony, given the ancient Native roots of stickball and baseball, one of the themes underscoring the plot of *Miko Kings.* Ezol explains how stickball was used to train warriors, and base-and-ball was a game used to promote diplomacy between southeastern tribes (40). She claims that the latter "was played on every ancient square ground in the southeast. It had two intersecting lines that crossed at the mound where the pitcher stood. . . . From the mound, a pitcher was the embodiment of the center pole that could access the Middle, Upper, and Lower World" (39). As Howe notes in her essay "The Story of Movement: Natives and Performance Culture" that ceremonial pole is called the *iti fabassa,* which connotes "a kind of knowledge" (254). The pitcher, then, is important, not only logistically, but also spiritually. The name Hope is short for *Hopaii,* or prophet. Levine explains that, in Choctaw culture, "The highest ranking shaman was the hopayi or prophet" (394), a figure with the ability to communicate with spirit beings. Thus, when Hope has the vision of the *toli* player during his last hours at the nursing home, it is not surprising that he *becomes* the ball player, returning to the last game of the Twin Territories series in order to remedy the mistake he made by throwing that game more than fifty years before. The spirit he saw was, in fact, himself, after his own death, wearing the accoutrements of one of the warriors from whom Blip had claimed he received his power.

Fittingly, Hope's ceremony occurs on a baseball field, a "square within a circle," also "a medicine sign" (98). Winning the series against the Ft. Sill's Seventh Cavalrymen is about more than simple competition. Henry Day's attempt to rile up the crowd underscores what is really at stake for the Miko Kings in this game: "I have only three words for the Major General Thornton: *Custer's Last Stand*" (193). The US Seventh Cavalry was notorious for its role in the nineteenth-century Indian Wars; in fact, the Twin Territories Series takes place less than twenty years after the Wounded Knee Massacre on the Pine Ridge Reservation. Day's invocation of the Native American rout of Custer's men at the Battle of Little Big Horn is meant to inspire both the team and the Indians in the crowd, reminding them of their strength in an era of disillusionment, the end of Indian Territory. Don L. Birchfield describes how the Choctaws were forced by the US government in 1866 to allow the construction of railroads through their nation, resulting in an influx of whites who wanted the land upon which they were squatting to become a state. Birchfield explains:

> In 1907 those intruders got their wish, when the illegal state of Oklahoma was created by the United States Congress, in violation of Article IV of "Treaty with the Choctaws, 1830," when the Congress caved in to the pressure from its constituents, betraying the Choctaw people for the second time. Choctaws, and all other members of the so-called Five Civ-

> ilized Tribes . . . were forced to accept the individual allotment of farms and were declared to be Oklahoma citizens. The tribal estate (ownership of land in common) was thus broken up and Indian nations were declared to be dissolved. (121)

John T. Kilpinen describes the effect of allotment on Indians as transforming them "from sovereign national units to wards in the eyes of the state" (484). LeAnne Howe represents the injustice of this second loss of land by the Choctaws on a personal level in the conflict between Henri Day and a squatter who takes up residence on his land, ultimately stealing it from him (*Miko Kings* 178).

The Twin Territories Series occurs on the eve of Oklahoma statehood; a defeat of the Cavalrymen by the Miko Kings would have eased the pain of this second historical loss of Choctaw homelands, coming less than a hundred years after their Removal from Mississippi. As a result of Hope's decision to throw the game, the pain of his people becomes embodied in him, when Blip cuts off his hands as punishment. Both Hope and the Choctaws are deprived of the healing power in his hands. To ameliorate this history, Hope enacts a ceremony at the moment of his own death, in the presence of Kerwin who has tried to heal him and the *toli* player who takes him back to the ballpark (215).

As Ezol explained to Lena early in the novel, baseball is a game that is "*past time*" (44), or has no time limits. Thus, Hope's connection to the sacred returns him to the 1907 Twin Territories Series, where he makes a different decision the second time around: "Hope winds up, looking straight up into the Sun as if in prayer to *Hashtali,* the Choctaw's source of power. He disappears inside it. When he pulls out of the light he throws everything he's got at the Cavalry" (218), striking out his last batter. Hopaii has given hope to the Choctaws, whose jubilant celebration "can be heard all the way back to Ft. Sill, where, after twenty-two years, Geronimo, honored leader of the Apaches, is still a prisoner of war" (218). The ceremony enacted by Ezol and Lena, the recovery of the Miko Kings story, is interdependent with Hope's ceremony, rewriting the loss of the Twin Territories series. Their collaboration has changed history, as evidenced by the blog created by Lena, in which people are sharing their knowledge of the Miko Kings and their 1907 Twin Territories championship win. Ezol, Lena, and Hopaii haven't changed the history of Native American land disenfranchisement, but they have recovered a lost story, empowering their people through hope. The novel's last line reflects its ceremonial nature: "Such is the sacred made manifest in the flesh of the page" (221).

Like Ezol Day, Shakbatina is the *alikchi* of *Shell Shaker* whose healing ceremony comprises not only events in the novel but also the story itself. Shakbatina first sacrifices herself for her daughter, and later, her spirit dances in a ceremony that resonates across centuries to save her female descendent, Auda Billy. This act also unites history and the dispersed bands of the Choctaw tribe. Shakbatina's narrative frames the novel—sections of which are set in the present, while others are set in the eighteenth century—and establishes parallels between characters from both eras.

As head of her clan, Shakbatina is responsible for leading trading expeditions to other Choctaw villages; however, she contracted smallpox from trading with the English: "They had traded me disease for our corn. It was in their blankets, the ones I brought back to Yanabi Town. This disease destroyed many of our people and knapped my body like a piece of flint" (10).[11] Since she is unable to barter with the Red Fox people, she sends her daughter Anoleta instead. Anoleta, one of the wives of Red Shoes, is wrongly accused of murdering another of his wives, a Red Fox woman, leading to rising hostility with the possibility of war between the two villages. As a member of the *Inholahta* moiety,[12] Shakbatina seeks peace within the tribe, so she offers her own death in place of her daughter's to assuage the tensions (5). Pesantubbee explains the nature of this Choctaw value, the maintenance of harmony within individuals and communities: "In the case of unnatural death such as murder, balance was restored through restitution. The one who caused the death forfeited his or her life for the deceased. In that way the one who killed restored balance to the family, the community, and the moiety that had lost someone" (150).

Shakbatina struggles to follow the *Inholahta* way, as she is bitter and desires revenge against her enemies. She urges Anoleta to enlist the aid of Jean Baptiste Bienville in their war against Red Shoes and the English, a deepening of the alliance between the French and the eastern bands of Choctaw. She also fantasizes about making the English pay for the pain she has endured from the smallpox: "I'd often dreamed of hanging [their] intestines in the trees so everyone could see their shit"

(10). Such an act would unveil the evil she believes exists within the English to all who might judge otherwise from exterior appearances. As a child, Shakbatina had painted her face red in the tradition of a warrior, much to the shame of her mother, who works to instill in the child her heritage of peacemaking. Yet, Shakbatina cannot forget her warrior beliefs, and when she offers her body as sacrifice to the Red Fox clan, she wears white, the color of peace, and paints her face red, the color of war. She has split herself in two, a foreshadowing of the coming split of the Choctaw people during Removal. She believes that representing herself in this way is a message to her people: "we must fight to survive" (15), a message to ensure tribal survivance.[13] Shakbatina's division of her identity may also be another kind of foreshadowing rooted in the eighteenth-century Choctaw belief that people had two spirits, "one that went to the afterworld and one that remained on earth restlessly wandering about its former habitation" (Pesantubbee 161). If a spirit did not have all it needed for the journey to the afterworld, it might stay behind in order locate those items. In this case, what Shakbatina needs is for her people to be united, which is the goal of *Shell Shaker*'s textual ceremony.

Shakbatina's division of self gives her the power to transcend time. Common in eighteenth-century Choctaw culture, a bone-picking ceremony follows her death. Bone-picking emphasizes the holiness of the bones of the dead, signifying the individual's lived past and eternal existence (*Shell Shaker* 178). Horatio Bardwell Cushman, author of *History of the Choctaw, Chickasaw, and Natchez Indians,* argued in 1899 that "no people on earth paid more respect to the dead, than the Choctaws did and still do; or preserved with more affectionate veneration the graves of their ancestors" (191). This sentiment is echoed by *Shell Shaker*'s Father Renoir, a French priest who renounces his vows to live with Shakbatina's daughter, Neshoba (178). Bone-picking also suggests the symbiotic relationship between people and the earth. Howe explains, "Things are made right when we are returned to the earth as food for the planet. Life continues" ("The Story of America" 36). Before her death, Shakbatina pledges that she will not leave her people: "When released by the bone-picking, I will grow and sprout up like green corn. From the mound I will watch over our people. Do not cry for me, I am a fast grower" (*Shell Shaker* 8). Shakbatina's speech links her to the power of *Ohoyo*

Osh Chisba, or Corn Woman. The bone-picking ceremony that follows Shakbatina's death is one of the most striking moments in a novel replete with the violence of war, murder, and rape. In "Repugnant Aboriginality: LeAnne Howe's *Shell Shaker* and Indigenous Representation in the Age of Multiculturalism,"[14] Monika Siebert describes the multifaceted language of the scene, concluding,

> Howe offers plenty of opportunities to assimilate what is taking place, even to deeply appreciate the terrifying—and sublime—beauty of the ritual. At the same time, however, she thwarts such assimilation, giving unrelenting play to the gruesomeness, potential horror even, of the traditional Choctaw practices she describes. She forces her readers to visualize crushed skulls, half-decayed bodies coming apart in other people's hands, and necrophilic sex. (110)

For Siebert, the bone-picking ceremony is designed to upset attempts at cross-cultural understanding, a goal of multiculturalism, instead, creating a kind of "epistemological gap" (112) that resists full comprehension of Choctaw rituals by a mainstream audience. This is an interesting point, given the types of balancing acts many American Indian writers perform when envisioning an audience for their creative works;[15] however, I would argue that Howe's objective in her explicitly detailed representation is less about obfuscating ritualistic practice for non-Native readers and more about centering the text within a Choctaw worldview. In particular, the necrophilic elements of the ceremony underscore a relationship between fertility and death that begins with *Ohoyo Osh Chisba.*

True to Shakbatina's pledge prior to the bone-picking ceremony to remain with her people, her spirit arrives on the 1991 Autumnal Equinox to help Auda, who has been raped by her former lover and the current Choctaw tribal leader, Redford McAlester. Shakbatina extends herself to her descendant, uniting colonized present and tribal past, in a shell-shaking ceremony: "Auda watches the spirit woman with turtle shells strapped to her ankles. She's big-breasted and wears a deerskin dress, bloodied at the neck and hem. Smoke rises from the turtle shells and forms a constellation on the ceiling. Auda knows the dance. Every spring she shakes shells with the other Indian women in Southeastern Oklahoma" (18). The ceremony has already linked the women symbolically through its continued practice, but Shakbatina's dancing creates a physical link between the two. Shakbatina's presence will help Auda heal the tribal wounds of yesterday and today by collapsing past and present, like Ezol's intervention in her descendant's life.

Shakbatina's shell-shaking ceremony also connects her own history and that of her descendent back to a much earlier female ancestor. The first conflict between Choctaw peoples and Europeans alluded to in the novel is the 1540 battle between Hernando de Soto and the Choctaw leader, Tuscalusa (Howe, "Author's Note" 226). Howe's fictional representation of the meeting is a creation story, in which a woman becomes the first shell shaker, both mythic and powerful, through her ceremonial act of love. Shell shakers are traditionally women in eastern woodland tribes who "stomp dance" at various ceremonies, providing rhythmic accompaniment to the singing and dancing with their turtle-shell leg rattles (Howard and Kurath 1).[16] The first shell shaker, of whom Howe writes, is the wife of Tuscalusa and who Shakbatina calls Grandmother of Birds. Because Tuscalusa has heard that de Soto is a dangerous enemy, an *Osano* (bloodsucker), he prepares for a battle with the Spanish in order to lure the invaders away from his people.[17] According to Shakbatina, Grandmother of Birds danced "for four days and nights . . . extolling the heroics of the man she loved" (2). Grandmother's ankles bleed from the continuous dancing, and this sacrifice moves *Miko Luak,* the fire's spirit, to take her prayers to the Autumnal Equinox, *Itilauichi,* who in turn, gives her a song to "make things even" (2). This ceremony is passed down matrilineally through the novel and operates as a tool for "evening" out personal, social, and cultural injustices. In the case of Tuscalusa's battle with de Soto, the Choctaw men were defeated and their bodies mutilated. Grandmother does not mourn her husband; rather, she sings the song given to her by *Itilauichi,* and she and her sisters take flight in the form of birds to found the seven original Choctaw towns. She also begins a tradition of peace-making, and her descendents are known as *Inholahta* (6).

Shakbatina's shell-shaking ceremony gives her the ability to transcend time for the purpose of healing and can be linked to Hope's return to the Twin Territories game more than half a century after the fact. LeAnne Howe explains the similarity between ceremonial dancing and baseball: "This counter-clockwise direction is how southeastern Indians dance around a fire. Counter-clockwise is also the direction a baseball game is played. Baseball is a game without time" ("And Here Too Comes an Echo" 212). Shakbatina's arrival in the present leads to the final death of Red Shoes, as embodied by corrupt politician Redford McAlester. One theme of the novel is that the historical division of the tribe has led to a continuous process of division among the Choctaw. Shakbatina confesses to killing McAlester through Auda's body, repeating history, yet also healing Auda/Anoleta. Shakbatina's dance sets into motion a series of events which leads to a spiritual encounter between McAlester and Auda, or Red Shoes and Anoleta, in which the original crime that led to Shakbatina's death is confessed: Red Shoes is the killer of his Red Fox wife (200). These two characters are not the only contemporary embodiments of historical figures. Nearly every member of the Billy family has a role in the original civil war between the Choctaws, and Auda's family helps her to deliver the spirit of Red Shoes to the *Nanih Waiya,* the cradle of Choctaw civilization (161). The burial of Red Shoes is the final act of Shakbatina's ceremony, which will begin to heal the wounds inflicted on the Choctaw people by colonizing Europeans in much the same way that rewriting the Miko Kings' story brings hope to communities divided by US settler colonialism.

Central to the healing ceremony in *Shell Shaker* is the figure of the *Imataha Chitto,* the Choctaw leader who would unite the tribe. Despite his claims, Red Shoes's actions prove that he is not this figure; in fact, his relationship with the English actually divides the tribe. His contemporary doppelganger, Red McAlester, sells out his people through his dealings with the Mafia. Given the power of women in Choctaw society, Shakbatina believes the *Imataha Chitto* would not be a man (185). Though tribal traditions have changed as a result of colonization, Isaac notes that his sister Susan, Auda's mother, still follows the matrilineal tradition by caring for the personal possessions of their powerful ancestor, a shell shaker (60). Howe's presentation of strong female figures reclaiming their roles as leaders in Choctaw society is a subversion of colonial patriarchy. The murder of McAlester following his act of sexual violence against Auda suggests that Choctaw women will not succumb to a colonizing male superstructure, just as the actions of Ezol and Lena imply that they also will not succumb to a language and history imposed by colonial power.

Delores Love is the *Imataha Chitto,* uniter of her tribe, and another of *Shell Shaker*'s *alikchi* figures. She has experienced her people's varied stages of history: tribalism, dispersal, colonization, and decolonization. In the eighteenth century, she is Mantema,[18] the *Imataha Chitto* who is bayoneted to death in the battle against Red Shoes and the *Inkilish Okla* (English people). During her childhood in the twentieth century, she first runs away from a government boarding school and then again away from her tribe in Oklahoma with her sister. Delores and Dovie become actresses in California who bill themselves as "The Love Maidens of The Five Civilized Tribes" (117). Even though Delores despises her Indianness (155), she is willing to exploit it, buying into the role of a Hollywood stereotype, for material gain. That changes when her mother dies, and she returns to the tribe and learns the funeral traditions from Nowatima, Susan, and Isaac Billy's grandmother, a descendent of Shakbatina. The matrilineal sharing of this knowledge speaks to the connection between women and death rites through their traditional association with corn:

> The roots of corn reached into the Below World, the world of fertility (or life) and death. For the Choctaw the Below World was not a world of punishment, of hellfire, but one of power that was also dangerous. Women were associated with that power because Ohoyo Osh Chisba, a woman, became corn, and women of This World were responsible for the cultivation of corn as well as other plants. They also embodied the power of fertility and death through their menstrual cycles. (Pesantubbee 152)

After Delores learns the pole-pulling ceremony[19] and traditional songs from Nowatima, she conducts her mother's funeral and begins to sing for others, creating a resurgence of interest in Choctaw traditions. Delores has come full circle from her tribal self, through an internally colonized self, to a decolonized self, inspiring others in her tribe to embrace their cultural beliefs. Delores believes that "her role as modern *foni miko,* bone-picker, is the only useful thing she's ever done" (146). This faith in her cultural traditions leads to her vision of what must be done with the body of Redford McAlester.

Delores receives her vision as she kneads dough, the dough becoming the fertile mud of the *Nanih Waiya* and the surrounding area, "the cradle of Choctawan civilization" (161), suggesting an Interstate South which can simultaneously exist within and outside the geographical boundaries of the Southeast. In the vision, Delores sees ancient ancestors at the moment of creation and realizes that McAlester's body must be buried there, in Mississippi, in order for tribal healing to commence. Delores takes the body to the sacred ground of the *Nanih Waiya.* Like the novelistic healing ceremony of *Miko Kings,* Delores's ceremony requires the interdependence of the community. She is accompanied by Isaac, who possesses a stone containing the spiritual essence of both Grandmother of Birds and Tuscalusa (147). Like Shakbatina, they, too, had split themselves in order to ensure the survival of their people. In addition to Isaac, Tema's son, Hoppy and his friends have also come to the ceremony to provide assistance. Hoppy, like Hope in *Miko Kings,* is a prophet figure as suggested by Divine Sarah's nickname for him, "prophet boy" (68), and his intuitive understanding of his family's internal and external conflicts; he will eventually inherit the stone containing his ancestors' essences. The Oklahoma Choctaws are met by relatives from the Mississippi Band of Choctaws. Echoing the actions of Grandmother of Birds, seven shell-shaking women aid Delores in the ceremony, one which also includes burying Red Shoes/Red McAlester with numerous material possessions so that his spirit will remain in the mud of the *Nanih Waiya.* According to Pesantubbee, it was not uncommon for Choctaws to be buried with possessions and even spouses and friends who would accompany them to the afterlife (153). In the case of McAlester, Delores Love and Isaac Billy will be his companions, sacrificing themselves to guard over his spirit.

The journey eastward, upon which Delores, Isaac, and many other Choctaws embark, is one that represents a community united with the goal to make itself whole, rather than one divided by death, disease, and enemy arms. It is significant that Delores learned the traditional funeral songs from Nowatima, who was also keeper of the oral history of her people's displacement from their homelands. At the same time that Delores gains the knowledge to bury the dead, she learns of the terrors of the Trail of Tears, on which her ancestors suffered from disease, malnutrition, hopelessness, and death (*Shell Shaker* 148). McGowan argues that Removal failed, citing the fact that southeastern Native peoples maintain communities throughout the region (62). Though this is true in the sense that the Southeast was not entirely ethnically cleansed of its Indigenous peoples, it is also true that Removal succeeded, as evidenced by the many populous tribal communities in Oklahoma, what was to be

"Indian Territory." *Shell Shaker* demonstrates both the failure of Indian Removal and performs a "strategic counter-removal" (Anderson, "On Native Ground") by representing the journey back East to the mother mound in the original Choctaw homelands.

In *Reconstructing the Native South,* Taylor takes issue with such an optimistic reading of the return of Howe's characters to the *Nanih Waiya,* making the cogent point that Delores and Isaac are "killed by the casino overlords who follow them in pursuit of the dirty money they have taken from Redford's stash" (64). Yet, Taylor's focus on the novel's failure to "slay the demons of materialism" (62) misses the mark when considering the novel's spiritual dimension. At least two major characters in the novel are actually spirits, and nearly all the major characters are linked across the centuries by spiritual aspects of themselves that transcend whatever material body they may inhabit. If we consider Pesantubbee's description of an earlier Choctaw belief that a spirit would not begin a journey to the afterworld until it had everything necessary to do so, then clearly, Shakbatina's descendents, the Billy family, and Redford McAlester were spirits with unfinished business, and that business could not be completed until the novel's eighteenth-century wrongs were righted in the twentieth. Isaac and Delores are aware that their deaths are self-sacrifices in order to "help [Red McAlester] stay put" (212) in his burial mound, saving the tribe from his greedy spirit.

As *Shell Shaker* suggests, unification of the Choctaws in the eighteenth century would have been the most dangerous scenario for the English colonizers; Shakbatina's survivance has made this unification possible in the twentieth century. The implication is that a contemporary unification of the Choctaws is one step toward decolonization. At the novel's end, Shakbatina acknowledges, "My story is an enormous undertaking. Hundreds of years in the making until past and present collide into a single moment" (222). Like Ezol Day, Shakbatina has found a way to transcend time and space in order to heal her descendents individually and communally. *Shell Shaker* is a novel comprising numerous ceremonies, all of which work toward the larger ceremonial event of the novel itself.[20] Shakbatina's (and the novel's) final words are "*Hekano,* I am finished talking" (222); thus, language signals the ceremony's end. Similarly, *Miko Kings* conflates language and ceremony in its last line, "the sacred . . . manifest in the flesh of the page" (221).

LeAnne Howe's representations of the community roles of Choctaw women, men, and *Ohoyo Holba* both resist a Western tradition of patriarchy and gender binarism and recuperate cultural practices overrun by colonialism. Like her theory of tribalography, Howe's works "seem to pull all the elements together of a storyteller's tribe, meaning the people, the land, and multiple characters and all their manifestations and revelations, and connect these in past, present, and future milieus" (Howe, "The Story of America" 118).[21] Within such a framework, ancestor spirits such as Ezol Day, Shakbatina, and the *toli* player have as much agency as any living character. These powerful Choctaw ancestors provide an interesting response to dominant cultural depictions of Indian ghosts in American literature. Renee Bergland has argued that, in the early nineteenth century, "Indian ghosts shaped the nation and the national literature, constructing America as a haunted community rather than a simply imagined one" (102). Annette Trefzer made the point that in modernist southern fiction, specifically, "Native American presence is eclipsed and yet rendered in the signifier of the mound grave as a historical spirit that leaves its imprint on the land and its people" (3). In these contexts, it is significant that LeAnne Howe's ghosts are not haunting Euro-Americans; instead, they are helping to heal Choctaw communities haunted by a history of genocide and the continuing implications of US settler colonialism.[22] Achille Mbembe's conception of necropolitics or "contemporary forms of subjugation of life to the power of death . . . [that] profoundly reconfigure the relations among resistance, sacrifice, and terror" (39) is a powerful paradigm through which to consider the South's reliance on slavery and Indigenous ethnic cleansing to solidify its nation-building efforts. Significantly, Mbembe enumerates examples of necropower such as the plantation and the colony, in which inhabitants are a kind of "*living dead*" (40), citing the current occupation of Palestine as "the most accomplished form of necropower" (27).

Howe's depiction of a Choctaw journalist losing her Palestinian boyfriend to a terrorist bomb and then immediately choosing to return home to Oklahoma in *Miko Kings* is an urgent linking of diverse global sites of necropower. Byrd extends this argument to Native Americans, claiming "Indians [are] the original necropolitical affect of the living dead brought back to haunt cosmopolitan colonialism," and it is only through the decolonizing works of LeAnne Howe and other Indigenous American writers and thinkers that "settler, arrivant, and native [can] apprehend and grieve together the violences of U.S. empire" (*The Transit of Empire* 229). For Howe, one way to work through that grief is to represent specifically Choctaw gendered sites of power in the face of these violences, such as the healers in her novels. As the author observed, "I'm trying to write myself healthy . . . by losing the wounds of the past three hundred years" ("The Native South" 139).

CHAPTER THREE

Interstate Simulations and Postindian Warriors

> Nobody played an Indian like Portland. I mean, he is Indian, but that's different. Just because you are an Indian doesn't mean you can act like an Indian for the movies.
>
> —THOMAS KING, *Green Grass, Running Water*

In 2007, LeAnne Howe appeared on Jon Stewart's satirical comedy news program, *The Daily Show,* in a segment called "Trail of Cheers." She was interviewed by Aasif Mandvi about the former University of Illinois Native American mascot, Chief Illiniwek, who had been retired the previous winter, per the Board of Trustees' decision. Howe represented the university's American Indian Studies Program, supporting the board's decision and discussing why the mascot was offensive. Two of the university's students were also interviewed, one who was in favor of the decision, describing the mascot as a "race-based stereotype," and another who disagreed with the decision and who was, not surprisingly, wearing face paint in support of the "chief." The latter student was labeled a "Fighting Illini Tribesman" by the program, and his position was lampooned by the show. Just prior to his interview, a map of the United States, focused on the Southeast, was displayed, as Mandvi's voiceover described how "Native American mascots once flourished across this great country," but that they had been "forced from their ancestral lands." The ironic comparison of the genocidal impact of Indian Removal and the progressive shift away from employing Native American sports mascots highlights the ludicrous and demeaning position of those who continue to support the use of these "race-based stereotypes." Howe's appearance on the show is doubly significant, considering that she is a descendent of two tribes who were forcibly removed from "their ancestral lands." Yet, Howe was gracious and funny throughout the interview, such as when Mandvi describes her as "an expert on all things Indian," and she gives him an "Indian burn," presumably to demonstrate that expertise. This willingness to arm herself with "humor, new stories, and survivance" makes LeAnne Howe an example of Gerald Vizenor's vision of a postindian warrior (5).

Vizenor argues in the preface to *Manifest Manners: Postindian Warriors of Survivance* that the word "indian" is "an occidental misnomer, an overseas enactment that has no referent to real native cultures or communities" (vii). For Vizenor, the postmodern interventions into a culture dominated by the ideological legacy of Manifest Destiny, or "manifest manners," are "postindian warriors." Defying the simulation of Indianness in culture and in its artifacts, such as Western movies, sports teams' mascots, and new age spiritualism, postindian warriors arm themselves with "humor, new stories, and survivance" (5). Vizenor points out, however, that "postindian warriors and missionaries of manifest manners are both responsible for simulations" (13), the former providing "new stories of tribal courage" (4) and the latter the absence of the "tribal real" (4).

Scott Romine's *The Real South: Southern Narrative in the Age of Cultural Reproduction* similarly investigates authenticity, arguing that "[t]he South is full of fakes—Civil War reenactments and plantation tourism, to name two" (2). Though Romine's study doesn't address American Indian representation, there are many examples of his argument that "the fake South . . . becomes the real South through the intervention of narrative" (9) in the history of non-Native southerners' representations of Removal such as the Leake County, Mississippi, Tri-Racial Festival of 1951. Theda Perdue relates how "Choctaws played stickball and danced, and African Americans sang 'Negro spirituals,' but whites owned the past. In a pageant portraying the negotiation of the Treaty of Doak's Stand (1820), whereby Mississippi unscrupulously obtained 'some of its richest and most populous land,' white men played the roles of Pushmataha and Mushulatubee" ("The Legacy of Indian Removal" 27). Perdue notes how this and other examples of a "hijacking of the history of removal by whites" (28) has affected Native peoples historically and in the present, leading to "depression, suicide, alcoholism, violence, and a host of antisocial behaviors" (29) associated with historical trauma. Yet, Romine's conception of cultural reproduction, particularly his focus on narrative reproduction, suggests that a body of work such as LeAnne Howe's can displace narratives such as those of the paternalistic whites who thought it was a good idea to pretend to be Pushmataha and Mushulatubee when they were in the presence of actual Choctaw people. One of the most compelling elements of Romine's argument is that "the South [is] in play as a site of negotiation and mutual navigation" (236–37), opening a door to "different Souths" (237), Native or otherwise.

My model of an Interstate South concerns the circulation of Indigenous cultures within the region that became known as "the South" and the way that contemporary Indigenous people travel within, into, and out of the Southeast, a form of resistance against colonial spatial constructs. We have seen an overlap, at times, between Native and Interstate Souths. Choctaw culture and peoples circulate between Oklahoma and Mississippi, with further movements of the culture in Hollywood film as well as the presence of Hollywood film in the Choctalking texts of LeAnne Howe. These circulations create representations of "different Souths," whether they are in Oklahoma or Romania, as a result of Howe's connections to Choctaw history and culture, with its birth and continuation on southeastern land.

In light of its ties to a third space of sovereignty, the Interstate South manifests opportunities for other forms of colonial resistance, particularly ideological. Within a larger context of her characters' movements outward from Choctaw homescapes, Howe complexly renders American Indians and non-Native people playing Indian, including the material gains and emotional losses that result from such simulations. "Playing Indian," as Philip Deloria terms it in his critical volume of the same name, an example of Vizenor's "manifest manners," leads to an "indeterminacy of American identities [that] stems, in part, from the nation's inability to deal with Indian people" (5). Howe's work resists the dominant cultural ideology, both by parodying stereotypes and by portraying a number of characters who can be considered postindian warriors.

In her collection *Evidence of Red,* Howe presents a series of parodic poems, the organization of which suggests that all of the stereotypes represented are spin-offs of the original simulated Indian: Noble Savage. In the series's introductory poem "My Name Is Noble Savage," the speaker claims to be "built for iconography" (76), producing "Children you sketch / and photograph, / Catalogue, / But soon abandon." Noble Savage describes the archaeological and anthropological interest in America's Indigenous peoples as a discipline of study underscoring this message: the dominant culture values Native peoples only for their usefulness. This usefulness is manifold, however, as Noble Savage explains: "You killed me / In order to bring me back to life / As your pet, a mascot" (76). Indian Mascot, then, is one of the children produced by Noble Savage.

Aside from scientific interest, what is the usefulness of simulations like Noble Savage and Indian Mascot, first to European and then to dominant US culture? Philip Deloria summarizes the ideology born from Enlightenment philosophy: "[Noble] savagery both juxtaposes and conflates an urge to idealize and desire Indians and a need to despise and dispossess them. . . . Two interlocked traditions: one of self-criticism, the other of conquest" (4). Howe satirizes the simulations produced by this ideology in the poems that follow the first of the series, detailing Noble Savage's heartfelt confessions to his therapist, Pocahontas's desire for Noble Savage, Indian Mascot's desire for Noble Savage, and Indian Mascot's stint with the Village People. Parody becomes allegory when Indian Mascot is decried by Native Americans and eventually shot by a young Indian boy. Noble Savage has, at the last minute, come to his rescue, and the simulations die together.

The final poem of the series, "What happened to Indian Mascot and Noble Savage—After the shooting?" simply answers the title's question: "Nothing. / They were never real. / This is Hollywood" (85). Howe uses Hollywood, the center of American cultural simulation production, as a symbol of the Western ideological impetus to project fantasies of Native American life, culture, values, and identity. American Indian representation in Western films is, of course, one of the most pernicious examples of simulated Indianness, providing non-Native American audiences with what Vizenor describes as "vicious encounters with the antiselves of civilization, the invented savage" (7). This simulated Indianness parallels Romine's analysis of the ubiquity of *Gone with the Wind* in which he describes Tara as "ground zero of southern cultural reproduction: the site at which the real South is simultaneously exploded and regenerated—re-covered and recovered, ad infinitum and in many respects ad nauseam—in what amounts to an endless loop" (27). Hollywood provides a similar "endless loop" of savage Indians, outside of which actual Native peoples exist. In LeAnne Howe's "What happened to Indian Mascot and Noble Savage—After the shooting?" the death of Noble Savage and Indian Mascot within a framework of Hollywood simulation, by a young Indian boy, undermines the typical image of white conquest of the American West by exploding that loop; as a result, the poem operates as a symbol of hope that a young generation of Native Americans, postindian warriors, can destroy these cultural stereotypes.

Noble Savage and Indian Sports Mascot[1] make another appearance in Howe's oeuvre, with some significant variations, in her play, *The Mascot Opera: A Minuet,* commissioned by Minneapolis's Mixedblood Theatre.[2] The play more consciously takes aim at the continued use of American Indian sports mascots, conflating the practice with Hollywood simulations of Native savagery in Western films. The stage directions call for scenes from "John Ford westerns" (2) and shots of "dancing and prancing" (2) Indian mascots to be displayed on screens behind the actors. Significantly, in the play, Indian Sports Mascot "must be Caucasion" (2). Given the numerous stage directions suggesting that the actors take a cue from the University of Illinois's former official mascot, Chief Illiniwek, it is clear that Howe's years teaching in the English and American Indian Studies departments at Illinois were troubled by this particular simulation of Indianness. In an interview with David Davis for the *Society for the Study of Southern Literature* newsletter, Howe explains that, after the ban on Chief Illiniwek as official mascot, students continue to wear T-shirts with his image to class in defiance. Even more alarming, "The American Indian Studies building on the Illinois campus is periodically threatened. Someone calls and leaves a voicemail threatening to blow our building to smithereens. Swat teams came to our building in 2007, and in 2011, our director of American Indian Studies, Robert Warrior, and his family were threatened by a voicemail left on our office phone." Such verbal violence is enabled by the university's hypocritical stance on the retired mascot. According to C. Richard King, the University of Illinois licenses "throwback jerseys" (138) with Chief Illiniwek's image and allows space for students and alumni to celebrate the mascot at events such as homecoming.

The Mascot Opera: A Minuet expands upon the interplay between Noble Savage and Indian Mascot, offering a third perspective that varies from those in *Evidence of Red.* When Noble Savage says "She's too intense for me" in *The Mascot Opera* (5), he's referring to American

Indian Girl, who is actually the first speaking character of the play, an activist fighting stereotypical depictions of Native peoples. When Noble Savage makes the same comment in the poem "Noble Savage Sees a Therapist" in *Evidence of Red,* he is referencing the speaker of the previous poem, "Disney's Pocahontas Longs for Noble Savage," who says she will "fuck 47 / Make love to thousands more / Birth a nation of sons and daughters" before declaring, "They will all be a substitute for you" (77). This "marriage" of Noble Savage and Disney's Pocahontas suggests the proliferation of simulated Indianness based in romanticizing European and Euro-American ideologies. The shift of antecedents to the pronoun "she" from *Evidence of Red* to *The Mascot Opera* could not be more significant. American Indian Girl is an intellectual, and more importantly, an actual Native person. She is also "a young and earnest college student" (3). As Fryberg et al. have noted, "Exposure to American Indian mascot images has a negative impact on American Indian high school and college students' feelings of personal and community worth, and achievement-related possible selves" (215–16). By positioning this character as college-aged, Howe offers hope to younger generations that a status quo of whitewashed history and American Indian "vanishment" can be overcome. Like the young Indian boy who shoots Noble Savage and Indian Sports Mascot, American Indian Girl is a postindian warrior, resisting the cultural stereotypes thrust upon her, yet her resistance seems to fit better with Vizenor's vision: rather than responding with violence, humor and intellectualism are her weapons.

She fights the ignorance that creates the mythologies of Noble Savage and Indian Sports Mascot with Vine Deloria's 1969 publication, *Custer Died for Your Sins: An Indian Manifesto.* She quotes the book, "reading loudly, as if the words are bullets" (13), emphasizing the idea that Native peoples must fight their battles in the ideological realm. Deloria's words literally kill the fallacious characters, yet as in the series of monologues featuring Noble Savage and Indian Mascot in *Evidence of Red,* Hollywood will continue its function of projecting cultural fantasy: the last image is a video still of a wooden Indian. Despite its damning of multiple Native stereotypes, *The Mascot Opera: A Minuet,* clearly focuses more intently on American Indian mascots, which as C. David King argues, "matter to all of us, for only in coming to terms with mascots can we begin to come to terms with the legacies of colonization and start to unravel the racism that dehumanizes and divides all of us" (140). This issue obviously matters to LeAnne Howe, who, at the beginning of her documentary *Playing Pastime* about fast-pitch softball in southeastern Oklahoma Indian communities, asks the question, "How did American Indians become the mascots for a sport they may have invented?" By the end of the film, she declares that her work is devoted to undermining the hegemonic ideology of Indian vanishment.

In light of LeAnne Howe's writing on American Indian mascots, it is significant that the most public interview she has given—on *The Daily Show*—linked the subject of mascotting to southeastern Indian Removal. "Trail of Cheers" parodies the name "Trail of Tears," the latter one of the best-known historical events associated with Native Americans, certainly for non-Natives. However, it is not well known that there were multiple removals (or "Trails") in the Southeast and across the Americas. The satirical suggestion that ending race-based mascotting is somehow oppressive to the fans of those sports teams they represent underscores a skewed logic of colonialism—that resistance to hegemony is its own form of hegemony. In this case, those who support the continued use of American Indian mascots fear their own power will be removed, as if that is somehow equivalent to the unjust and illegal land grabs experienced by southeastern tribes in the nineteenth century.

Howe's coauthored play *Indian Radio Days* also satirizes Native American stereotypes and takes place in a bingo parlor in which a radio show is being recorded (Stanlake 21). The radio show narrates the histories of American Indigenous peoples from their origins to a time in the future when Indians are "[establishing] new homelands" (144) on Mars in order to escape a colonized planet. The play attempts to encapsulate the antagonisms that resulted from European and US settler colonialism by focusing on key historical moments. The most obvious and amusing critiques of manifest manners are the representations of commodified Indian images used as product advertisements such as "White Cloud Indian Toilet Paper" (113), "Red Woman Chewing Tobacco," and "Cheap Cherokee" (119). Though the ironic names of these products touch a nerve because they are so close to actual commodified Indian images, the advertisement for a series of films based on *Star Trek* presents a more painful historical parody with titles such as *Star Track: The Trail of Tears* and *Star Track II: The Wrath of Andrew Jackson.* The commercial even advertises a new television show spoofing *Star Trek: The Next Generation* including the characters "Captain Pick Hard, a descendent of French fur traders," and "Elijah, the animated wooden Indian who longs to be human" (144).[3]

Though all of the advertisements used in *Indian Radio Days* poke fun at the commodification of Native Americans, the references to the sale of tobacco are particularly poignant because they signify one of the earliest trading relationships between America's Indigenous peoples and Europeans. The wooden cigar-store Indian presented an immutable simulation, one that was useful only in its ability to support the production of capital. Howe has poked fun at cigar-store Indians in other ways, in *The Mascot Opera,* of course, and most notably in the author picture on the back of *Evidence of Red,* in which a smiling Howe salutes the camera, mimicking the pose of the wooden Indian behind her. I have previously argued that Howe's mocking salute undermines the idea that Native peoples have been "conquered" considering the way these statues denigrate the sovereign element of the earliest trade relationships between Indians and Europeans (Howe, "Choctawan" 211). Howe, the living, breathing Indian, stands beside the statue, clad in a loincloth of stars and stripes, advertising "Cigars Cubains." The T-shirt in the background of the picture reads, "Montreal," suggesting the location of the tourist shop in which Howe, the contemporary American Indian, stands in contrast to the mute historical caricature beside her. Stars and stripes juxtaposed with French language and Cuban cigars demonstrate the global quality of Indian-European trade relationships. This parody is funny and symbolic: the authentic Native person posing as the simulation.

Yet, in *Indian Radio Days,* Elijah's character—a play on *Next Generation*'s Lieutenant Data, a machine who desires to be a man—illustrates the dehumanizing quality of stereotypes and other such simulations. Elijah is based on the character of Lieutenant Data, an artificial life form who seeks to grow beyond his programming and become human. This parallel poignantly underscores constructed images of Native Americans by Europeans and the dehumanizing quality of wooden Indians designed to sell material goods. No longer are Natives active participants in the exchange of goods such as in the early transactions to which such statues allude; instead, their historically inaccurate images are frozen in time. The muscled, dramatically clad wooden Indian on the back of *Evidence of Red* seems more significant than the product being sold, exoticizing the potential transaction while eliminating the difficulty of cross-cultural exchange. Like Data, the wooden Indian can be fully controlled by humans; Data can even be turned off when he poses a danger to himself or others. Data's emotion chip and artificial consciousness provide him with something like humanity, causing viewers to consider the notion of what makes a human being. Unlike an artificial life form, the wooden Indian has no self-determination; his desire to become human will never be achieved. The implication is that, while such wooden Indians continue to be used as tools of advertising, Native peoples will be viewed as dangerous "others," acceptable only in mute and unchanging forms.

Indian Radio Days also represents simulated Indianness in the form of white people playing Indian. One of these is a character interviewed by the radio-show narrator named "Princess Wanna Buck," a New Age diva "well known by new pagans, old hippies and self-aware non-Indian advocates" (134), who offers a workshop called "Know Your Indian Inner Child" (135).[4] The interview demonstrates Princess Wanna Buck's charlatanism through her claims of being able to connect people to their "native prebirth self" (135), her fixation on money, and her affiliation with the "'FORE REAL' PEOPLE TRIBE" (135). This humorous depiction is reminiscent of an anecdote about a Euro-American man giving a workshop on "Plains Indian Spirituality" during the late 1990s, as shared by Shari Huhndorf in *Going Native: Indians in the American Cultural Imagination.* She explains that

> [such] New Age fascinations with Native America reveal a series of disturbing problems. In New Age practices, "Native" traditions generally reflect a heavily European ethos. In this particular case, the fixation on self-discovery and self-healing articulate the very Western ideologies of bourgeois individualism. At the same time, the teacher's selling of "Indian" knowledge and experiences manifests a profoundly capitalist mindset. (163)

Ultimately Huhndorf argues that such misrepresentation and exploitation of Native culture by the New Age movement "represents another, newer phase in European America's colonization of Native America" (163). Given the play's emphasis on colonialism and its concomitant conflicts, *Indian Radio Days*'s depiction of Princess Wanna Buck is making a similar argument.

The play lambasts another example of whites playing Indian with its portrayal of Kevin Costner at an imagined 1995 movie premiere to the sequel of *Dances with Wolves, Son of Dances with Wolves.* In the play, Costner is self-absorbed and self-congratulatory for his relationship with American Indians in the first film, exposing himself as another kind of flaky New Ager for having made the decision to do the sequel after communing with nature in Sedona, Arizona. Through this representation, *Indian Radio Days* critiques the reception of *Dances with Wolves* by the mainstream film industry as a movie that departs from early representations of American Indians as savages. As Huhndorf points out, *Dances with Wolves* "seems neither original nor a radical departure from conventional depictions of Native Americans. Like earlier Westerns, it tells a story that leaves stereotyped visions of Native life intact and the radically unequal relations between European Americans and Native Americans unquestioned" (3). The movie's Sioux characters inhabit the "noble" side of the Enlightenment binary, while the Pawnee characters fulfill its expectations of "savagery." Most significantly, the protagonist, Costner's character, the white man, assumes a Sioux identity and becomes the tribe's savior, affirming white superiority, a required underpinning of manifest manners.

Howe's first play, *Big PowWow,*[5] also coauthored with Roxy Gordon, explores the problem of whites "playing Indian" more deeply than *Indian Radio Days,* given the latter's formal structure as a series of vignettes. The three-act play presents a conflict between two women: Brooke, a former hippie and social worker, and Blossom, an impoverished, single Choctaw mother of three young children. Intervening in this conflict is Tullock-Chish-Ko, an ancient ancestor of Blossom's, "born a thousand years ago" (2).

In the first act, Blossom is presented as "chubby," with "a rotting front tooth," hair that is "long and dirty" (2), living in a trash-filled Oklahoma City apartment. Brooke wants "to help" (6), but rather than listening to Blossom's repeated requests to retrieve her children from one of their grandmother's homes, Brooke instead chastises Blossom's lifestyle. She wants Blossom to assimilate into mainstream American culture, claiming, "We're all just Americans now" (5). Blossom has internalized the racism of her surrounding society, claiming she is a "no good" Indian (4) and wants little to do with Brooke's desired changes, instead focusing on her children. Brooke believes she is "not just another white woman" (9) because she has studied some American Indian history and "got caught up with some AIM supporters" (10) during her hippie days. Not surprisingly, when Tullock-Chish-Ko appears, Brooke believes she is having "an Indian spiritual awakening" (13) while, ironically, Blossom translates the spirit's Choctaw words to her. Tullock-Chish-Ko operates much like Vizenor's "postindian warrior," using humor to resist the history of "manifest manners," yet his age suggests he might be better called a "preindian warrior." The spirit subverts Brooke's expectations of traditional American Indian culture by speaking in coded quotes from popular music, such as this display of nationalism: "This land is my land—from California to the New York Islands. From the Redwood Forests to the Gulf Stream waters. This land was made for me and Blossom" (18). He also criticizes Brooke's assumptions about how and why Blossom should change, arguing that she just wants the Choctaw woman to assimilate into dominant culture (16).

Most significantly, Tullock-Chish-Ko brings to light a fact Brooke had withheld from Blossom: that she had had three abortions. Thus, Brooke and Blossom are presented as twinned figures: one woman who denied motherhood because she had the means to make that choice and the other who accepted it because she had no other choice. Tullock-Chish-Ko also introduces one of the most significant themes of the play through his repeated claim that "Everythin is everythin" (24). Howe has discussed the idea of interrelatedness as a Choctaw epistemology in various works, linking it to the idea of *nukfokechi* in "The Story of America: A Tribalography." *Nukfokechi* means "brings forth knowledge and inspiration" (30), and the ancestor uses the term to contextualize a story about the importance of hawks for Choctaws, a story that "brings forth knowledge and inspires us to make the eventful leap that one thing leads to another" (32). Tullock-Chish-Ko also demonstrates in this act that Blossom is not so much of a mess as Brooke thinks because, according to his beliefs, the "[responsibility] of humans is to maintain life" (15), which Blossom clearly wants to uphold, given her decision to retrieve her children without Brooke's help.

Despite and as a result of Tullock-Chish-Ko's continued presence, both Brooke and Blossom have gone through extensive transformations in the second act of *Big PowWow*. The act is set in a fitness club where

Blossom obsessively works out in "color-coordinated tights and exercise clothes designed by Jane Fonda sportswear," and Brooke watches her, now dressed in "a tasteful designer buckskin skirt and blouse," wearing a "leather headband," "bone jewelry," and "buckskin boots" (32). It seems that Blossom has taken Brooke's act 1 assimilationist advice to an extreme, telling the social worker, "I don't care about my ancestors. I'm trying to get to know *your* ancestors" (34). Brooke, who has been having encounters with Tullock-Chish-Ko for several months (presumably the reason for her appropriative changes), declares, "I fucked her up. I can't talk to her now about spiritual things. I have committed the same crime my entire race has committed" (35).

At this point in the action, Tullock-Chish-Ko appears stage left, interjecting occasional comments. As in the play's first act, the spirit's presence seems to amplify the tension between the two women. Blossom appears no longer concerned about her children; rather she is interested in her appearance and sexual conquests. Their conversation devolves when Brooke once again tries to define authentic Indianness:

> Brooke: You're a real Indian, you cannot lose the old ways.
>
> Blossom: *(Shocked. Long pause)* There aren't any real Indians, Brooke.

This scene speaks to Taylor's discussion of the ways in which studies of authenticity by Romine (the South) and Paul Chaat Smith (American Indians) intersect: "Substituting what appears to be a 'real' . . . version of Indian identity becomes a crucial mechanism for maintaining cultural distinction in a world that equates indigeneity with anachronistic pageantry" (20). In the second act of *Big PowWow,* Blossom rejects the "anachronistic pageantry" that Brooke has now adopted. Their tense exchanges continue until Brooke calls Blossom a "cheap Indian bitch" (43), and the women begin screaming at each other, ending the act.

The final act of *Big PowWow* resolves the conflict between the Choctaw and Euro-American woman by foregrounding Choctaw cultural practices and beliefs. This not only undoes Blossom's assimilationism, but it also converts Brooke from her position as consumer of faux American Indianness to practitioner of Choctaw religion. The act takes place in Tullock-Chish-Ko's original time and in the Choctaw homelands at the *Nanih Waiya.* Brooke, who has fantasized that she is in love with the spirit, is shocked by what she sees and by the expected gender roles of the era. Tullock-Chish-Ko explains that he was "tired of the way you two was actin'. I brought you here to show you what you was talkin' about" (45), which he goes on to say is "bein' NDN." Brooke gets another lesson in "bein' NDN" when she asks about why the Choctaws built mounds, and the spirit declares that "[they] get you closer to the sky" (50). Brooke assumes that being in the sky equates to being close to a Christian Heaven, but Tullock-Chish-Ko replies in the negative, explaining that he wants to "be with the hawks" (51). Again, Brooke's stereotypical assumptions about Native cultural practices are subverted when she assumes that he means "eagles," and he confirms that he means "hawks" (51). In her essay, "Embodied Tribalography: First Installment," Howe explains that "[red-tailed] hawks embody special meanings for southeastern Natives, especially Choctaws. The red-tailed hawk is a solar bird, one of power and strength, and the tail feathers are bright red in sunlight. Red signifies lifeblood and is sometimes a powerful metaphor for war" (180).

Blossom's character again transforms significantly in act 3. Though she had been running from her Choctaw identity, she slowly grows accustomed to the ancient world in which she has been thrust. Eventually she begins drinking with Tullock-Chish-Ko, and an intimacy develops that enrages Brooke until the three engage in a ménage à trois. Afterwards, the spirit begins a ritual act that upsets both Brooke's and Blossom's expectations about indigeneity. Tullock-Chish-Ko dons the "claw-like fingernails" of a traditional bone picker,[6] erotically handling and cleaning the corpse of one of his friends. Though Brooke is fascinated by the ceremony, Blossom is distraught because seeing the bone-picking unveils her own internalized colonialism and its affiliated cultural loathing. She confesses, "People are always putting us down, making fun of us. I didn't want it to be like this. I didn't want them to be right. I didn't want us to be like animals" (58). As Blossom has a breakdown, Brooke approaches Tullock-Chish-Ko to ascertain the ceremony's meaning. Again, the spirit reiterates, "Everythin' is everythin'" (60). When Brooke presses for an explanation, he explains that there is a connection between humans and animals and ancestors, and that as a bone-picker, "[he picks] away at the present to get to the past" (60). Bone picking, then, becomes a symbol for getting "into life. The heart of the matter" (62). In the case of Blossom, she needs access to her cultural past in order to improve her present. Tullock-Chish-Ko is giving her an alternative to assimilation. Yet, Blossom rejects his offer because she is appalled by the ceremony, telling him, "You're not my ancestor and I am not a part of you. We bury our dead" (62). Despite his attempts to make her understand, she says, "You're disgusting. I hate you. I won't be like you" (63). To which he responds, "No, you're disgusting. I hate you. I won't be like you. You don't know what love is. We pick bones because we love. We don't give our relatives to strangers who defile their bodies, tryin' to make them look alive like yesterday's meat" (63). The scene takes an even more visceral and erotic turn when Tullock-Chish-Ko offers part of the corpse for Blossom to smell, claiming, "To smell death is to smell life" (63). The play ends with all three characters smearing rotted corpse flesh on their bodies and chanting "Love is, life is, death is, love is, life is, death is, life is, love is, death is" (64). This chant, a variation on "everythin' is everythin'" speaks to the cyclic nature of life in the same way as Koi Chitto's ejaculation on Shakbatina's corpse during her bone-picking in *Shell Shaker.*

As is often the case in an author's earliest work, *Big PowWow* lacks some of the more sophisticated nuances of Howe's later writing, yet within the play lie the seeds of her future production. Obviously, her continued work as a playwright has been informed by this first piece, as well as the sexualized bone-picking scenes that appear in her short story "Danse d'Amour, Danse de Mort" and her novel *Shell Shaker.* What might be most telling about this work within Howe's oeuvre, however, is the presence of the ancestor spirit come to heal the contemporary Choctaw woman. We see this kind of *alikchi* figure in both *Shell Shaker* and in *Miko Kings.* Considering *Big PowWow* within the larger issue of simulated Indianness, we have a white woman and a Choctaw woman debating questions of authenticity. Unlike the other white characters who "play Indian" in Howe's works, Brooke is given a chance to try to understand Choctaw culture through a central ritual; her response is to embrace what Monika Siebert has termed "repugnant aboriginality" (1). Even more notably, Blossom accepts a history she had reviled, not because it's something that she has been told she should do; rather, because she finally understands a central tenet of Choctaw cosmology: interconnectedness.

In Howe's novel *Shell Shaker,* Choctaw people play Indian for various ends. One example is Isaac Billy, who successfully pretends to be an inarticulate "John Wayne Indian" (54) in order to avoid being questioned by reporters about his niece's arrest. This humorous scene shows Billy's wily tricksterism, as he exploits non-Native stereotypes of Indians for his own self-interest. Isaac Billy is, in fact, a complex figure who, as a teenager, was the lover of a much older Delores Love, and who could both "[doctor] horses" and sing "ancient warrior songs" (167).

Representations of simulated Indianness in the novel offer a more multifaceted investigation of the emotional challenges of assimilation and an individual's attempts to resist it through Delores's character. Delores and her sister, Dovie, had a youthful career as Hollywood actresses billed as the "Love Maidens of the Five Civilized Tribes," participating in a process that Indigenous film theorist Michelle Raheja has termed "redfacing" (xii). Their niece, Auda, reflects on their silver-screen personae: "How their long black hair must have whipped in the wind as they rode bareback on Paint ponies, parading their history in skimpy loincloths" (117). This simulation of a sexualized Native American womanhood can be traced back to early colonial writings in which an Edenic American continent "constituted a gendered territory of mystery that required—and even desired—exposure, penetration, and possession by European men" (Householder 14). Yet, as Raheja notes, such roles for American Indian actors provided economic, social, and political opportunities not available within the confines of reservations, disempowered spaces of a larger US colonial project (13). Delores remembers her acting career as a period in which she adored European colognes and actors in cafés, a time when she was a "double-faced woman" (149). This description speaks to the ambivalence of dual identities experienced by people of color within colonized societies as theorized by W. E. B. DuBois,[7] and taken up by contemporary scholars of postcolonial theory.[8] Raheja propels this argument further, claiming,

> For Native Americans the twentieth-century "problem of the color-line" would be further complicated by the fact that the "amused contempt and pity" focused on Native Americans is coded as always already in the past. Native American actors and directors were forced to examine themselves through the eyes of others, but this necessitated a looking backward through the mists of history because Indigenous peoples had been written out of the present and the future of the United States through various forms of discursive genocide. Thus they are ascribed the value of absence

> through assimilation and disappearance and the value of excess through the compulsion in Hollywood media to return continually to the scene of Indian-white contact. (15)

Thus, Delores and Dovie are assigned sexualized roles romanticizing the pre-Removal era of southeastern Natives, oddly accentuated with the Plains Indian costumes monolithically dispensed by Hollywood for Native actors. Delores acknowledges that becoming an actress was the result of running away from the boarding school that alienated her from her cultural traditions and, ultimately, from her family (149). While she is still reeling from the death of a young Ponca girl at school, she begins to menstruate for the first time. Having to learn about this significant moment of early womanhood from a stranger shames her, and she declares that she "doesn't want to be Indian anymore" (154). What Delores doesn't understand as a girl is her conception of being Indian is intertwined with the cultural breakage forced by Indian boarding schools and other forms of colonial violence. Even though she knows her mother could have healed the Ponca girl, this knowledge does not overcome her internalized colonialism. As an adult, when her own mother is dying, Delores cannot maintain an assimilated identity; thus, she and her sister abandon their Hollywood lifestyle, returning to Oklahoma to pursue vocations that serve the Choctaw community. When Delores Love learns how to conduct the pole-pulling ceremony and traditional funeral songs from Nowatima, she feels as if it "is the only useful thing she's ever done" (146). In fact, she is the novel's *Imataha Chitto,* or greatest giver, who will unite the tribe, both in the novel's present and past time; rejection of her vocation simulating Indianness is a critical step in her evolution toward this role, another form of "postindian warrior."

Miko Kings also depicts numerous examples of simulated Indianness specific to the turn of the twentieth century, during the period just before the abolishment of Indian Territory and the establishment of Oklahoma statehood. Miko Kings team owner Henri Day's burgeoning romantic feelings toward Miss Bennett, a young white woman from St. Louis, are quickly tempered when he learns that she has come to visit family and "see wild Indians in tipis" (114). When he turns their conversation toward the 1904 World's Fair, sharing his enthusiasm for the "new inventions" like the Wright Brothers' "contraption" (114), he is once again disappointed to hear that her favorite exhibition was

Geronimo, who was selling pictures of himself and arrowheads he had made. In the era just after the Indian Wars, Geronimo's imprisonment was a coup for the US government, or as Day describes, "a living war trophy for the U.S. Cavalry" (115). Geronimo's position as an object of display reinforced beliefs of Euro-American superiority and created a less fearsome simulation of the former war leader. The *Miko Kings* scene ends with Day paying for purchases with a newly minted penny which, to his consternation, displays "an Indian in a headdress" (116). These exchanges are synecdochical of the issue for Native Americans in a culture of "manifest manners": how can Indigenous peoples be recognized as humans while being constantly surrounded and bombarded by stereotypical projections of themselves invented by dominant culture?

In *Miko Kings,* Howe portrays a similar ambivalence toward Hollywood representations of Native Americans as in *Shell Shaker,* when Hope Little Leader decides to quit his acting role in the film *His Last Game,* in which he is forced to wear a wig "to make him look traditional" but which is woven "like a girl's braids" (7). The film, which is to depict two rival teams, one of which is the Choctaw Indians, is supported by Henri Day, who is interested in the profits it may yield. Predictably, Hope is "made up to look like an aging, stoic plains warrior" (7) and another teammate wears a Plains-style headdress and leather-fringed war shirt. Though Hope quits the film, deciding "[It's] bad luck to play make-believe" (10), the director convinces him to return. This decision foreshadows what is to come in the novel: Hope's betrayal of his team and the loss of his gifted pitching hands. The editors of *Seeing Red: Hollywood's Pixeled Skins* explain how *His Last Game,* the first silent movie about baseball, was filmed in 1909 and "was supposedly set in 'Indian Territory,' with a Choctaw 'Noble Savage' dressed in braids and buckskins" (xiv). Howe's decision to represent the filming of the movie upsets the simulations of Indians present in the film by fleshing out the actors' individual personalities, conflicts, and decisions.

A more painful example of Native people "playing Indian" is depicted in the documentary *Indian Country Diaries: Spiral of Fire,* written and narrated by Howe, in which she visits Cherokee, North Carolina, in order to learn something of the culture of her father, a man she never knew. The initial scenes of Howe taking in the touristy streets of Cherokee highlight her revulsion at what she describes as a "tourist spectacle."

She contrasts the "visual paradise of Great Smoky Mountain National Park" with the "stoic wooden Indians, cheesy dreamcatchers on sale in every store, Pocahontas dolls—the worst Hollywood stereotypes—all marketed by Cherokees themselves." The complexities of Indians playing Indian are revealed when she interviews Chief Henry, the elderly Eastern Band of Cherokee man who dresses in a feather headdress and charges tourists to be photographed with him. She asks him, "How come you haven't thought of dressing up like a Cherokee?" He explains that Hollywood movies created expectations about the way that Native people should look and live, and he learned to "capitalize on what they were showing the American people on movies." He also describes how much more lucrative and appealing this occupation was than his other options in the mountains of Southern Appalachia, and is certainly better than his first job, "carrying two five gallon cans of diesel fuel to a bulldozer building the Blue Ridge Parkway." As Taylor has noted, "In a depressed Appalachian countryside where travel and tourism have replaced logging and hunting as primary forms of subsistence, the Cherokees adapt to the changes and play the role that will most help them 'survive'" (130). Despite LeAnne Howe's distaste for the many examples of the tribe exploiting American Indian stereotypes for profit in the town, she learns that most of the tourists believe that the man in the feathered headdress "is the only Indian [they have] seen" (*Indian Country Diaries*).

Chief Henry's testimony suggests a seemingly willful resistance by non-Natives to acknowledge Indigenous presence even when they are standing in the midst of it; Philip Deloria's thoughts on Native American participation in such masquerades provides a helpful context: "It would be folly to imagine that white Americans blissfully used Indianness to tangle with their ideological dilemmas while native people stood idly by, exerting no influence over the resulting Indian images. Throughout the long history of Indian play, native people have been present at the margins, insinuating their way into Euro-American discourse, often attempting to nudge notions of Indianness in directions they found useful" (*Playing Indian* 8).[9] Chief Henry lives in a doubly marginalized southern cultural space: Appalachian Native America. His vocation does not make a political statement about American Indian cultural identity; rather, it makes a political statement about a disparity of economic opportunity. Raheja's claim about filmic "redfacing" could also be considered in this case, the Cherokee man's masquerade providing "a means of protection as a kind of . . . visual prophylactic that keeps Native American cultural and spiritual practices somewhat sacrosanct, or at least hidden from the white tourist gaze" (22).

Howe's story "Carlos Castaneda Lives in Romania" in her 2013 memoir/travelogue, *Choctalking on Other Realities,* shows the author's ability to engage in the conversation about simulated Indianness with humor, grace, and wisdom. Though the story's plot follows her and her husband's 1998 trip to Romania to speak at a seminar in Resita, its theme continuously cycles around how Native American cultural authenticity is prescribed to Howe by the Europeans she encounters. Dean Rader's observation about another piece in the collection is also true of this story: "[Howe] trades easy antagonism for a kind of wry bemusement" ("Foreword" iii).

Throughout the narrative, there are numerous examples of Europeans who are purportedly interested in Native American culture, yet what has sparked this interest is reading the questionable anthropological writings of Carlos Castaneda. The first such encounter occurs in Vienna's Demel Shop in which Howe and her husband, Jim Wilson, have stopped to enjoy the chocolatier's confections. When their waiter learns that Howe is an American Indian, he immediately launches into his knowledge of Castaneda's work, making broad assumptions about Native culture and shamanism. Wilson quickly curtails the conversation so that, as he puts it, they would not be there "all day debating Carlos Castaneda and his books" ("Carlos Castaneda Lives" 128). This scene sets up the story in significant ways. There will, of course, be many more moments depicted in which Europeans assume they know something about Native Americans from what anthropologist Richard Price has called Castaneda's "forgeries" (139), and in each of these moments, Howe's reticence to seriously discuss Castaneda is quickly dismissed by the Europeans who have taken his stories of Yaqui shamanism to heart. This scene is also important for another reason: chocolate. As Howe notes, even though "tourists around the world believe chocolate is *Old World*" (127), it is indigenous to the Americas. She underscores this point with an anecdote about how Moctezuma and Cortes drank "a local concoction, hot chocolate mixed with vanilla" (127).[10]

Howe brings "indigenous gifts" (126) to share with those she meets along her journey, suggesting her own position of diplomacy. This role places Howe in a long line of American Indians who "were engaged in diplomacy from the moment of First Contact" (Weaver, *The Red Atlantic* 136). O'Brien notes that, for southeastern Natives in particular, gift exchange was an important element of formalized diplomatic practice since at least the Mississippian era (ca. 1100–ca. 1600) through the French colonial era ("Protecting Trade" 104). Howe continues the tradition, bearing chocolates: "individually wrapped . . . cowboy boots, peanut-cluster cowpatties, and the ever-popular Pocahontas-on-a-stick" ("Carlos Castaneda Lives" 127) made by Cherokee chocolatier Edna Sixkiller in Ada, Oklahoma. The Pocahontas-on-a-stick is doubly significant, given the global Disneyization of Matoaka, the Indian woman of the Powhatan confederacy who became Lady Rebecca Rolfe. Weaver details the ways in which Lady Rebecca's engagement with English culture, including at the court of James I, aligned with Chief Powhatan's diplomatic aims (*The Red Atlantic* 144–50).

Despite Howe's skepticism about Castaneda's writings, one of the best-known topics he describes, nagualism, or shape shifting, occurs upon her arrival in Romania. She describes the space in which the customs officials wait at "Checkpoint Charlie" because it "feels like a highly charged border crossing in which anything can happen" ("Carlos Castaneda Lives" 132). What happens is a gender-bending scene shift to *Casablanca,* Howe playing the role of Rick Blaine, her husband playing Ilsa Lund, and the Czech officials opposing them as Captain Renault and Major Strasser. The information exchanged in the scene intertwines the Hollywood film with Howe's own life, such as her birth "in a home for unwed Indian women" (133). The tension escalates until of one the Czech officials decries Castaneda's writings about nagualism, at which point Howe breaks the illusion, declaring, "My name is LeAnne Howe. . . . I am not Humphrey Bogart" (137). As Howe and her husband enter Romania, she thinks they have "passed a kind of cosmic test of the non-ordinary variety" (137). Yet, the "non-ordinary" nature of this story has been evident from the first paragraph, in which Howe's Toyota RAV4 was run off the road in Iowa by a "fierce gust of floral winds" (125). Howe sees the wind as a harbinger, having been told that "cosmic forces such as a violent invisible wind often announce great change" (125). This passage and the subsequent strange journey upon which Howe and her husband embark bear a resemblance to another classic Hollywood film in which a young woman is propelled by a strong wind to a faraway place. Ken McCullough (62–63) notes a similar allusion to the *Wizard of Oz* in *Shell Shaker* when Delores is "taken up into a whirlwind" (160) and flies over *Nanih Waiya,* describing it as "an emerald city" (159).

Over the course of the story, Howe's exchanges with Romanians about Castaneda's writings will evolve until the moment when she meets the "wizard" himself. Her first exchange with a fellow seminar speaker, Vlad, a physicist, turns to Castaneda after Howe mentions that she has brought books by American Indian authors to leave at the Center for Complexity Studies, which is hosting the event. Though Howe tries to explain the controversies surrounding Castaneda and his supposed informant, Don Juan, Vlad becomes insistent, arguing that "life and death and multiple realms of Otherness exist simultaneously" ("Carlos Castaneda Lives" 139) and that Howe should understand these ideas as a tribal person. He wants her to agree that her teachings are like those of Don Juan, and though she disagrees, she instead asks him about his own research, which, not surprisingly, concerns the possibilities of shape shifting.

Howe begins to understand the appeal of Castaneda's writings after her lecture, when she is asked extensive questions about Indigenous American survival and considers the legacy of communism, particularly Romania's impoverishment. She describes her accommodations at the seminar, sleeping under piles of her clothes for warmth, since there were no blankets on the beds, and breakfasting on green peppers and radishes with "fresh bread and hot tea" that "made it a feast" (142). She also reiterates how travel teaches us "more about ourselves than . . . the Other" (142). Howe's ruminations on Romania and travel affect her interactions with the many people who try to engage her in conversations about Carlos Castaneda and Yaqui shamanism. In a humorous series of encounters labeled by number (34, 43, 52, 61, and 70), she shares snippets of conversation which often begin with questions about her own Native authenticity, include comments about Castaneda, and end with her diplomatically offering an Indigenous American gift (the chocolates she brought from Oklahoma) made by "real Cherokees" (142). In encounter 52, however, the tone of the exchange evolves when Howe refers to Castaneda's book as a "tribalography" (143).[11] Encounter 61 hearkens back to the lessons of *Big PowWow*'s Tullock-Chish-Ko when Howe's response to a Don Juan reference is "Everything is everything?" (143). Howe's final reply in encounter 70 is a quote by her *Big PowWow* and *Indian Radio Days* coauthor, Roxy Gordon: "Everything exists and everything will happen and everything is alive and everything is planned and everything is a mystery, and everything is dangerous, and everything is a mirage, and everything touches everything, and everything is everything, and everything is very, very strange" (143).[12] These rejoinders suggest that Howe herself is finding connections between Choctaw beliefs and the ways the Romanians she meets are interpreting Castaneda for their own spiritual needs.

If Howe is in any way writing herself as a Dorothy figure into her travelogue of Romania, then it is inevitable that she will meet the man behind the illusions she has encountered. Castaneda appears in the final scene to talk about Howe's "home." He tells her that she "can't outrun [her] birth mother's story" (144) which was revealed during her *Casablanca* shape shifting. Castaneda helps Howe view the actions of her birth mother from a new perspective:

> She didn't abandon you when you were born, she died when you were born. Imagine, she had to walk out of that home for unwed Indian women as Other. Excluded. Different and indifferent. Who do you think bequeathed you the strength to become the Other, a mouth with fingers that will write the stories of Grandmother of Birds, a fierce warrior, baseball players, dying soldiers, and even Humphrey Bogart? (144)

Castaneda's words are a balm for her earlier anger, when she claimed her birth mother "didn't bother to check whether I was male or female. Just walked out on me pretending I never happened" (133). What Howe learns from Castaneda's teaching is that her birth mother gave her the ability to shape shift, to see through the eyes of Others, and to write their stories.

"Carlos Castaneda Lives in Romania" is much less about Carlos Castaneda and even the obsession for his work Howe encounters there than it is about a moment of understanding one of the most central skills of being an artist, embodiment,[13] and how it can reveal previously inaccessible realms. From a biographical perspective, the final scene between Castaneda and Howe suggests a sea change in her own understanding of her birth. This may not be so clear when reading *Choctalking on Other Realities* from beginning to end because the collection's prologue, "My Mothers, My Uncles, Myself," describes Howe's birth and the circumstances surrounding it more sympathetically and in much more detail than "Carlos Castaneda Lives in Romania." Yet, the fictional name of the boarding house in which Howe was born, "Auntie Mm's" (1), binds the prologue to the *Wizard of Oz* allusions of Howe's Romanian journey, underscoring the theme of finding one's home, regardless if that home is physical, intellectual, or spiritual.

Whether they are American Indian college students, Choctaw elders, or the author herself, LeAnne Howe's representations of postindian warriors resist the ideologies of manifest manners, including simulated Indianness, creating a body of work in which Native peoples can see themselves reflected honestly and respectfully. In these works, Choctaw culture travels from *Nanih Waiya* to Oklahoma City to Hollywood and back again, demonstrating an Interstate South as a nexus of relationships to place with a potential for ideological and other resistances. Not only do Native and Interstate Souths overlap, "Carlos Castaneda Lives in Romania" moves Howe's work onto a global stage in which tribalography travels to Eastern Europe, after taking a short detour through Castaneda's imagined Yaqui country.

CHAPTER FOUR

Choctalking Global (Dis)Connections

> Once, in a story, I wrote that Indians are everywhere.
> Goddamn right.
> —SIMON ORTIZ, "Travels in the South"

As LeAnne Howe's stories, poems, plays, and critical writings operate within Native and Interstate South frameworks, their characters and themes (and the author herself) circulate on the global stage. In *Grounded Globalism: How the U.S. South Embraces the World,* James Peacock defines the US southern global experience as one that is grounded in a "place-based context" (257). He argues that "grounded globalism summarizes an anchoring and embodiment of a global process" and that "the South epitomizes that grounding" partly because it "[retains] a regional identity and also [defines] its own global identity" (258). Peacock's concerns intersect with those of Chadwick Allen, whose study *Trans-Indigenous: Methodologies for Global Native Literary Studies* describes the reticence of Indigenous intellectuals to accept "global comparative frameworks for Indigenous studies" (xiii) particularly in light of the American Indian literary nationalism movement. Allen accurately describes the anxiety: "The local, having fully won a place at the academic table, becomes engulfed (once again) in the name of the global" (xiii). Yet, Allen himself seeks to "develop a version of Indigenous literary studies that locates itself firmly in the specificity of the Indigenous local while remaining always cognizant of the complexity of the relevant Indigenous global" (xix). Howe thinks of her own work similarly, describing *Shell Shaker*'s characters Redford McAlester, Tema Billy, and Adair Billy in her essay in *Reasoning Together*: "All have traveled widely, traded information, adopted new tools, and then returned home with new ideas that are both dynamic and destructive. They are international and intertribal, reflecting a larger worldview that would have been as important in the past as it is in the present" (330).

Thus far, my analysis of Howe's body of work has been limited to geographical boundaries established by settler colonialism in the United States. To investigate her work globally, it is important to "[remain] always cognizant of the complexity of the relevant Indigenous global," as Allen notes above. Yet, such a study must be "grounded" in local contexts, Choctaw homescapes. Consequentially, while considering LeAnne Howe as a writer of the Global South, I will cycle back to sites in Mississippi and Oklahoma and cycle beyond US borders to Japan, Israel, Jordan, and even outer space.

In *Indigenous Peoples and Globalization: Resistance and Revitalization,* Hall and Fenelon describe globalization as "economic, political, and cultural patterns that are involved in a close and complex process of interaction" (2–3). Their central claim is that Indigenous peoples have resisted and survived these complicated global processes for centuries[1] and continue to do so: "In forming alliances with Greens and globalization-spawned movements, indigenous peoples are doing what they have been doing for millennia: adapting, adjusting, and adopting to changing circumstances to maintain their sovereignty" (146). Though globalization can be traced back centuries, the authors make a clear distinction between capitalism in a world economy and a global economy, arguing that in the latter, transnational production, exchange, and consumption replace state-to-state relationships (2–3). LeAnne Howe's Choctalking texts demonstrate the ways that globalization connects and disconnects cultures economically, politically, and culturally.

Shell Shaker represents both the economic and political ramifications of globalization, particularly in its depiction of a casino capitalism that ultimately affects Choctaw sovereignty. Legal scholar Angela R. Riley discusses the relationship between globalization and sovereignty, arguing that the former "promises (or threatens) to connect us across time, space, and borders . . . minimizing the nation-state, and concomitantly, its relevance" (1057). Gore Battiste, Auda Billy's attorney in *Shell Shaker,* makes a similar argument when he tells his client that she has been fighting for the sovereignty of her people by resisting Redford (Red) McAlester's administration, corrupted by his dealings with the Mafia. He asserts, "It was only a matter of time until international gangs, or the corporate Mafia, found their way onto Indian land by loaning start-up money for casinos. These are the new Indians wars . . ." (114).

Like his historical counterpart, Red Shoe,[2] Red McAlester engages in a dangerous game of siding with whichever faction benefits him at the time. He claims that he is working on behalf of the Choctaw peoples, but his actions suggest that his motivations are much more selfish. When Auda first meets Red, he seems genuinely concerned with the welfare of the Choctaws, and their relationship blooms into what appears to be an ideal romantic and business partnership. What comes between them is the construction of the Casino of the Sun, the profits from which Red used to launder money for the Genovese crime family (90–91).

Despite *Shell Shaker*'s negative depiction of the Choctaw casino, Jessica Cattelino's study of the impact of gaming on the Florida Seminoles suggests that Indian gaming can have positive financial impacts for tribes, considering the fungibility of money within a model of casino capitalism. Because money is simply exchanged for money, "gambling does not fit into a model of production, distribution, and consumption" (191). Cattelino argues that, given money's fungibility (that is, units may be interchanged without altering their purpose), "revenues from casinos can be used for educational scholarships or economic development, and individual family income can originate from either casino dividends or wages, without any necessary effect on the social meaning or function of that money" (191). The use of Indian gaming profits are limited by the 1988 Indian Gaming Regulatory Act, which requires revenues to be spent on programs that benefit the welfare or economy of the tribe, philanthropic donations, or funding local government organizations outside of the tribe (194). Red McAlester's use of casino revenues to launder money for the mob and the payoffs he receives for his services not only violate the Indian Gaming Regulatory Act, but they also threaten the Choctaw people's sovereignty through this criminal alliance.

However, like Red Shoe, Chief McAlester has fickle loyalties. His crony, Carl Tonica, remembers how when Red "felt the Italians squeezing him, he switched alliances to the Irish" (139). From a historical perspective, this is a fitting partnership. The Choctaws and Irish were both ravaged by English colonialism, and their relationship was strengthened with a monetary gift by the Choctaws to the Irish in 1847 to alleviate the suffering of the potato famine.[3] This gift was twice commemorated in the early 1990s, first in Ireland where Choctaw dignitaries were invited to an annual walk in memory of a starvation march during the Famine in County Mayo. That year, the walk was dubbed the "Trail of Tears" in honor of the guests. Two years later, a group of Irish citizens came to the United States and walked the five hundred miles from Oklahoma to Mississippi; later that year, Irish President Mary Robinson was named an honorary Choctaw Chief (O'Donnell).[4] Not only does Red's shifting alliance reflect the Choctaw-Irish connection, but so does the theme song of Delores and Dovie Love's acting days, "Arrah Wanna," an early twentieth-century Tin Pan Alley production in which an Indian maid is courted by an Irishman. Moloney argues that the song's love affair points to the extent of Irish marginalization in the United States (395).

Red's alliance with the Irish, however, is not merely one of cross-cultural good fellowship. It is, in fact, an act of vengeance, explained by Divine Sarah: "McAlester stole millions from the Mafia and gave it to the Irish Republican Army to kill Englishmen for crimes they committed against the Choctaw two hundred and fifty years ago" (141). Though Red's motivation appears as if it might be based in concern for his people's welfare, the conversation coma-bound Auda has with his spirit at novel's end suggests otherwise. First, Red tells Auda he wants her to use the nine million dollars he stole from the mob to buy the *Nanih Waiya* from the state of Mississippi.[5] Speaking in the voice of both Red Shoes and Red McAlester, he makes another attempt to justify his illegitimate dealings: "It was my dream to have all the advantages the foreigners brought into our nations without surrendering to their rules. It was the same with the casino business. . . . Whether it was Bienville and the *Filanchi,* or the D'Amato brothers and the Italians, it's just the trappings of time that have changed for the Choctaws" (200).

Red's desire for foreigners' material goods suggests his own internalized colonialism, a point which Adair discusses earlier in the novel when she says, "the English and the French taught the Indians to love foreign things above all else" (162). To prize such objects over one's own land or culture is to denigrate oneself and one's people. Thus, Red is buried with not only the nine million dollars but also with other material goods he had greedily sought such as his clothes and computer (194). Howe has commented on the practice of burying elaborate material items in graves, arguing that the desire to hoard such goods is "selfish" and that archaeologists have misread the meanings of such burial mounds ("Choctawan" 214). Instead, burying Red's prized possessions with him will ensure that no one else will contract his diseases of evil and greed (*Shell Shaker* 194).

Another problem with Red's approach to leadership of the Oklahoma Choctaws concerns the question of "good governance." Riley argues for the necessity of "cultural matching" or a reflection of "a tribal community's ideas regarding the proper use and scope of authority" (1087) in its governing bodies. This is clearly not the case under Red McAlester's tenure as chief, considering that, when Susan Billy challenged his dealings with the Italians at a tribal council meeting, he barred public discussion at such meetings and decided to conduct all future tribal business within the confines of his own offices (58). Riley also asserts that, even though Indian nations have a right to determine tribal membership, the banishment of tribal members simply for voicing dissent is highly problematic; an example of this is the "de-tribing" of the Billy family (57). Granted this occurs after Red McAlester has been shot to death, but since only Auda and Susan have been implicated in the crime at that point, the "de-tribing" of Isaac and other family members seems excessive, at the very least. For Red, his administration, and his criminal business partners, the Billys represent a powerful link to Choctaw history, and they threaten a government more concerned with pleasing "foreigners" than with taking care of the tribe.

One more questionable aspect of McAlester's leadership, a result of his corruption by outside influences, is his decision to build the Casino of the Sun in the first place. As Cattelino points out, one criticism aimed at tribes by non-Indians is that gaming leads to cultural inauthenticity (191). This kind of critique also seems to be leveled at Red McAlester's administration from within the tribe when the spirit of Auda's ancestor, Shakbatina, says, "*I did not come back here to be Grandmother to a tribe of entertainers at the Casino of the Sun*" (*Shell Shaker* 141). The very name of the casino suggests the extent to which McAlester is willing to sell his out his culture for the sake of financial gain. Carson describes the importance of the sun within Choctaw spiritual beliefs:

> The sun god had chosen the Choctaws as his people and the land around the mound [*Nanih Waiya*] as their world, and so long as they followed his law, they would remain on the bright path to a righteous life. Should they

> stray from the path, however, and follow the dark one, the monsters who haunted the boundaries of their world would invade their land, bringing destruction and despair. (*Searching* 8)

The name of the casino suggests a reverence for the sun god; in fact, McAlester has brought "destruction and despair" on his people, presumably from following the wrong path, one of greed and selfishness, ultimately letting monsters invade the Choctaws' lands in the form of a criminal gang looking to profit from the tribe's financial success.

Howe's play *Indian Radio Days* depicts a far different attitude toward Indian gaming, set in the distant future, in an age beyond globalization, envisioning a kind of intra–solar-system casino capitalism. In this iteration, Indian gaming has been lucrative enough to finance an *Indians in Space* project. Harvey Little Green Man, a biotechnician for the off-world project, is asked how Native peoples will deal with a shipload of Earth pioneers headed for their new homelands on Mars: "We kept telling the OTHERS to stop their polluting ways or Mother Earth would be uninhabitable. Now, looks like we're gonna have to build another chain of high stakes bingo palaces and casinos so we can get away from those folks again" (145). In this example, gaming has provided the financial means to escape a history of colonialism and oppression on Earth and provide Native peoples an opportunity to start fresh without the influence of the "OTHERS," presumably Western culture. Interestingly, the image of earth's citizens fleeing a polluted planet toward a colony created by American Indians suggests a dependency on the latter by the former. Both this and the classification of non-Indians as "OTHERS," subverts the hegemonic discourses of Indian-white relations in the Americas.

Howe's works also critique the commodification and appropriation of Native Americans and their cultures within the context of globalization. Such commodification and appropriation of Native cultures as a result of globalization are depicted in the short drama *The Unknown Women*[6] in Howe's collection *Evidence of Red.* This one-act play features four female characters: First Character (the Spirit, Ohoyo Chish-Ba Osh), the Unknown Woman (Corn Woman), Red Woman, and Choctaw Woman. Each woman has a monologue, at times interacting silently with each other through stage directions, and finally coming together at the end, urging the audience to tell stories in order to "create people and author tribes" (20). The Unknown Woman's monologue includes the story of how corn came to the Choctaws and its sacred relationship to earth and sun. The personification of corn (in the being Corn Woman) underscores the violence of colonialism through an Old World God obsessed with the "metal and machinery" of technology (13). In his presence and through the acts of his followers, a growth process that was once so sensual that each kernel of corn "represents an orgasm" (13) ultimately deforms her. She says, "Sometimes I am tortured with acids that swell my body beyond grace. Eventually, the son of God sends Agronomists disguised as Angels to study me. They take field trips and write exhaustive notes about their experiences with corn. I am no longer beautiful, nor represented as food for thought" (14). Instead, she becomes commodified, a product of global capitalism, exported to Romania to be boiled with potatoes, to Egypt to be eaten as a breakfast cereal, and to Turkey, a country that claims that it originated the vegetable (12).

Beyond the economic and political ramifications are the cultural implications—connections and disconnections—posed by globalization in the body of Howe's work. Howe's neologism "Choctalking" is related to a particularly Choctaw point of view, the term first manifesting in a short story in *Evidence of Red,* "Choctalking on Other Realities." Given the original story's subject matter and the fact that Howe also titled her globetrotting memoir/travelogue *Choctalking on Other Realities,* another dimension of "Choctalking" is a form of transcultural communication. If we do, indeed, read "Choctalking" as an elision of "Choctaw code talking," then the language's globalized function in the two World Wars suggests the possibility of both alliances and enmities.

Examples of global (dis)connections are most evident in three pieces from Howe's collection *Choctalking on Other Realities:* "Choctalking on Other Realities," "I Fuck Up in Japan," and "Yaa Jordan, Yaa 'Ayouni." Aesthetically and structurally, they all can be described as tribalographies, which Howe explains come from "the Native propensity for bringing things together, for making consensus, and for symbiotically connecting one thing to another" ("The Story of America" 42). In these three texts, Howe brings Choctaw culture, and southeastern Native cultures more broadly, into conversation with those in Asia and the Middle East. Dean Rader's discussion of the aesthetics of *Choctalking on Other Realities* is also useful to consider, given the tribal specificity of the texts therein: "One memory leads to another memory, which leads to an observation, which leads to a family story, which leads to a comical encounter overseas, which illuminates a Choctaw mode of being in the world, which leads to yet another observation about Oklahoma, which prompts another memory, and the narrative spins on, always turning on the axis of Choctaw history and culture" ("Foreword" i). I discuss "Choctalking on Other Realities" as fiction here because its first appearance, in *Evidence of Red,* groups it as one of the collection's "stories." Even though the collection, *Choctalking on Other Realities,* is marketed as autobiography, the ambivalent space in which the piece exists is demonstrated by Howe's reference to it in her January 2009 blog entry: "While I continue to call Choctalking 'fiction,' there are many elements of the story that have been taken from events in my life. But isn't that the truth of fiction, anyway? Ourselves, but always in disguise?"

"Choctalking on Other Realities" is a powerful collection of vignettes[7] connecting the oppression of Jewish, Palestinian, Choctaw, African American, and Vietnamese peoples through the experiences of the unnamed narrator. The story is framed by the image of a Palestinian woman running from Israeli soldiers in Jerusalem after a peaceful protest march turns violent. The image of the running woman resonates with the Choctaw narrator, who witnesses the scene, and who flashes back to a childhood memory of running away from a Christian kindergarten. She is pursued by the white teacher, who locks her in a broom closet as punishment (45). By story's end, the Palestinian woman is also captured and imprisoned, linking the violent histories of US settler colonialism to the creation of the state of Israel. This connection between Palestinians and Native Americans is not exceptional in Howe's work. There is the previously mentioned love affair between the narrator of *Miko Kings,* Lena, and Sayyed, a Palestinian man killed in a terrorist attack, as well as Auda's comparison of Indian Removal to the displacement of Palestinians in Jerusalem in *Shell Shaker* (45).

In contrast to her other, more surface pairings of Indigenous Americans and Palestinians, "Choctalking on Other Realities" is a complex tale of the connection and disconnection between various cultures. In the prologue to the collection, *Choctalking on Other Realities,* Dean Rader describes Howe's narrative style as "a metaphor for the connectedness among appearing disconnects" (ii); similarly, in her essay "Making It Work: A Model of Tribalography as Methodology," Jill Doerfler notes that "an important aspect of tribalography is its emphasis on connections" (68).[8] Given the linkages between American Indians and Palestinians, it is not surprising that a conversation between the narrator and a Jewish shopkeeper becomes tense, but it is a tension born out of an attempt to reach cultural understanding. In fact, as this particular vignette begins, the narrator describes her desire to "place [the Jewish woman] in our past, to put myself in her beginning, and intertwine our threads of history—for we are nothing without our relationships. That's Choctaw" ("Choctalking on Other Realities" 50). The shopkeeper's story is already intertwined with broader Native American history, or at least she claims it to be, citing a Cherokee great-grandmother. As Hobson, McAdams, and Walkiewicz point out in *The People Who Stayed,* "it has become commonplace to regard stories of Cherokee grandmothers and great-grandmothers [by non-Natives] with suspicion" (8), and Howe pokes fun at this phenomenon in *Indian Radio Days* when one character claims, "It's been twenty years since I met a human being who wasn't a Cherokee" (143). Despite her skepticism, the Choctaw narrator listens to the woman's story about her family's immigration to the United States and later immigration to Israel before sharing stories of her own history.

It seems that the Jewish woman and the Choctaw woman will find common ground when the narrator explains that her people are also immigrants (to Oklahoma) and describes the emergence at *Nanih Waiya* and the Gulf Coast homelands of the Choctaw. Their fundamental disagreement begins when the shopkeeper claims that Jerusalem was meant to be a city of unity, and the narrator asks, "Then why, every day, do Jews and Arabs try to kill one another?" The woman counters with, "Why did Indians sell Manhattan to the Christians?" ("Choctalking on Other Realities" 52). The falling darkness is a metaphor for the pain within each woman that arises from their violent cultural histories. The shopkeeper tries to ameliorate the situation by telling the story of her great-grandfather's love affair with the Cherokee woman in North Carolina, both social outcasts, he for his exile, and she for being a "conquered" person (52).

The Jewish woman's assertion that Native peoples are conquered elevates the tension level, and despite the narrator's protestations, she continues to argue that the 1971 surrender at Alcatraz Island proves that Indians had lost their courage to fight. What follows is the narrator's story of the Treaty of Dancing Rabbit Creek and the Trail of Tears, ultimately drawing this comparison:

> Oklahoma or Indian Territory was a forerunner of Israel. Choctaws were the first to be removed there, other Indian tribes from around the country soon followed. We were supposed to live together in peace. Form relationships. It wasn't easy, but for the most part we did it because we did not idealize war. However throughout the nineteenth century more and more whites moved into Indian Territory. . . . on April 22, 1889 the American government opened the unassigned lands to the whites. . . . It was estimated that twenty thousand immigrants were waiting at the border to stake their claims. (54)

Finally, the narrator explains that Indians hadn't lost their courage; rather, they were "overwhelmed" (54). The Jewish woman, who thought she knew something about Native American history, no longer argues with the Choctaw woman, suggesting that she may have begun to consider an alternate perspective.

The complexity of "Choctalking" reflects the processes of globalization in which histories are intertwined and linked in sometimes surprising ways. The Palestinian woman captured at the story's end is called "Nina," and the narrator makes clear that she is the exact same Nina from an earlier vignette, a Russian, Ukrainian Jew who had survived the notorious World War II massacre by Germans at Babi Yar near Kiev (47). The face of the Jewish woman is overlaid on the face of the Palestinian woman, drawing together their ironically twinned histories of oppression.

Even more telling is the setting of this first vignette in which Nina, the Jew, appears. The narrator is much younger than when she meets the shopkeeper in Jerusalem—only nineteen years old (the year of the Alcatraz occupation)—and waitressing in the café at the Oklahoma City airport. The location signifies the global space in which the cultural and political conflicts of "Choctalking" play out. The young Choctaw woman's colleagues include Susan B. Anthony, an African American woman, Nina, and Gretchen, a German Catholic who fled Nazi Germany in World War II. An argument breaks out between Nina and Gretchen for reasons that are unclear, but old antagonisms from the war surface, and the two women's distrust of each other nearly ends in violence. The narrator intercedes, feeling it to be her duty as union representative for the International Brotherhood of Hotel, Motel, and Restaurant Workers of America. The fight is averted, and it is clear that both women are scarred from their war experiences.

Superimposed upon the trauma of World War II is the trauma of Vietnam; the young protagonist has eschewed her previous ties with Christianity, having been "baptized many times" (46) within different Christian denominations, in favor of socialism. Though her new loyalty may be a result of the college scholarship provided by the AFL-CIO, she reflects upon the classism of the Vietnam draft: "It's not news at the airport café that the Vietnam War is being fought disproportionately by the poor. Every Monday through Friday we serve red and yellow, black, and poor white boys their last supper as civilians. They're on their way to boot camp. . . . I want to tell them to run. But don't" (47). What prevents her from doing so is her own personal trauma, the memory of being locked in a closet by the Christian teacher when she ran away from kindergarten, a white woman who warned her, "*No one gets hurt if they do what they're told*" (47).

The narrator overcomes this childhood trauma in the last vignette of the story, titled "I Am Still Running," when she urges the Palestinian woman who is also Nina the Ukrainian Jew to "RUN!" finally understanding the lie she had been told by the teacher so many years before when she hears the same words spoken by an Israeli soldier (56). The narrator turns to spirituality at the story's end when she sees a member of the Israeli Parliament, and she imagines he is saying a prayer for women who have been the victims of all sorts of historical traumas: Jews at Babi Yar, Palestinians at Deir Yassin, Vietnamese at Mi Lai, Mayans in Chiapas, and African Americans in Alabama. She also imagines the prayer is for all her ancestors, important because the man she imagines praying has "palms facing toward the Sun," suggesting the Choctaws' worship of Hashtali. For the narrator this is a turn away from the colonizing religion of the Americas, toward Choctaw spirituality, that which will save "The People" (57).

"Choctalking on Other Realities" is about global oppression, whether it is rooted in political or economic power struggles. Rather than condemning any one group, the narrator ultimately seeks a balm for the scars left by the complicated and intertwined histories of twentieth-century military and political wars with a turn to the spiritual, a localized

Choctaw spirituality springing from southeastern Indigenous lands, wherein a healing may begin. I read this spiritual turn as hopeful; similarly, Dean Rader has called the collection *Choctalking on Other Realities* "highly optimistic" ("Foreword" vi), though he focuses on the use of humor in the text. Like "Choctalking on Other Realities," Howe's essays "I Fuck Up in Japan" and "Yaa Jordan, Yaa 'Ayouni" end on seemingly positive notes, combining humor and spiritual elements to illuminate the global connections and alleviate the disconnections of Howe's travels.

"I Fuck Up in Japan" is a painful and beautiful rendering of Howe's 1993 experience representing American Indians at the International Forum on Anti-Discrimination and Human Rights as part of the United Nations' "International Year of the World's Indigenous People" in Japan. She was to stay with various families across the country as part of the larger cultural exchange, and she wryly relates this to the colonial era in which Europeans were "doing immersive family experiments in our [Choctaw] homelands" (96). Despite the ravages of colonialism, she jokes, "I know, *I know,* it didn't work out for Choctaws or other American Indian tribes, but since this was the end of the twentieth century, I hoped for a better outcome" (96). As in Romania, Howe acts as an American Indian diplomat during her Japan stay. Yet, unlike her mostly measured responses to cross-cultural conflict in "Carlos Castaneda Lives in Romania," which details a journey that took place five years after her Japan visit, "I Fuck Up in Japan" is a raw accounting of what the title states bluntly.

As Rader notes, Howe "is hardest on herself" (iii). The "fucking up" concerns her own inability to see outside of her cultural boundaries, and she notes that "Oklahoma could not have prepared [her] for the Far East" (99). Yet, Howe is contrite by story's end, and it is clear how she was, in fact, set up to "fuck up" by a convergence of public and personal histories along this journey. The narrative of Howe's cultural missteps in Japan is punctuated by a series of alternate stories in alternate timelines that reveal underlying tensions. Howe acknowledges that she felt "haughty" (99) about her position representing American Indians in Japan, and she also felt the experience would somehow make up for the loss of her job in the securities industry, which she blamed on Japanese economic policy (99). She also wanted to know if Japanese people think they are related to American Indians, based on information she had learned in the sixth grade (101). More painfully, she relates how her uncle, Loy Billy, was killed at the age of nineteen in World War II (108), a memory that is inevitably connected to her grandmother smashing her Japanese china plates after Pearl Harbor was destroyed (100).

Given these underlying tensions and Howe's confession that she did little linguistic or cultural preparation for her journey in Japan, the conflicts that occur seem inevitable, yet Howe's use of humor and honesty give them a poignancy that sets "I Fuck Up in Japan" apart, not just from other stories in Howe's collection, but also from the larger genre of travel narratives. Howe's confusion over a variety of unfamiliar toilets is a metaphor for her overall lack of comfort in Japan, even during the most intimate and essential human functions. The initial, quite hilarious toilet narrative, occurs when Howe, on her first homestay, encounters a fur-covered, yet electrically heated toilet seat. She has had to remove seven layers of clothing because the house in which she is staying is frigid, so she is left nearly naked, panicking about a potential electrocution while using the unfamiliar toilet. Despite her fears of being found dead like Elvis Presley, she wishes the toilet "Good evening" in Japanese and bows as she has been taught, before taking her chances (99). The next toilet incident occurs later in the journey, after Howe has spoken at the International Human Rights Forum, and this one is not so funny; in fact, it shames her homestay family because Howe actually has to receive training in the proper use of the toilet. The toilet incident is precursor to her homestay host, Mr. Fugimoro, throwing his chopsticks in anger across the dinner table when Howe asks to spend the following night in a hotel to "have a day's rest" (120). Despite attempts to explain that her request had nothing to do with her hosts' hospitality, the homestay has been ruined. She stays the night, but when she leaves, "There were no ceremonial good-byes. No one bowed" (121).

The toilet narratives bookend "I Fuck Up in Japan" and serve as more ridiculous examples of Howe's transcultural mistakes. Central to the essay is a poignant example of Howe's own cultural insensitivity, ironic within a larger collection showing the author as most often the brunt of others' insensitive questions, claims, and assumptions about American Indians. Howe's gaffe occurs in the company of Professor Mitzuhito Kanehara, a specialist of ethno-literature translation, who hosted her during her first week in Tokyo hotels. One of the places they visit during that time is a Buddhist shrine in Kanagawa Prefecture. On the day of the visit, their conversation includes a comparative discussion of American Indians and Burakumin, the historical "untouchable" caste, who engage in "undesirable" occupations such as being craftsmen and artists (105). They find common ground between the groups, Kanehara concluding "All roads lead to social constructions" (106). Ironically, what follows this cultural connection is a distinct disconnection, when the discussion turns toward American Indian writers. As in "Carlos Castaneda Lives in Romania," there is a gap in international understanding of "ethnic frauds," in this instance about Jamake Highwater, whose books had apparently been translated into Japanese in the guise of Native American literature. Despite Kanehara's "pensive" (106), "thoughtful" (107) silence, Howe becomes angry and can't "stop talking about ethnic frauds and how they were the modern equivalent of nineteenth-century Indian agents" (107). She is unaware that she is disrespecting a sacred space, the site of the statue of the Great Buddha of Kamakura:

> I yammered on and on like some kind of manic. I don't excuse my irreverence at the temple site except to say I wasn't seeing the statue of Buddha. Nor was I seeing the other tourists there. I was seeing the Choctaw people in the Lower Mississippi Valley in 1738. Smallpox blankets arrived in the east and were traded west, along with the smell of oblivion—gifts from hairy-fingered foreigners. I was seeing our warriors fall and get up, fall and get up, then walk through a door that centuries later I would emerge from, my fists clenched at birth, screaming who wants to fight? I was seeing myself, a warrior engaged in a desperate battle I will not win, enemies on all sides. Then suddenly I awakened in the sunlight, surrounded by lush greenery and hackberry trees, frightened by the raging woman I'd become at the Buddhist shrine. (108)

This scene is important for a number of reasons. Rader notes how in other stories in *Choctalking,* Howe "is punished for not being Indian enough or for being the wrong kind of Indian . . . [or simply] for her Indianness" (ii). Yet, at the site of the Buddha, "*LeAnne Howe,* not some clueless Anglo, is the one committing the faux pas" (iv). The scene is ironic within the larger narrative, yet it is also poignant and brave: Howe reveals that we are all sometimes incapable of seeing beyond our individual assumptions and biases. Through her later actions, she also shows us how we can accept our missteps with grace. The other significant element of this scene is Howe's reference to herself as a warrior; near the outset of the story, Howe mentions her "red beaded warrior coat" (96), and allusions to it appear in other stories in the collection as well. More telling is the picture of Howe on the collection's cover, wearing the coat and posing ironically in front of a shop called "Red Indian," presumably raising her hand in the Hollywood Indian gesture that typically precedes the fake greeting "How," much like her ironic pose on the back cover of *Evidence of Red.* Howe's identity as a warrior links the stories in *Choctalking on Other Realities* through the artistic motif of the red warrior coat at the beginning of each chapter. This is another example of Howe as a postindian warrior who continues to fight the simulations of manifest manners with humor.

After her tirade about ethnic frauds, Howe immediately feels shame for the way she has treated her host and the way she has disrespected the Buddha, and she spends time quietly reflecting on her actions. She remembers the stories of her uncles who served in World War II and how painful it must have been for Schlicht Billy to pick up the body of his brother, Loy, who was killed in action. Howe notes, "Carrying the memory of it is hard" (109), clearly a reference to all the painful stories she carries, such as those that bubbled up as she stood before the Great Buddha. Yet, her response to the event later that evening offers her readers a way to think about cultural disconnection and the possibilities for reconciliation. After coming across a pamphlet in her purse about the Great Buddha (while searching for a tissue, suggesting her emotional state), Howe reads the Buddhist teachings therein, and accepts all that has happened: "'*Itadakimasu,*' I said, quietly as a prayer, both hands on my heart. 'I humbly receive'" (109). As in the story "Choctalking on Other Realities," spirituality, this time Buddhism, heals the pain of cross-cultural conflict.

Yet, there are many more moments of connection between cultures in "I Fuck Up in Japan." Early in the piece, Howe relates the story of how her poor sixth-grade education in Oklahoma led to her belief that Asians thought they were genetically related to American Indians. She explains that, upon her return from Japan, she researched the use of the term "Mongolian" as a signifier of race and learned how it had been applied to American Indians and Arctic Natives. She then muses, "Maybe that's why the US government forced American Indians onto reservations—to suppress the Mongols. I know, *I know,* a ridiculous idea. But after Pearl Harbor was attacked on December 7, 1941, Japanese Americans were sent to internment camps on or near Indian reservations" (102). A moment of disconnect, born out of a colonial education, becomes a moment of connection based in the two cultures' histories of oppression.

The most compelling global connections of "I Fuck Up in Japan" occur when Howe speaks at the International Human Rights Forum, along with the three other representatives of global Indigenous cultures: "Mr. Eeda, Ainu [Japan's Indigenous peoples], from Hokkaido; Alan Brown, Koorie, Aborigine from Australia; and Illia Janovich, Sinti Roma from Austria" (115). As Howe notes, at that time, the global population of Indigenous peoples was 300 million, spread across seventy countries (115). Howe's lecture focuses on a proposed hazardous-waste dump site that the Mississippi Band of Choctaws' chief had agreed to build on their land and the subsequent vote by the tribe that ensured the dumpsite would not be built, after all. This historical event echoes the populist resistance against Red McAlester in *Shell Shaker.* Mr. Eeda's talk about the Ainu contains numerous links to American Indian history: how they had been known as "savages," how they weren't given the right to vote until 1924, and how they were currently "fighting the Japanese government in the courts for placing hazardous waste dumps on their land" (116). Alan Brown discusses his aunt's role in founding Aboriginal Health Services in his region, and Howe notes that, unlike Indian Health Service clinics in the US, Aboriginal people fully manage these clinics. Similar to the story of American Indians as Mongols, Brown explains that the Australian "government and anthropologists tell Aboriginal peoples that they've only been in Australia for 40,000 years. 'The question we ask is . . . why this isn't long enough to establish indigenous residency'" (117). He also describes the germ warfare waged on Aboriginal peoples by the English via smallpox-infected blankets, which Howe associates with the historical incident in which Lord Jeffrey Amherst permitted smallpox blankets to be traded to American Indians in 1763 (117). After Illia Janovich speaks of the forced removal of Sinti Roma from Germany in 1940 and the continued struggles by his organization to educate their children, Howe notes that the audience and the speakers weep: "Perhaps it was the power of all our stories that made them cry. We made ourselves cry. Indigenous peoples are still struggling to survive; that's the story" (117).

These transcultural connections stand apart from others in *Choctalking on Other Realities* because they focus on globalized Indigenous experiences, invoking Chadwick Allen's advocacy for the importance of trans-Indigenous studies. Trans-Indigeneity stands in contrast to a transnationalism that can never be separated from "the violent histories and destructive legacies of settler colonialisms" ("A Trans*national* Native" 17). Allen argues that within Native American and Indigenous studies "centering the Indigenous has become the new standard" (18), and his methodology outlines a "global literary studies (primarily) in English that . . . [acknowledges] the mobility and multiple interactions of Indigenous peoples, cultures, histories, and texts" (*Trans-Indigenous* xv).

Certainly Howe's comparative representation of global Indigeneity demonstrates how trans-Indigenous studies can illuminate the connections between peoples damaged by shared histories of colonial violence and scientific racism. It can also offer hope through the sharing of trans-Indigenous experiences. Yet, despite the trans-Indigenous connections made at Japan's International Human Rights Forum, the day ends painfully, when the speakers are shuttled off, given no opportunity to spend time together, due to their busy lecture schedules. Despite their roles as international representatives of their peoples, the Indigenous speakers have no agency in the situation. Howe describes Mr. Eeda's poignant move of solidarity when he "turned away from his handlers and raced toward the car I was in. As the driver started the engine, Mr. Eeda put his hands on the back windshield; he was crying. I quickly put my palms against the glass to show that I was feeling what he was feeling. Mr. Eeda ran a few steps alongside the car and I wanted to get out and run with him, but the car sped off" (118). Despite this brutal goodbye, Howe realizes that their stories will continue to be the connective tissue that links them.

"I Fuck Up in Japan" closes by pairing anecdotes that exemplify the cultural (dis)connections therein. The section is called "This Is the Story I Didn't Want to Tell," a title that could have encompassed the essay in its entirety. During a visit to a small town in the countryside, Howe meets a man who had been held as a prisoner of war by Americans in World

War II. He feels ambivalent toward the United States and is curious to know if attitudes toward the Japanese have changed. In particular, he wants to know if the term "Jap" is still used negatively. Howe explains to the reader that it was a term she had heard used profusely growing up and also when she worked in securities, but since this was the end of a journey in which she had unwittingly insulted her hosts on numerous occasions, she lies to the man. Her lie is transparent, creating even more discomfort, but she explains that she is emotionally exhausted from her previous cultural missteps. The essay ends as Howe prepares to leave Japan. She writes in her journal, "*Green, green, I've never seen such / vibrant emerald mountains and fields, / set against a titan blue sky. / Magnificent, even in winter. / Yakne achukma, good land in Choctaw*" (122). Her emphasis on blue and green is reminiscent of Ezol Day's discussion of *okchamali* in *Miko Kings,* and the term's connection to life, specifically the Choctaw peoples' Mississippi homelands and emergence place, another "good land."[9] Despite Howe's desire for forgiveness for her disrespect of the Great Buddha of Kamakura and her mistakes along the journey, she finds hope in the idea that "our bodies are the epic landscape that carries the story of human existence, of our ancestors, of ourselves, of memories without fixed finality" (122). Central to the issue of indigeneity are land and human relationships with it; Howe's embodiment of land is one positive way that she and other Indigenous peoples can continue their struggles against oppression, despite colonial violence historically, and in the present.

"Choctalking on Other Realities" turns on the possibilities of spiritual union between cultures engaged in seemingly perpetual conflict, and that spirituality is rooted in Choctaw religious traditions of the US Southeast. "I Fuck Up in Japan" interweaves Choctaw spirituality and Indigenous land issues with a subtle comparison of Japanese land to the *Nanih Waiya* to conclude a complex tale of cultural (dis)connections. Howe's representations of Choctaw cultural practices in a global context are a form of grounded globalism, particularly when we situate indigeneity as central to the US Southeast in terms of land and culture. Her short story "Yaa Jordan, Yaa 'Ayouni" is probably the best example in *Choctalking on Other Realities* of the global circulation of both Indigenous and mainstream southern culture.

Like the two previously discussed works, "Yaa Jordan, Yaa 'Ayouni" is a tribalography, a complexly told tale of Howe's journeys through Jordan from 1993 to 1994, interweaving past and present and linking seemingly unrelated details. It is unique within the larger collection for its screenplay format. This authorial decision may be as a result of Howe's early revelation that she dies in Amman, Jordan, in November 1993, one of several deaths; the piece's formal structure creates emotional distance from this painful topic. Another reason for this formal choice may be the way that, like theater, the screen emphasizes orality. Christy Stanlake notes the affiliation between American Indian drama and creation stories: "The interrelated concepts of the power of language derive from numerous Native origin stories that link the winds with human breath, and the acts of speech and thought with that of creation" (109). Similarly, the Choctaw word *nukfokechi* "represents a kind of creation" since *nuk* or *nok,* a prefix, concerns "the power of speech, breath, and mind" (Howe, "The Story of America" 123). The formal structure resonates more strongly given that this particular piece is about the creation of the author, through her deaths and rebirths.

The uniqueness of "Yaa Jordan, Yaa 'Ayouni" also lies in its numerous moments in which mainstream US southern culture finds its way into Howe's travels through the Middle East. The screenplay begins with a scene in which Howe is refused a visa to enter Syria because she is a practitioner of Choctaw religion.[10] Border crossing operates as a multidimensional metaphor in the piece, demonstrating the ways in which borders can be blocked or the ways in which they can be crossed and recrossed, even the border between life and death. The voiceover that transitions from the first scene to the next elaborates on the theme of death:

> Before the Middle East, before Jordan, before the incident at the Syrian embassy, I'd long been attracted to the idea of death and what's beyond our recognition that those at death's door witness. Does the earth itself fade away as we encounter our origins, or is it someone else's origins we see? I die three times during the year I am in the Middle East, and each death buries much deeper into the past than the previous dying. I suppose I'm looking for an answer to a simple question: Why am I here? (147).

The second of Howe's "deaths" occurs on a road trip with her friend Mindy, a Texan also living in Jordan in early 1994. Their journey begins when they decide to drive to Beirut for dinner. Howe notes, "Only

Texans and Oklahoma Indians say such things. . . . One of the reasons for [our] friendship is that we shared a warped vision of space and time" (147). The background music for their trip includes Garth Brooks's "Friends in Low Places" and Willie Nelson's *Live from Austin, Texas,* creating a Texahoma soundscape across Jordan and Syria. Their mode of transportation is Mindy's Florida-plated 1989 Cadillac Seville, and their plan is to drive 188 miles and cross two national borders in order to eat *Kibbeh nayyeh,* a lamb dish that Howe had first experienced in Fort Worth. She muses, "Perhaps my love of the Middle East really begins at Hedary's Restaurant, talking with Mr. Hedary and his Lebanese customers and seeing posters of their homelands" (149). Howe's taste of Lebanese culture in Texas leads her and her Texan friend on a journey to rediscover that experience in Beirut.

At the Jordan-Syria border, Howe chooses to lie about her religion, given her previously denied access to Syria, self-identifying as a Christian. Howe details how "Jews, Christians, and Muslims are 'people of the book,' meaning they may go to war with one another, [and] they acknowledge each other's beliefs and practices" (151); they only know the stereotypes Hollywood has reproduced of American Indians. Despite the lie (or because of the lie), the women's paperwork is accepted, and they successfully receive visas to enter Syria. The moment of triumph is dampened when Mindy asks "Do you think Brownsville's Port of Entry would give visas to Mexicans wanting to cross into Texas?" (153), and they somberly reflect on the hypocrisy of US pride in being a country of immigrants and its concomitant history of racism and segregation. The scene illustrates the tension of border crossings and their inherent dangers for minority cultures everywhere.

Disaster is foreshadowed when the Cadillac crashes to a stop on the Syrian steppe after Mindy attempts to avoid killing a stray sheep that had wandered into the road. Everything seems to be in working order until, after a brief stop for dinner outside of Damascus, the car's brakes go out. Howe's journal details how they got towed and slept in the car, and then it takes a more serious turn: "*Fell asleep in the backseat / Stopped breathing. Died. Learned nothing. / Revived by a stranger / that pumped my heart / seventeen times. / No vision, just blue waters.*" As at the end of "I Fuck Up in Japan," the watery landscape of the Choctaw homelands intercedes in a faraway place, when Howe seems to need its calming effect most. Immediately preceding this scene, Howe described the restaurant where they ate dinner, sharing the space with an Arabic man and his three beautiful wives. In an attempt to understand how it might feel to be a third wife, Howe remembers her birth mother's story of an old Choctaw man who had married two sisters. Howe's mother cleaned house for them, but she quit when it seemed that they desired for her to be the third wife. This near-transcultural connection becomes a disconnection when Howe explains, "No scene I will ever write for film could evoke how my mother felt about her life. Though she was the embodiment of stoic, she shuddered at the thought of being a third wife" (159). Though much of the road-trip section of "Yaa Jordan, Yaa 'Ayouni" details Jordanian or Syrian customs and peoples, it is also one of the best examples of the way Howe juxtaposes her own personal history, along with the peoples and cultures of the US South, to those she encounters in the Middle East.

As in "Choctalking on Other Realities," a Cherokee princess makes an appearance in "Yaa Jordan, Yaa 'Ayouni." Howe humorously begins the scene by defusing readers' disbelief in such a bizarre manifestation of southeastern Indigeneity in Jordan by claiming, "I swear to the *Almighty* this is true," more southern colloquialism than Christian belief. Like the shopkeeper with whom she has a tense conversation in Jerusalem, a Jordanian librarian tells her that her great-grandfather brought home a Cherokee wife. She also claims to be a descendent of Pocahontas, which demonstrates a globalized lack of knowledge about the diversity of southeastern tribal peoples. Howe's response to the librarian reflects an openness that we see throughout *Choctalking on Other Realities* to the possibilities of global connections: "the remarkable thing was that everything about that story, *sans* Pocahontas, was plausible" (167). Howe uses the anecdote to educate her readers about the realities of Matoaka's life and her tribe. She also makes an interesting point about the relationship between Cherokee and Powhatan peoples:

> I think Pocahontas's tribe gets twinned with Cherokees because Virginia and North Carolina are close in proximity. The Cherokees developed a trading relationship with the British *aka* Virginian traders as early as 1690. Cherokee women did marry with men from the Empire. Soon afterwards "princes and princesses" were running around barefoot in the Southeast descended from British fathers and Native mothers. This is the

> story of contact in America. Claiming a Native identity through ancestry allows non-Indians to own American Indian history, be entitled to it *and* our homelands, yet have no actual responsibility for any of it. (168)

Positioning this story within a global context shows the extent to which actual American Indian history has been subsumed by the myths of colonialism. Yet both the Israeli shopkeeper and the Jordanian librarian carry a particularly southern story. As Taylor has noted, "The romance of the Cherokee princess grandmother is more common in southern families than elsewhere in the nation, and understandably so" (13) given the location of the Cherokee homelands and the east-west movement of European colonialism across North America.

The third of Howe's deaths in "Yaa Jordan, Yaa 'Ayouni" comes in the final scene, and it represents the author's life by first fading into a picture of Earth from outer space, then depicting a photomontage of all the locales visited in *Choctalking on Other Realities.* The scene echoes Howe's prose-poem "Indians Never Say Goodbye," which significantly is the final piece in *Evidence of Red,* in which she remembers being in the hospital with rheumatic fever as a child. In the earlier version of the story, a vision of her Ain't Sally sings a healing song to her, and she remembers how the elderly woman with whom she shared the room died. In the screenplay version of the scene, Howe dies with the woman. She describes them as "twinned" (172), and they cross the border between life and death to visit unknown places. Describing herself as a "changed being," Howe waves "hello and good-bye to both my mothers and all my future descendants swimming in the waters of the blue green orb" (172). As in "Choctalking on Other Realities" and "I Fuck Up in Japan," "Yaa Jordan, Yaa 'Ayouni" ends in a Choctaw spiritual space. Howe positions herself within a matrilineal system, acknowledging her mothers and her own position as mother. She also invokes the "blue green" of *okchamali,* the sacred emergence place.

Despite its depiction of the commodification and appropriation of American Indian people and cultures, *Shell Shaker,* like the works examined from *Choctalking on Other Realities,* also speaks to the life-affirming cultural cross-currents present in the globalized era. One of the more cosmopolitan characters, Tema, an actress who has lived in England and who is married to an Englishman, believes that Choctaw religious beliefs have echoes in other world cultures. She explains, "When I performed in *The Conference of the Birds,* I realized how much the Sufis are like Choctaws. . . . Sufis believe that there is only one God, and all things emanate from that energy. Mankind's distinctions between good and evil have no meaning in Sufism because the two are connected to the unit that is God. . . . The Sufis must be Choctaws at heart, don't you think?" (151–52). Tema's represents both the intersection of English and Choctaw culture and Sufi and Choctaw spirituality.

Howe's allusion to *The Conference of the Birds,* written by Peter Brooks and Jean-Claude Carriere, and based on a collection by Persian poet Farid ud-Din Attar, is just one of many examples of a larger motif in her writing about the power and significance of birds as communicators and spiritual beings.[11] Another is her October 13, 2010, blog entry entitled "Amman, My Life Among the Birds." Howe describes her apartment on the top floor of a building as being surrounded by birds: "there are pigeons practicing yoga on the rooftops, crows gossiping on my windowsills, and some variety of tiny songbirds . . . flying around the balcony each morning singing happy tunes" ("Amman"). The blog goes on to detail her observations of a particular rooster that crows at the most inopportune of times, connecting all this bird activity to Choctaw beliefs. She writes,

> Birds are very important messengers to American Indians. The eagle is a powerful symbol of protection and valor in warfare, and highly revered, and there are hawks, ravens, also beloved for their variety of interactions with native peoples. Even the owl is a special kind of messenger. I should also mention that our tribal newspaper at the Choctaw Nation of Oklahoma is called, *Biskinik,* meaning the newsbird. ("Amman")

In addition to these cultural connections, the Jordanian birds provide Howe with a bridge to her own personal history: a grandmother who kept chickens, and the figure "Grandmother of the Birds,"[12] in *Shell Shaker.* While grounding her reflections on birds in her own culture, Howe acknowledges that the birds outside her apartment sing in Arabic. She relates how the frozen chickens in the markets are killed "in the Islamic tradition, halal, 'by the hand with a large knife,'" later describing how she purchased one of those chickens and fried it up southern style with cream gravy, potatoes, and peas. These juxtapositions of and intersections between Jordanian and Choctaw cultures demonstrate Howe's attempt to find common ground between the two, without privileging one over the other.

Howe once again references *The Conference of the Birds* in her February 4, 2011, blog, in which she ponders the impacts of the Egyptian demonstrations which ultimately led to the toppling of President Hosni Mubarak. As she wonders what will happen to Egypt, she realizes that is the business of the Egyptian people, not hers or the US government's; she hopes that the Egyptians will find themselves at the end of their struggles toward self-determination just as the "birds find at the end of their journey, only themselves, their reflection" ("The Conference of Birds"). The Persian poet's words are so meaningful to Howe because they speak to the interconnectedness of all beings, yet she is also trying to find a balance between such connection and the sovereignty of individuals: "*See why I return again and again to The Conference of Birds? We're separated; we're connected; we're separated; we're connected. Which is it?*" ("The Conference of Birds"). LeAnne Howe's oeuvre suggests that the answer to the question she has posed in her blog is "Both."

At first blush, Wai Chee Dimock's description of American literature might seem applicable to Howe's work: "a crisscrossing set of pathways, open-ended and ever multiplying, weaving in and out of other geographies, other languages and cultures. These are input channels, kinship networks, routes of transit, and forms of attachment—connective tissues binding America to the rest of the world" (3). Dimock's planetary model relies on deep time and a connectivity that transcends the nation-state, linking people linguistically, politically, economically, culturally, and familially (258). However, despite the obvious globalized elements within LeAnne Howe's writing, reading her within this framework would not take into account the tribally specific implications of her position as a Native literary nationalist rooted in Choctaw homescapes. In her essay in *Reasoning Together* she explains, "In the beginning there are Choctaw stories. There are Cherokee stories. There are Diné stories. There are Lakota stories. I am trying to say that we, the people, are derived from creation stories. We are people of specific landscapes, and our specific stories are told about our emergence from a specific place" (333). This place-based cultural argument underscores the nationalist aspect of what it means to "Choctalk" and its concern with the role of an individual, within a particular Choctaw perspective, engaging with and trying to understand other cultures. Romero has similarly argued that, in Howe's works, the "alliance-building and cross-cultural knowledge work to strengthen Choctaw sovereignty" (22).

Howe's position seems akin to that taken by Jace Weaver in his 2011 essay, "The Red Atlantic: Transoceanic Cultural Exchanges" in which he claims to "take a cosmopolitan turn," "without abandoning, rejecting, or betraying [his] nationalism in any way" (4). Weaver's 2014 monograph, *The Red Atlantic: American Indigenes and the Making of the Modern World, 1000–1927,* demonstrates a long history of Indigenous American engagement in the Atlantic world, including "how they thought about it, conceptualized it, and articulated it" (xiii). In a similar vein, LeAnne Howe's articulation of "Choctalking" gives voice to a tribally specific perspective of the globalized era in which her characters live. Weaver convincingly argues that even though "[some] scholars see in the cosmopolitanism and hybridity of Indians and their cultures a loss of indigenous authenticity . . . [such] a position fails to account for the fact that Natives and their cultures had always been highly adaptive, appropriating and absorbing anything that seemed useful or powerful" (30). To revisit Hall and Fenelon, this willingness to take on the cultural processes of globalization and its implications is more evidence of Native people "adapting, adjusting, and adopting to changing circumstances to maintain their sovereignty" (146), which would certainly seem to be true in the case of LeAnne Howe's Choctalking global stories.

CONCLUSION

Native Southern Literary Studies

Where Do We Go from Here?

> I . . . remember mounds assembled,
> basketful by basketful—the building.
> Various earths carefully compiled
> commemorating dead immortal
> underneath compelling skies.
>
> —ALLISON ADELLE HEDGE COKE,
> "Waiting for the Last Lunar Eclipse, 2004"

I have situated LeAnne Howe's work at the intersection of southern and American Indian literary studies, considering Native, Interstate, and global Souths, adding my voice to the burgeoning field of Native Southern literary studies. I have also examined the various ways in which LeAnne Howe's literary productions "Choctalk." My theorizing of an Interstate South marks southeastern Indigeneity as dynamic in its physical and cultural circulation, including the waves of Indian Removals that wracked the region; it also underscores the continuing resistance and presence of Native peoples in the Southeast. Like other southernists, I am concerned with the history and culture of the South; however, I am attempting to infuse southern studies with a good dose of work being done in Native American and Indigenous studies. LeAnne Howe is one of the most important American writers of the twenty-first century, given her complex themes and rigorous interventions into our understanding of history. We need more in-depth studies of individual American Indian authors and their relationships with the South. Robert J. Conley and Allison Hedge Coke immediately come to mind as writers with bodies of work that would be excellent candidates for such analyses, though there are scores of others whose writing can be read at the convergence of Native and southern studies, including Janet McAdams, Geary Hobson, Marilou Awiakta, Joy Harjo, Craig Womack, and Karenne Wood. We also need more investigations of nineteenth-century literature of the Native South, including work on *The Cherokee Phoenix* and a sustained unearthing of archival materials, as James Parins has done in *Literacy and Intellectual Life in the Cherokee Nation 1820–1906*. Continued production of tribally specific literary studies of southeastern Native peoples such as Craig Womack's *Red on Red: Native American Literary Separatism* and Daniel Heath Justice's *Our Fire Survives the Storm: A Cherokee Literary History* will also advance southeastern Indigenous groundwork.

Though Native Southern literary studies comprises a relatively small group of scholars, I am always surprised by the diversity of approaches when I encounter the work of my colleagues at scholarly conferences and through their publications. Annette Trefzer's *Disturbing Indians: the Archaeology of Southern Fiction* (2007) innovatively examines American Indian influence on Southern Renaissance writers. Melanie Benson Taylor has consistently made significant contributions to the field, mostly notably in *Reconstructing the Native South: American Indian Literature and the Lost Cause* (2012), in which numerous American Indian authors' works are treated alongside African American and white southern writers. Keith Cartwright provides a particularly lively examination of southeastern Native folktales, history, and literature as part of *Sacral Grooves, Limbo Gateways: Travels in Deep Southern Time, Circum-Caribbean Space, Afro-creole Authority* (2013). Rain Prud'homme-Cranford and Gina Caison are both at work on promising book-length projects. Cranford's *Gumbo Banaha Stories: Louisiana Indigeneities and Decolonizing the Transnational South,* seeks to place literary and cultural artifacts created by members of Louisiana's Native and Creole diasporas within the southern literary canon. Caison's project, *Red States: Indigeneity, Settler Colonialism, and Southern Studies,* pairs Native and non-Native texts in order to demonstrate the ways American Indians confront ongoing colonialism and continue to be present in the South.

Eric Gary Anderson, whose seminal work has been so important to my own understanding of what a Native Southern literary criticism might look like, is also breaking new ground in his research on southeastern earthworks. His keynote address at Mercer University's 2014

Native South Symposium, "Reading and Writing Earthworks," argued that "earthworks stand as evidence of Native literacy, Native technology, and Native angles of vision." In a more recent article, "Earthworks and Contemporary Indigenous American Literature: Foundations and Futures," Anderson engages in a close reading of both Allison Hedge Coke's *Blood Run* and a number of LeAnne Howe's pieces that reference earthworks, most notably four essays published between 2013 and 2015[1] which Anderson describes as "a four-part suite, a kind of earthworks jazz that explores many layers and variations on performance but that also, taken together, forms one larger composition" (15). These essays are products of a collaborative research project in which Howe has been engaged since 2011 called "Indigenous Knowledge, Contemporary Performance." Her team members include playwrights and theater scholars, and the project "involves developing new Indigenous performance models based dramaturgically on Indigenous cultural texts" ("Embodied Tribalography: First Installment" 178). Along with Monique Mojica, Howe is developing a dramaturgical model based on earthworks' structures. In the same way that land is layered in mound-building, Howe and Mojica are layering stories. The end product of their collaboration is a forthcoming play called *Sideshow Freaks and Circus Injuns,* which will certainly add another text to the rich collection of Native Southern literature.[2]

Though the development of a new Indigenous dramaturgical model is exciting, what I find most interesting in Howe's "four-part suite" of earthworks essays, is her conceptualization of embodiment. Howe first elaborates on this idea in the last chapter of *Choctalking on Other Realities,* "Embodied Tribalography: First Installment," tracing a new evolution of tribalography, her aesthetic theory and methodology which has inspired numerous Native and non-Native scholars and writers since 2002. She asserts that "what is missing from the 'Story of America' is a discussion of reciprocal embodiment between people and land as part and parcel of a tribalography" (173). In her original iteration, tribalography ties together "all the elements . . . of a storyteller's tribe, meaning the people, the land, and multiple characters and all their manifestations and revelations, and connect[s] these in past, present, and future milieus" ("The Story of America" 42). The critical difference between this idea and embodied tribalography is that Howe is attempting to demonstrate how tribal peoples may embody the land from which they come. She notes that in *Miko Kings* there is a reciprocal relationship between the land and Native characters, which then drove her to begin research on the earthworks on which ancient ball games were played ("Embodied Tribalography: First Installment" 174).

One of the most compelling examples that Howe uses to demonstrate the idea of Native embodiment of land is the 3,600-year-old Bird Mound at Poverty Point, Louisiana (179). She describes how 238,000 cubic meters of soil were moved in approximately ninety days to create the mound (180). The time frame is important: approximately ninety days is the period of time between which a red-tailed hawk is born and leaves the nest.[3] Howe asserts that "Bird Mound at Poverty Point is possibly a performance mound that embodies the story of the red-tailed hawk from birth to first flight—the story of its creation. I suspect that the people who came together, from many directions, to write the story of Bird Mound into the land must have considered her an important symbol for their communities" (181). She discusses many ways that Bird Mound would have had meaning for its creators, including its calendar function, iconography, and how its creation suggests both the Vernal Equinox and the Summer Solstice, significant ceremonial cycles for the Choctaw. Bird Mound, of course, is not the only example of Native embodiment of land. In her coauthored essay "Life in a 21st Century Mound City," Howe argues that we should "think of mounds as linked chapters in the novel of Indigenous North and South America. With different characters and points of view that de-emphasize chronology and plot, but give voice to a plethora of storytellers writing on the land, we may find that earthworks are mnemonics designed to help Natives *remember* to return home for solar and lunar ceremonial events" (6). Again and again in her work, Howe notes the relationship between land and the Choctaw people, whether that land is the creative mud of *Nanih Waiya* or a flaming prairie in Oklahoma.

An overt illustration of Indigenous embodiment of land from Howe's oeuvre is her story "Indians Never Say Goodbye," in *Evidence of Red*, in which Ain't Sally first appears, a piece clearly grounded in the Texas landscape. The story is set in Hayrick, Texas, "outside of Dublin" (99). We are told that the place was "[o]nce a base camp for nomadic tribes following buffalo" (99) and that Hayrick took its name from "a solitary mountain standing in the breadth of open grasslands" (99). The rural roads of West Texas "were two lanes of dust and dirt," and one could see "stagnant, green-belted river beds and one-lane bridges" (100). There are also nine references to snakes or Snake People in a story of three pages.

"Indians Never Say Goodbye" is the first depiction of Howe in the hospital during her bout of rheumatic fever, in which Ain't Sally chants words of healing. This visit provides the frame for the memory of meeting Ain't Sally in Texas as a child. In the memory, the two share a vision of the Snake people eating "the intestines of [her] uncle's butchered cow" (101). Ain't Sally explains that when she was a child "they blew across this place like red dust devils on flat neutral plains" (100). Ain't Sally never reveals the identity of the Snake people, but she does share two pieces of knowledge with her niece: "The ghosts of your ancestors will visit you there" and "Indians never say goodbye," foreshadowing the hospital visit. This story would seem to be solely about the passing of Indigenous time/space knowledge from one generation to the next were it not for the final two paragraphs when Howe reveals that, twenty-five years later, she learns "[t]o make the sign of the snake means: Comanches are here." Through her numerous allusions to snakes and Snake people and by ending "Indians Never Say Goodbye" with these lines, Howe marks West Texas as Comanche land: the mountain, the plains, the "stagnant, green-belted river beds" (100). Like other female ancestor spirits in Howe's works such as Shakbatina in *Shell Shaker* and Ezol Day in *Miko Kings,* Ain't Sally's words enable her descendent to heal. Also, like Shakbatina and Ezol Day, Ain't Sally embodies Choctaw beliefs about the permeability of time and space. Yet the subtext of "Indians Never Say Goodbye," with its repetition of Comanche presence, can also be read as a lesson on tribal embodiment of land.

Embodiment of land is the point of departure for Howe's vision of embodied tribalography. Yet, as a methodology, embodied tribalography is more complex. In *Choctalking on Other Realities,* Howe as world traveler embodies immediate family members, ancient ancestors, and even non-Natives such as Humphrey Bogart, invoking the connectedness of Howe's original tribalographic theory. Despite Howe's cultural missteps in "I Fuck Up in Japan," an embodiment of land provides a path to healing. In "Carlos Castaneda Lives in Romania," the explicit theme of cultural authenticity artfully shifts once more to healing, this time through embodiment of the stories of others. Also, in "Carlos Castaneda Lives in Romania," an embodied tribalography is more personal, specific to Howe's family history, yet it simultaneously illuminates a key element of her creative process. Similarly, at the end of *Choctalking on Other Realities,* Howe comes back to *Miko Kings,* the novel that spurred her to begin researching earthworks and notes the way embodiment has affected her creative process: "Ezol Day is the metaphorical *iti fabassa,* the center pole of the story[4] of *Miko Kings,* ever-in-motion, connecting multiple worlds at once. In a way, I guess Ezol Day embodies me, not the other way around. I have her to thank for teaching me how to express the embodied stories presented here" (192–93). In this rhetorical move, Howe conflates herself and her character, which is one of the elements of her travelogue that clearly differentiates it from her other works. Yet, this also suggests an even more personal definition of "Choctalking": LeAnne Howe's individual Choctaw-talking perspective and its expression through poetry, drama, fiction, nonfiction, critical theory, and whatever new genre the author might invent.[5]

Though I have attempted a comprehensive analysis of the products of LeAnne Howe's more than thirty-year writing career, much remains to be done. Her work is rich, and she is prolific, with no signs of slowing down. In addition to two new plays, *Sideshow Freaks and Circus Injuns* and *Savage Conversations,* and a documentary, *Searching for Sequoyah,* Howe is also hard at work on *Memoir of a Choctaw in the Arab Revolts of 1917 and 2011,* which she has described as "a new form of trans-Indigenous novel" (Howe and Etheridge). Along with its innovative trans-Indigenous elements, which will depict relationships between the Choctaw and two Middle Eastern tribes, Howe is also experimenting with form. She explains that the novel "will have film, memoir, fiction, songs, and imagery in e-book form" ("The Native South" 144). Howe's experimentation with digital forms in her 2015 production of an animated video poem, "Noble Savage Learns to Tweet," is another example of her pioneering aesthetic.[6] Thematically, the piece continues the adventures of Howe's contemporary, parodic "Noble Savage" from *Evidence of Red,*[7] manifesting in this piece as a social networking, Wall Street trader (traitor?). On the page, the poem takes the form of a Twitter feed; in the animation, Noble Savage's tweets are given a depth and context that underscores the line "comedy 2 horror" ("Noble Savage Learns," 99

Poems for the 99 Percent 43). When Noble Savage tweets that he is on a "first-name basis with Wall Street culture," the images of faceless Native people being hung from a gallows follow. The next image, a sign that reads "CHRISTMAS SALE / DAKOTA LAND / PRICES TO SKYROCKET," alerts the viewer that Noble Savage's alliance is with the same nation that simultaneously hung thirty-eight Dakota men on December 26, 1862.[8] Noble Savage's other questionable Wall Street alliances include Lady Gaga, whose animated figure strips his suit away to reveal a stereotypical loincloth, and "suicide girls" who wear Plains Indian headdresses as fashion statements. Given her exciting new works, I certainly intend to continue investigating LeAnne Howe's writing and look forward to what others have to say about it. And there are many other writers of the Native South whose work needs further analysis and explication.

I have been heartened to observe what appears to be the beginnings of a turn toward the South in Native American and Indigenous studies. The presence of LeAnne Howe, Craig Womack, and Allison Hedge Coke at the 2008 Society for the Study of Southern Literature Conference was but one of several hopeful occasions. Jace Weaver gave one of the keynote addresses at the 2014 Society for the Study of Southern Literature Conference on his recent publication, *The Red Atlantic,* and though that volume is about the entire Atlantic world, he notes many key exchanges that begin in or involve Indigenous peoples of what becomes the South including the diplomacy of Matoaka (Pocahontas), the Croatan chieftain Manteo's disappearance along with the other members of the "Lost Colony," and the treaty negotiated by Tomochichi to found the Georgia colony. It has also been encouraging to see leading scholars in Native American studies accept positions at major research institutions in the South, including Weaver's directorship of the Institute for Native American Studies (INAS) at the University of Georgia, Craig Womack's professorship at Emory University, and LeAnne Howe's appointment as Eidson Distinguished Professor of American Literature at the University of Georgia. These developments are particularly exciting because southern scholarship and institutions have traditionally focused on black/white relations, but as Weaver shared with me in an e-mail interview, he was recruited specifically "by an associate dean who wanted to confuse the Southern binary of race being about black and white and who felt that given Georgia's history it was important to have such a program." In fact, since the INAS program began operating in 2004–5, it has played an important role both locally and nationally. As Weaver notes, "In 2008, INAS organized and hosted the meeting at which the vote was taken to form NAISA [the Native American and Indigenous Studies Association]. We maintain a robust agenda of community-based scholarship, as well as programming. We have an undergraduate certificate program with approximately 35 students and a graduate certificate program with between 12–15 students." North Carolina also has options for students desiring to study in the field, including an American Indian and Indigenous Studies Program at the University of North Carolina at Chapel Hill, Western Carolina University's Cherokee Studies Program, and the American Indian Studies Program at the University of North Carolina at Pembroke, which offers specific courses on southeastern Indian peoples. The University of Florida offers a minor in American Indian and Indigenous studies. These kinds of programs are important for the future of Native American literary studies because they underscore the continuing presence and significance of Native peoples in the South, where we are haunted by the legacy of Removal.

In her recent *American Quarterly* essay, "A Return to the South," Jodi Byrd presents the clearest answer I have yet seen to the question: where do we go from here? Byrd's article engages with new southern studies, particularly Tara McPherson's postulation of a "non-South" which contrasts to the "many Souths" model born from transnational and creolization studies (609–10). Spurred by Taylor's assertion that "[the] Native South is a space rarely considered an active geography within Indian country at all, even by Native scholars" (11), and Newton's assertion that the Caribbean is also not accepted as an Indigenous space (121), Byrd makes this claim: "As an archetypal non-South, Native Souths are negated, and indigeneity itself provides the negative space through which arrival becomes intelligible" (611). Despite the erasures of Native peoples materially and ideologically from the Southeast, not simply via Removal, but through a settler colonialism that is maintained "as a structure rather than an event" (Wolfe 390), Byrd suggests a way for a "return" through one of the most familiar geographic spaces in southern literature: *Yokna (yakni)/patawpha (patafa). Yokna/yakni* means "land" in Chickasaw, and *patawpha/patafa* means "furrowed," "plowed," or "split open" ("A Return" 618).

Byrd cites another Chickasaw scholar Phillip Carroll Morgan's 2013 study of nineteenth-century Chickasaw governors, particularly the story of Cyrus Harris, elected five times between 1856 and 1872 (Morgan 68). Morgan presents significant support to argue that the name of Faulkner's fictional Yoknapatawpha County most likely was a result of family knowledge: Faulkner's great-grandfather had lived close to Harris, whose family home, *Yakni Patafa,* was built "atop an ancient Indian ceremonial mound near Pontotoc, Mississippi" (86).[9] The point of Morgan's historical and literary analysis is that Faulkner's popularity and its critical importance "reflect the power of the place in which his stories were conceived and written, and that the place is inseparable from its indigenous inhabitants and their traditions" (111). Jace Weaver has argued that Yoknapatawpha operates metaphorically for the way "the land that was once wholly Natives' has been split from them" ("Splitting the Earth" 67). For Byrd, *yakni patafa* could signal a new critical praxis that sutures past divides into calls for indigenous homecomings and (re) occupations:[10]

> What if, rather than remain a sui generis place-name within a fictional or even a geographic archive of deferral and loss, *yakni patafa* might signal a practice for us across time and through time? What if we imagined the land, the regions, the Souths and non-Souths discretely and in aggregate as not only split open but furrowed in an attempt to provide some deeper understanding toward the continual return of exegesis? And finally, what if Indians were able to return to these spaces as agentic participants capable of determining their own pasts and futures beyond those of the vested and occupying nation-states? (619).

Byrd has already demonstrated how *yakni patafa* as critical praxis might work, through the example of Phillip Carroll Morgan's analysis of Faulkner's texts and relationship with north Mississippi land. Yet the possibilities of this practice for Native Southern literary scholars seem infinite. Certainly, the investigation of earthworks, either as represented by Native authors or through a mound-layering aesthetic, could be another form of a "furrowed land" hermeneutics. Given that *yakni patafa* is a Chickasaw phrase, there might be other tribally specific approaches connected to southeastern Indigenous lands. My "Choctalking" reading of LeAnne Howe's works could be one such illustration, particularly when I focus on Choctaw words related to land, such as *Nanih Waiya* and *okchamali.* Byrd's discussion of *yakni patafa,* however, suggests more than a hermeneutic approach: the returns she imagines are also material and political. *Yakni patafa* could be read as another kind of "*Indigenous groundwork* [marking] Indigenous epistemologies that inform identities, resistances and survivals," both countering and seeking hegemony (Clark and Powell 5). In the case of Oklahoma-born Choctaw LeAnne Howe, her return to the South as an endowed chair at a major southern university reflects her own position as an "agentic participant," creating texts that determine Native pasts and futures from a tribally specific yet globally conscious perspective.

APPENDIX

THE NATIVE SOUTH, PERFORMANCE, AND GLOBALIZED TRANS-INDIGENEITY

Conversation With Leanne Howe

My second interview with Choctaw writer and professor LeAnne Howe was conducted on March 23, 2013, at the Dakota Nation's Mystic Lake Casino in Minneapolis, Minnesota, during the annual Native American Literature Symposium. Howe and I first met in 2008, when I interviewed her at the Society for the Study of Southern Literature's biennial conference in Williamsburg, Virginia. At that time, I was finishing my dissertation, one chapter of which examined spirituality in Howe's 2001 novel, *Shell Shaker.* That interview was eventually published in the journal *MELUS (Multi-Ethnic Literature of the United States)* in 2010.

KS: You were interviewed in the fall 2012 issue of the newsletter for the Society for the Study of Southern Literature in which you spoke at length about the burgeoning field of Native Southern studies and about how you and other southeastern tribal peoples self-identify as both Native and southern. So, as an extension of that, do you consider your writing to be southern literature? Would you classify it that way?

LH: Yes. Absolutely.

KS: Would you say that "Choctalking on Other Realities" is just as southern as *Shell Shaker,*[1] considering the difference in their settings, because they're coming from that same original space of people from Mississippi, or the place before Mississippi?

LH: Right.

KS: So, the classification for you is always connected to land.

LH: Always. I have this collection of short stories coming out, *Choctalking on Other Realities: New and Selected Stories.* Years and years ago, I'd written a lot more on the Global South. In fact, there's "The Chaos of

Angels." I don't see it as the Global South, but others may. I see it as the South, and there's a fight between a character, a Choctaw woman and an African American woman, and she later morphs into Haiti because Choctaws were once exported as slaves there in the 1700s, I believe. So, with the aid of the Chickasaws, a lot of our men were exported to work in the sugar plantations of what would become Haiti. So, I wrote this story, trying to intervene. It's set in Louisiana, in New Orleans, where we are everywhere, and we are nowhere. There's a line in *Shell Shaker* about that. But, the South and southern studies had so long, has so long—this is a raging point for me—ignored us, in fact, excluded us. Natives from the Five Tribes could not be in this conversation because the South was about black and white. Now, there are people like Eric,[2] and a whole slew of really good scholars who are saying, "Well, perhaps we should we think differently about this exclusion?" and I'm appreciative of their work, but I'm really railing against that earlier southern literary tradition that wholly and completely left us out of the discourse, although I admit Faulkner invented southern Natives in narratives. So, when I met you at the conference,[3] I think I had said something to that effect. Craig Womack was there . . . I remember.

KS: Allison.[4]

LH: Allison was there. We were trying to intervene and say, "Look." And maybe the field has moved on, but I have remained unhappy about why it took so long to consider southeastern Natives in the discussions of the South. Natives have great allies in Eric Anderson and Annette Trefzer, to name only two. Historian Theda Perdue is another. Still it seems to me that our homelands establish us as original to the South, and for any discourse to exclude us is willful, intellectual amnesia. Rarely do scholars say, "Oh, I never knew there were Natives in the South." No, it's something much more dangerous. They say something like this. "Well, you are no longer in the South, so you can't be part of the discourse about the South. Alas." It's a willful desire to make us absent; to make us disappear. So many of the narratives with our beloved trickster rabbit come out of the South. It isn't African Americans who have excluded us though. It's typically been white southerners who have happily replaced Natives in the stories with their version of history. What should we call this purposeful act?

KS: Genocide.[5]

LH: Yes genocide.

KS: Which is a word that is still not widely circulated in reference to Indian Removal and other similar US government-sanctioned acts.

LH: I know. That word is reserved for Jews and Jewish history, but it can and should also refer to American Indians.

KS: I mean, it's circulated in Native studies, but it's not widely circulated in discourse about the South.

LH: That's right because you know, it's this idea of, "we didn't do anything wrong." And, "You guys were interfering with progress." In *The Mascot Opera: A Minuet* for instance, I made Andrew Jackson, Andrea Jackson. His character would morph into this beautiful woman and then morph back to him as we are being replaced in the South. So, in that way I made him disappear. Kind of a tit for tat.

KS: When did this come out? I haven't read it.

LH: A long time ago I wrote *The Mascot Opera: A Minuet* as a ten-minute play for Minneapolis Mixedblood Theatre, but it was either too complex—it was a musical after all—or they didn't like it. [*Laughs.*] Whatever the case they didn't produce it. I think probably in the next couple of years we'll do something about it again at Illinois because we have so many problems with the school's former mascot, Chief Illiniwek.[6] So, the point to all this is that I wrote it as a response to willful amnesia. *Shell Shaker* is a response to the South's willful amnesia. The fight for our lands and lands in Oklahoma continues. For example when I was working on *Shell Shaker,* we were having our own warfare with our tribal chief.[7] He died in October 2011. He ended up going to prison. So, tribal people are having to fight outsiders, and they're having to fight insiders, and you have to do it simultaneously. I was very active in Choctaws for Democracy, and so was Jacki Rand[8] who was here yesterday at the conference. She presented on Mississippi Choctaws and violence against women, her current project. But Jacki and I and many others were a part of the Choctaws for Democracy, as was Scott Morrison, Doug Dry, Bob Burlison, there were hundreds of us during those years. At one meeting, I remember in Atoka, Oklahoma, there were nearly three hundred people gathered together concerned that some candidates running for chief were excluded from information they needed to run for office. The candidates couldn't get our tribe's voter registration records so they could contact voters to ask for their vote. The tribe's lawyer, who was also the lawyer for the Chickasaws, at that time, represented the tribe in order to insure that Choctaws running for office could not get the voter registered list. The stakes of that election were so high—it was like a Third World election. But things only got worse. At that time, our former chief was also accused of raping women, at work.

So in writing *Shell Shaker* I placed that stake in the ground in the eighteenth century in the Lower Mississippi Valley when things were tense for the southeastern tribes. In some ways, I think those events continued to haunt us into the twenty-first century. Because the Choctaws had a civil war that occurred because of Red Shoes in the eighteenth century, we had another kind of civil war in the 1990s. Choctaws for Democracy wanted to insure that we could have a fair election. That's what I believe Choctaws for Democracy was all about. To this day, I think I pay a price for being part of the organization. Scott Morrison, a Choctaw lawyer and activist, is dead. I think Doug Dry went to work for the Muskogee Creeks. (I'm not sure where he is working at this time.)

KS: Do you see Oklahoma as being culturally southern?

LH: Yes.

KS: Can you talk about that a little bit? There are two things I'm thinking about: one, you've got the Five "Civilized Tribes" from the Southeast, and they are located in Oklahoma. In our last interview you talked about Choctaws taking the physical dirt and the land and the place names and all of that, with them, on the Trail of Tears.

LH: Everything about southeastern Oklahoma is southern, the foods, our heritage, and cultural and ceremonial lifeways. The "cult of grandmothers" is strong in Oklahoma among Natives and even non-Natives, another cultural lifeway that I argue comes from tribal people. What I mean is that everyone looks to the families' matriarch for guidance, the oldest woman. Women control or "run" all kinds of businesses and community organizations in Southeastern Oklahoma. Another example is the way southeastern Oklahomans speak. If you listen to the way in which we speak, it's an extremely southeastern accent. And I think I mentioned this before, southerners do not speak with a drawl because it's something they brought from say, Ireland. I think it's because they were influenced by the Native pronunciation of vowels. We were talking yesterday with Gwen Westerman, who was raised in Oklahoma, and you know, she's Cherokee and Dakota. We were teasing her husband, and she said, "Say my name to him." And I said "Gwee-in, Gwee-in." And it has multiple syllables, and he just laughed because he hasn't heard that so much because they live in Minnesota. So we had this whole discussion on how our vowels and song-speak influenced southern speak. *I know, I know,* the linguists say otherwise. There's a scholar here from Ireland, Padraig Kirwan, and he and I laughed about how southern speak is supposed to be a derivation of Irish speech patterns. It's kind of funny when you think about it.

KS: Earlier you were talking about the "Chaos of Angels" and the message that Grandmother had for the Choctaw woman was, "You didn't get the joke. You responded with anger."

LH: "You responded with anger." Well, that character would be me. [*Laughs.*] I'm the one who is always angry. But to get at that anger, I use humor. And so, Isaac in the novel [*Shell Shaker*] is the humorous character. He's very funny in the story and the way he comes at political issues, and yet, he's the character that must sacrifice himself. So, you know, in my new play, *Side Show Freaks and Circus Injuns,* coauthored with Monique Mojica, I come out of Oklahoma, but the other characters I've created must go back to the mounds and crawl up through that cave in the mound and lose the wounds that centuries of colonialism have left on the body. My character is Panther Girl in this new play that we'll do in 2016. So the long and the short of it is I'm trying to write myself healthy, perform myself healthy, by losing the wounds of the past three hundred years. I believe the art I create in my lifetime can heal the anger I carry. I'm speaking here also about historic grief and trauma.

KS: You are an actress as well as a writer, professor, and critic. How do you see your experiences and worldview as a performer impacting your creative works? And what is the difference for you as an actress between writing drama or fiction and poetry?

LH: Well, I don't really think of myself as an actress.

KS: You don't?

LH: I wish I was.

KS: But you do perform, right?

LH: I'm a performer. Roxy[9] and I neither one, in our early plays—we never thought of ourselves as actors: we were performers. And somebody else would always have to do the heavy acting in our plays.

KS: Okay.

LH: So, Monique Mojica, who's my coauthor and co-performer, now she's a real actress because she can embody Shakespeare, she can embody, you know, characters on TV or by other Native playwrights—I can't do that. And, so, I could never say I was an actress because I don't think I have the talent to do that. I do embody the South. I embody my homeland, both metaphorically and physically. I'm just this short, stocky Choctaw woman, who, you know, came up out of those mounds just like everybody else. But when I say things are about land—of course I'm including more subjects that just "the land," I mean settler colonials want our bodies, our identity, our lifeblood, everything. But land is a thing I carry with me, just as my ancestors did when they carried dirt in their pockets from *Nanih Waiya.* And so by healing myself, metaphorically, we artists may end up healing the universe or spaces we inhabit. I'm trying to heal the space for my granddaughters. That they may grow into the healing is my highest desire for them. This all sounds like a lot of malarkey, I know. But there it is.

KS: You mentioned in the *SSSL Newsletter* interview, in regards to *Sideshow Freaks and Circus Injuns,* that you saw this work as revitalizing Native performance. How do you see that happening?

LH: Of course, *Indian Radio Days* is not that kind of play, and *Big PowWow* was set again at *Nanih Waiya* with the old ghost, a bone picker, which is an earlier play. Roxy and I were working through the past. We were reimagining an indigenous literary tradition and an indigenous performance tradition. I've written a paper that will probably be out this year on the Bird Mound at Poverty Point in Louisiana, how it was created in three months, which mirrors the three months' gestation for a red-tailed hawk. But *Sideshow Freaks and Circus Injuns* is a different animal, pun intended. It reveals, I think, a different meaning of indigenous performance.

KS: Can you talk more about the relationship between Bird Mound and performance?

LH: Red-tailed hawks embody special meanings for southeastern Natives, especially Choctaws. The red-tailed hawk is a solar bird, one of power and strength, and the tail feathers are bright red in sunlight. Red signifies lifeblood and is sometimes a powerful metaphor for war. These predator birds mate over a period of a few days in late winter or early spring. By March, the female lays her eggs, one every other day (two eggs in a nest can take up to four days to be laid). The incubation period for hawk eggs is typically thirty-five days. It generally takes another four days for the small nestlings to hatch out of their shells. Once out of their shells, the nestlings will spend another forty-six days or so in the nest before the baby birds begin to leave on short flights. The total time needed to create a red-tailed hawk, from mating to a fledgling leaving the nest, is approximately ninety days. Three months. Therefore, it would seem that Bird Mound at Poverty Point is possibly a performance mound that embodies the story of the red-tailed hawk from conception to first flight—the story of its creation. What were our ancestors trying to say in that three months building period? It was a performance of creation. So, we're trying to show through this process of embodiment, of embodying land, that story that comes up out of land. That bird mound is indeed influential to Choctaw people today because the red tail hawk is emblematic of our power as a group. That mound is five thousand years old, and knowing the mound's interaction with our culture is pretty remarkable. So, that southeastern embodiment, of knowing ourselves connected to the land still affects me as an artist. I'm still working through, not only our mounds, but understanding the performative aspect of many mounds. Hopefully that "knowing" will come out in the play *Side Show Freaks and Circus Injuns.* These days Native performers and writers are asking twenty-first-century questions. No longer are we content to write a victim's narrative. In *Side Show* we're trying to create a performance on the land, something our ancestors were trying to create five thousand years ago. Oh dear, more hubris, I know, *I know.*

KS: And so, to be dislocated, or disenfranchised from the land means losing an essential part of your lifeways.

LH: Right.

KS: You engage with that land. It's part of the story, but it's also a part of the body.

LH: It's part of the body. And it's part of the Native physical and political landscape. They've just found that the Rappahannock had an ancient mound. So, what we are doing is imagining a similar kind of process with this play, performing at mound sites all across Native North America. And it crosses many generations. My great aunt joined the circus in the late 1920s and "played Indian." It's my own narrative intertwined with many others from southeastern Oklahoma. Monique's writing about her family's experience in the circus. There are multiple collisions that make this play possible. My work is about land and all of the manifestations that have to do with "Southeastern-ness."

KS: We keep coming back to this theme. I'm really excited to hear you talking about this. This is what I sort of suspected, and you've said it in other ways. . . .

LH: And "Southeastern-ness" continues to influence my future work. We have a gang of people at work with us to help articulate the work through embodied performance, Chickasaw, Choctaw artists from Oklahoma, along with First Nations' artists. Can we heal ourselves? Can we be healed through art? *I think we can.* We're hopeful that, once the work is up, we can begin teaching from it—about historic grief and trauma. Then we'll see if the process is helpful. I hope. I hope.

KS: I read in your blog that you did "Choctalking on Other Realities" as a one-woman show a couple of years ago. I'm curious how that text changed when you changed form. Or did it? Or what did it mean to you?

LH: I didn't change the text. I was working with a filmmaker, Jim Fortier, who created nine short films, to enhance the visualization of a one-woman show. So, there are film cues that come up, and you'll see a child's feet for instance that morphs into a closet that morphs into the riot in Jerusalem, in East Jerusalem that happened when I was there, which was during the Intifada. The story circles back to the 1960s when African Americans were changing and calling for civil rights, and American Indians were doing similarly. During the show, nine short film segues flanked that performance. They served to bring the audience back into the restaurant, to the characters of those three women in the narrative that were Jewish, African American, and Choctaw. I played all the parts. That's the only difference.

KS: During the 2010–11 academic year, you were a Fulbright Professor in Amman, Jordan. What is it about Jordan and its culture that attracts you, and more broadly, how did you become interested in the Middle East?

LH: Tribes. I spent a lot of time with tribes in 1992 and 1993. I lived in Jordan from 1993 to 1994. The first time I went to the Middle East I was on a study tour in 1992 and we went to Jordan, and the occupied territories which included Gaza. And, when we went to live in Jordan in 1993, I realized there were literally hundreds of tribes there. Jordanians are extremely tribal. At that time social justice was meted out by judges within these tribes that cooperated with one another. For instance, someone had shot a man from a different tribe. So the judges in the tribes meted out justice. All the members of the offending tribe, whose member shot someone from the other tribe, had to leave town for fifteen years. I repeat, every member of that tribe had to pack up and leave town for fifteen years. It only seemed fair if you think about it. That the punishment is communal has a chilling effect on mayhem in the future. Tribes and tribalism in the Middle East fascinated me. Some things, lifeways, just made sense (to me). So, I fell in the love with the people and the deserts. They took us into their homes and lands and hosted us, and I responded. It was call and response. So, I had the piece, "Choctalking on Other Realities," and when I went back to Jordan as a Fulbright scholar, I just happened to be there during the Arab Spring, when the Middle East erupted. Hence, a new book. My Choctaw character goes to Bilaad ash Sham in 1913 and stays through the Arab Revolt. He gives up Christianity and becomes something newly created.

KS: He's a missionary, right?

LH: [*Laughs.*] Right, at first he is. But he gives it up for a newly created life.

KS: In the SSSL interview, you said that you were trying to birth a new form of trans-Indigenous novel. Can you talk about what that process is like and maybe how it is similar to or departs from your approaches in *Shell Shaker* and *Miko Kings*?

LH: Oh, this new book is a completely different animal and let me just say, I realize my new work could be a ginormous failure.

KS: Isn't that always true in a creative work, though? You're going out on a limb?

LH: Yes, but I've always thought that Natives are/were creating larger frames in their narratives. At least this is how I read American Indian, Indigenous, literature—that it is, indeed, a tribalography.[10] So, what does that really mean in praxis? I'm interested in answering that question. This new "novel"—if it works—will have film, memoir, fiction, songs, and imagery in an e-book format. So, I'm grabbing all the things that I work in, including poetry and song and writing and filming and performing, in a text. And it is trans-Indigenous and trans-genre. The epilogue will be interviews with the descendants of some of the Arabs that fought in that revolt. They will tell their own story.

KS: But you know what? I'm just curious, as someone who thinks about your work a lot—

LH: Oh God, I can't imagine that. Sounds terrible, is it?!

KS: Ha! Not in the least. So, one of the amazing things about *Shell Shaker* is how you move between centuries, and it pulls together some very diverse cultural and temporal issues. And you have some mixed media in *Miko Kings,* right? If you look at your work in an arc, can you see this novel as a progression of things you've tried? I realize it's a very new form that you're talking about by using digital media in a way that people still really aren't doing.

LH: *His Last Game* was a film, and it was incorporated into the story.[11]

KS: You had actual newspaper clippings too.

LH: Yes, newspaper clippings. And Ezol is traveling across time. She is the cosmos, in some ways. She's really telling a story of our math. She's really talking poetry. She also appears in *His Last Game* in the book. The book opens with, "This is a film. This is a book. This is a story." And so, I do see this as a progression that technology allows me to make. But I don't believe that Natives separate by genre, at least not in the storytelling. So it feels right to be able to do the work. But, you know, I know a lot of people who think that this is just outrageous. And my own graduate students are like, "Hmmm. But, it's a text, right?"

KS: Do you anticipate going in a similar direction after this book?

LH: Yeah, but I don't know what it is, yet. We were talking about this because I want to know where we're going as a field. Where are we going as a field? And, I want to be a part of that conversation, but I'm not quite sure what the conversation will be.

KS: So we were talking about the form as being the new element.

LH: Again, it could be failure. [*Laughs.*]

KS: I understand. But then you have also said "a new form of trans-Indigenous novel." Is that something that already exists? Are you thinking of that in a line like *Almanac of the Dead*? I just mean the trans-Indigenous part.

LH: No, I didn't invent trans-Indigenous because, you know, that's what Chad Allen talks about.[12] I'm saying that this work is new because by going across the ocean it links tribes in the East and tribes in the West.

KS: As opposed to all descendants of people of the Americas.

LH: Right. You know, Leslie, in *Almanac of the Dead,* goes to Asia.

KS: And there's the African connection.

LH: Right, she goes east, Africa, Mexico. Her novel is situating and is pivoting in this way, between North-South-East-West. So, in that way, perhaps I'm in conversation with what Leslie Silko was doing twenty years ago.

KS: You've also written about connections—and we've already talked about this a little bit—between Native Americans and Palestinians, with a character in "Choctalking on Other Realities" claiming that Oklahoma was the first Israel. How do you see Indigenous American issues intersecting with Palestinian issues, and what draws you to this particular example as opposed to other examples of settler colonialism around the globe?

LH: Land. And it was something that I saw firsthand. I saw it for myself. They were fighting over dispossession of one people for another group of people. This is just something that I saw, and I could make sense of in my writing.

KS: So much of your writing is meticulously researched and contains representations of historical figures and events. What do you feel is the relationship between fiction and history in your work? We just had a conversation today about actual historical events in relation to *Shell Shaker* and Choctaws for Democracy.

LH: I see history as story that historians tell. Yesterday I was just with two historians on the ethics panel. We had two historians at our table, and we come at story in very different ways. Jacki[13] said, "Well, history has to be objective." I think, "Is that really true though?" I don't think I'm telling an objective story so I guess that is one big difference. I'm telling a true story. Whether it's fiction or history. It's true that the world is created in a novel. In *Miko Kings,* the history of Oklahoma as Indian Territory and the baseball games were something that mainstream people in the late-twentieth century had never heard of. Crash Parr, who is a Cherokee from Oklahoma—from Tulsa—had written a lot on Baseball's Sandlots. He had given me a lot of research he had gathered. When I began to look at the newspaper archives, my God, Indians playing baseball in Indian Territory was just everywhere. But people had totally forgotten about, didn't know it, couldn't remember. A lot of the work that I *think* I do is recovering stories that are there. The story wants to be told. In my writer's hands the story must have a twist. And here's the thing: I don't think I seek the stories out. The story looms somewhere in the ether and finds me. Certainly this missionary character in my new novel goes to the Middle East. It's a story that wants to be told. I'm not sure I would have chosen it, even though I have loved living in Jordan. But I'm happy to be writing it. So, in that way, I am like a historian: only different.

KS: In *Miko Kings* there is this newspaper image—it's the front-page story on the San Francisco earthquake. What Ezol comments on is related to Choctaws in the community, and it's an interesting juxtaposition. That headline is just blaring "San Francisco Earthquake," and she's talking about this other history that is important and relevant to her experience and her uncle's experience. How do you manage to negotiate tensions between personal and/or individual histories and public or dominant cultural memories of history? Do you feel like you're trying to negotiate that?

LH: Yes. I tell you whom I rely on as one of my mentors, although he probably doesn't know it. Raymond Fogelson, an emeritus professor at the University of Chicago wrote a wonderful paper on the ethnohistory of events and non-events. The San Francisco earthquake was an epitomizing event, especially for the dominant culture, but it wasn't to folks in Oklahoma, so theoretically, I relied on his work to help me negotiate the questions I had about certain events in *Miko Kings.* Ray has been a mentor to about a million graduate students at the University of Chicago, and he's also been a mentor to American Indians. (Okay, I exaggerated the number, one million.) Ray worked with Will West Long (Cherokee), when he was a young scholar. Will West Long was a medicine person in North Carolina, Eastern Band of Cherokee Indians. So I quote Ray in "The Story of America: A Tribalography." In my work, I think I'm trying to recover southeastern Indian ways of being. Maybe that also comes from my grandparents because they were commenting and reading the paper twice a day, they listened to the radio every morning, they talked to the birds and small animals living in the trees around their house, they were interested in tribal things, and spirits, and they also sat with the dead when called upon for funerals. Their lives were a tribalography in which they were adding to their experiences.

KS: At this conference, they put me on a parody panel. I hadn't considered that I was writing about parody when I submitted my abstract, even though the paper is on Hollywood Indians and other simulations in your work. So I've been thinking about humor, and you've already talked a bit today about the way that you use humor as a coping mechanism. This morning I had a chance to read some of the introduction to *Seeing Red,*[14] the section about humor and trickster figures and dealing with these dominant cultural narratives about Indians. Can you just talk some more about the way that you use humor and satire and parody? Is it primarily a coping mechanism? Do you also see it coming out of a trickster tradition?

LH: You should talk to my colleague Harvey about that. Harvey Markowitz worked with the Lakota. He speaks Lakota. He wrote that section on humor in *Seeing Red: Hollywood's Pixeled Indians.* My relatives, my family, are, among other things, a bunch of jokers. Everybody was always joking. In fact, I joke a lot and sometimes my jokes fall flat. My editor for instance doesn't see humor in my work especially when I am a year late for deadlines.

KS: [*Laughs.*]

LH: They're very earnest people, editors. Seriously, I'm irreverent. I use vulgar language in my stories because it makes me laugh. I'm my own audience, I guess. I'm probably better at irony than straight-out humor. But the jokes in *Indian Radio Days* are pretty funny.

KS: I was looking at my paper last night and laughing out loud at the quotes that I had pulled out of the play because they're just so funny. And I realized I had couched some of it in this very serious, critical perspective. But you know, "Red Woman Tobacco" is not that far off from "Red Man Tobacco" or "Cheap Cherokee"/"Jeep Cherokee."

LH: Big Chief, and Little Brave condoms.[15]

KS: It is funny.

LH: Yeah, but when we went to the Smithsonian to perform *Indian Radio Days,* we'd have an all-white audience, and they didn't laugh at all. Some humor doesn't translate, but we'd go to Indian communities to perform and people would fall out of their chairs. They just fell out. Men, women, children laughing. So you know, "what plays in New York won't play in Poughkeepsie." Mainstream audiences at that time didn't feel they could laugh because we were supposed to be the "stoic Indians."

KS: I guess maybe we're getting past those cultural assumptions. I showed that clip to my students last semester of you on the *Daily Show* talking about the Chief Illiniwek controversy. This was after we had read *Shell Shaker,* so they had some contextualization, and when you gave Aasif Mandvi an "Indian Burn," one of my students couldn't quit laughing. He said, "I can't believe LeAnne Howe would do that."

LH: Why do I know how to do that? [*Laughs.*] Aasif said, "Give me the Indian Burn." [*Makes Indian Burn sound effect.*] He said "Oh, that really hurt!" I said, "Why do both of us know what that is?" And we laughed. Yeah, wasn't that wild?

KS: Yeah.

LH: Indians are pretty damn funny. I think it is a coping mechanism, but we're also funny people. It's surprising there are not more Native stand-up comedians. In my next life.

NOTES

INTRODUCTION

1. Dean Rader has described the first thirty-five pages of Howe's collection, *Evidence of Red,* as "a virtual anthology of Native genres" (*Engaged Resistance* 136).

2. I have heard Howe state on a number of occasions that she spent ten years researching and writing *Shell Shaker,* including at a reading she gave at High Point University on February 20, 2014. Though she is undoubtedly a twenty-first-century writer, her work also clearly overlaps with the Native American Renaissance.

3. *Big PowWow,* cowritten with Choctaw Roxy Gordon and performed in 1987 at Sojourner Theater Company in Fort Worth, Texas.

4. Kentucky has no state or federally recognized tribes. This is ironic, given its long history of Indigenous inhabitants; the state would not exist were it not for several treaties with the Cherokees.

5. The interview was published in the journal *MELUS* in 2010 as "Choctawan Aesthetics, Spirituality, and Gender Relations: An Interview with LeAnne Howe."

6. See Christy Stanlake's *Native American Drama: A Critical Perspective* (2009); Melanie Benson Taylor's *Reconstructing the Native South: American Indian Literature and the Lost Cause* (2012); Chanette Romero's *Activism in the American Novel: Religion and Resistance in Fiction by Women of Color* (2012); Keith Cartwright's *Sacral Grooves, Limbo Gateways: Travels in Deep Southern Time, Circum-Caribbean Space, Afro-creole Authority* (2013); Padraig Kirwan's *Sovereign Stories: Aesthetics, Autonomy, and Contemporary Native American Writing* (2013); and Monika Siebert's *Indians Playing Indian: Multiculturalism and Contemporary Indigenous Art in North America* (2015).

7. Horan and Kim have described the story "Choctalking on Other Realities" as "paradigmatic" (39), affirming Craig Womack's argument that the story's significance lies in the questions it provokes about indigeneity and geography ("Review of *Evidence of Red*" 158). I would argue that the piece is also paradigmatic of Howe's body of work.

8. Womack is responding particularly to the idea that English is the "enemy's language," such as in Joy Harjo's and Gloria Bird's 1999 collection, *Reinventing the Enemy's Language: Contemporary Native Writings of North America.*

9. Womack's argument echoes Acoma poet Simon Ortiz's claim in his 1981 essay, "Towards a National Indian Literature: Cultural Authenticity and Nationalism," that

"it is entirely possible for a people to retain and maintain their lives through the use of any language" ("Appendix" 257).

10. Coauthors of *American Indian Literary Nationalism,* as well as numerous individually authored pieces.

11. Edited by Womack, Daniel Heath Justice, and Christopher B. Teuton.

12. The material quoted by Anderson here follows his own reference to Warrior's *American Quarterly* piece, "A Room of One's Own at the ASA: An Indigenous Provocation." Cox's monograph puts into practice Warrior's proposal in *Tribal Secrets: Recovering American Indian Intellectual Traditions* that "critical interpretation of [writings by American Indian authors] can proceed primarily from Indian sources" (xvi).

13. This may be a reference to a language known as Proto-Muskogean, the parent language of the Muskogean language family, comprising the still living languages Choctaw, Creek-Seminole, Chickasaw, Koasati, Alabama, and Mikasuki (Haag 276).

14. A variation on this scene is depicted in Howe's essay "Yaa Jordan, Yaa 'Ayouni" in *Choctalking on Other Realities.*

15. See Parker, "Red Slippers and Cottonmouth Moccasins: White Anxieties in Faulkner's Indian Stories" (2002–3); Galloway, "The Construction of Faulkner's Indians" (2002–3); Weaver, Warrior, and Womack, *American Indian Literary Nationalism* (2006); Taylor, *Reconstructing the Native South: American Indian Literature and the Lost Cause* (2012); and Morgan, *Riding Out the Storm: 19th Century Chickasaw Governors, Their Lives, and Intellectual Legacy* (2013). The forthcoming collection of essays from the 2016 Faulkner and Yoknapatawpha conference, "Faulkner and the Native South," will also contribute to this growing area of scholarly concern.

16. Taylor's *Reconstructing the Native South* credits "a small but growing cadre of Native South scholars" such as Eric Gary Anderson, Annette Trefzer, Ellen Arnold, Geary Hobson, and Janet McAdams (x).

17. Taylor is citing a 1996 study by Theda Perdue and Michael Green.

18. See Deloria, "American Indians, American Studies, and the ASA."

19. Oklahoma or *okla humma* means "red people" in Choctaw (Haag 277).

CHAPTER ONE

1. Clark and Powell also cite roots for Indigenous groundwork in the writings of Vine Deloria Jr., Robert K. Thomas, Elizabeth Cook-Lynn, Taiaiake Alfred, and Daniel R. Wildcat.

2. The Mississippi Band of Choctaw Indians was federally recognized in 1945, and the Jena Band of Choctaw was federally recognized in 1995, though of course, their communities existed long before US government acknowledgment (Phyllis J. Anderson; "Jena Band of Choctaw Indians").

3. Kreyling's "The Fathers: A Postsouthern Narrative Reading" and Romine's "Where Is Southern Literature? The Practice of Place in a Postsouthern Age."

4. Trefzer suggests borrowing the term "palimpsest" from postcolonial theory which "allows us to see the complex textuality of [the South's] cultural traces and renders visible the histories of marginalized and colonized peoples" (29).

5. Betrayals by the fictional personages of Redford McAlester and Red Shoes and the historical personages Red Shoe and Greenwood LeFlore will be discussed later in the chapter.

6. Carson's classification of LeFlore as such is based on Caribbean theories of creolization focusing on "the processes whereby people who came to the Americas drew from the cultures of the people they encountered to weave together New World societies" ("Greenwood" 223).

7. I spoke with Jeffery Darensbourg, Alligator Band Council member of the Attakapa-Ishak Nation, who claims there is "NO evidence" of Attakapa cannibalism. Darensbourg explains that the tribe calls itself the "Ishak," or "human beings," whereas the Choctaws had called them "hattak apa," meaning "cannibals." Darensbourg thinks the name evolved because the Choctaws considered the Ishak "uncivilized as [they] preferred decentralized governance, a stark contrast to the highly hierarchal politics of the Choctaw." He also notes that there are conflicting historical accounts of Attakapa cannibalism ranging from Cabeza de Vaca's story that refutes the idea to Simon de Bell-Isle's description of it. He argues that accounts of cannibalism "[seem] to be second hand, and [were] useful as an idea to dehumanize and justify colonization and missionary activity" (Darensbourg).

8. In the century between these two divides, France was defeated in the Seven Years' War, ultimately losing its control in North America (DeRosier 16). Though New Orleans was under Spanish rule, Great Britain became the sole European power with whom the Native peoples could trade, a particularly difficult shift for the Choctaws since they had been accustomed to a system of diplomatic gift exchange with the French, and the English relied upon private enterprise and market values (O'Brien, "Protecting Trade" 104). The American Revolution created another disturbance in the trading dynamic between tribes and colonizers: since all of the larger Indian groups in the South, including the Choctaws, Chickasaws, Cherokees, and Creeks, had sided with Great Britain during the war, the United States viewed the tribes as "conquered" (O'Brien, "The Conqueror" 152). However, this perspective was challenged at the 1785 signing of the Hopewell Treaty with the newly formed United States government when "the Choctaws dominated the process of treaty making and assumed the continuation of their absolute sovereignty and control over their own destiny" (172). It was not until Jacksonian-era Removal that the politically and economically influential Choctaws' power base declined in the Lower Mississippi Valley.

9. Byrd translates "chaos" as "haksuba" rather than "huksuba" as does Howe.

10. Byrd argues that the "tattooed, blue-lipped Ancient Ones" the protagonist references at the beginning of the story operate as both an allusion to "Choctaw women's tradition of tattooing their lips with blue ink and a genealogical trace to the African and African-Choctaw ancestors of the Haitian woman" (*The Transit of Empire* xxviii).

11. The Dawes Act divided tribally held land into allotments with the goal of converting tribes from the communal method of hunting and gathering to the individualistic and capitalistic method of private farming. The allotments were to be held in trust and not to be taxed for twenty-five years so that the Native peoples could ease into a new economic system, but the Burke Act was passed in 1906, shortening the trust period for those deemed "competent." Competency resulted in the issuance of a fee patent, instead of a trust patent, which meant that allotments could be sold, leased, or taken away. The final piece of this disenfranchisement puzzle came with the 1917 "Declaration of Policy" in which Cato Sells, the commissioner of Indian affairs, declared that Native people with more than one-half white blood would be declared competent, resulting in fee patents for their allotments and US citizenship. This series of actions caused Native Americans to lose ninety-one million acres of land. Some of the losses resulted from people's inability to pay taxes when the trust period ended; some resulted from the swindling of people unaware of their land's value; and some was taken away as collateral on unpaid debts (Peterson 986–87).

12. Cartwright has criticized this privileging of Choctaw history in *Shell Shaker,* arguing that "[blacks] get removed from the historical narrative" (218). In my 2010 interview with the author, Howe noted that [there] are no non-Natives, almost none, in *Shell Shaker,* and that's on purpose, because this is a discussion that I wanted the Choctaw characters to have with one another" (213). She describes having removed a large section of an early draft because it focused on French history, but she clearly made other similar deletions. In her short story "Danse d'Amour, Danse de Mort," a precursor to the bone-picking and other scenes in *Shell Shaker,* black slavery is depicted, though not emphasized.

CHAPTER TWO

1. Wherever the Choctaw language has not been translated in LeAnne Howe's works, I have consulted Cyrus Byington's *Dictionary of the Choctaw Language.*

2. Simpson, "Land as Pedagogy: Nishnaabeg Intelligence and Rebellious Transformation."

3. This play is essentially the same, with some minor variation, as the piece "Unknown Women," embedded in Howe's critical essay "Ohoyo Chishba Osh," in *Preremoval Choctaw History: Exploring New Paths.*

4. Pesantubbee explains that the honor of "beloved" would apply to "any person who had distinguished herself in any number of ways, [but] the most common descriptions of women are those who had participated in councils or became peace leaders" (2).

5. The sacred aspects of stomp dancing and baseball will be analyzed later in the chapter.

6. One piece of linguistic evidence for Ezol's argument is the concept of an "unmarked" or "default" tense in Choctaw, which uses the suffix *-h* for "all nonpast events whether present or future" (Broadwell 172–73).

7. Catherine Rainwater's analysis of works by Anita Endrezze (Yaqui) and Leslie Marmon Silko (Laguna) considers "the fluid parameters of Indigenous time" in works which ultimately "change the past, and consequently, the present and the future" (2), much like the representations of time in *Shell Shaker* and *Miko Kings.*

8. Though this reading of the novel focuses on a specifically Choctaw conception of time/space, Chanette Romero has argued that Howe's novels engage in representations of nonlinear time that are similar to other women writers of color, classifying those ideas of temporality as circular time, healing time, spirit time, and embodied time (*Activism* 56–57).

9. In a similar vein, Gloria Anzaldúa scholar AnaLouise Keating has developed a theory of *poet-shaman aesthetics,* infused with Indigenous epistemologies, in which "words have causal force; words embody the world; words are matter; words become matter" (52).

10. Significant works on the intersections of gender, Queer studies, and Native studies in recent years include Driskill et al., *Queer Indigenous Studies: Critical Interventions in Theory, Politics, and Literature* (2011), *Sovereign Erotics: A Collection of Two-Spirit Literature* (2011); and Rifkin, *The Erotics of Sovereignty: Queer Native Writing in the Era of Self-Determination* (2012). A bit further in Howe's discussion of *Ohoyo Holba* in our *MELUS* interview, she makes clear that this Choctaw culture figure should not be conflated with the "two spirit" figure, given the cultural specificity of *Ohoyo Holba.*

11. Though there is evidence that some tribes were accidentally exposed to smallpox in trading situations, such as the Blackfeet (Vernon 182), there is also speculation that smallpox was used as a biological warfare technique by the British. Historian Francis Parkman published now infamous letters between English officer Sir Jeffrey Amherst and his subordinate Colonel Henry Bouquet in which they discuss the possibility of introducing smallpox to Indian tribes and the effectiveness of infecting blankets for that purpose in response to Pontiac's 1763 rebellion. Parkman comments that there "is not direct evidence that Bouquet carried into effect the shameful plan of infecting the Indians, though a few months after, the small-pox was known to have made havoc among the tribes of the Ohio" (649).

12. The *Inholahta* moiety of the Eastern Choctaw towns were peacemakers and associated with the color white, while the *Imoklasha* of the western towns were warriors, and associated with the color red (Galloway, *Choctaw Genesis* 355).

13. "Survivance" is one of Anishinaabe writer Gerald Vizenor's numerous neologisms, suggesting both survival and resistance, through "an active sense of presence, the continuance of Native stories" (vii).

14. This article was revised into a chapter in Siebert's 2015 monograph, *Indians Playing Indian: Multiculturalism and Contemporary Indigenous Art in North America.* In her book, Siebert shifts away from the phrase "repugnant aboriginality," replacing it with "gruesome authentic," which seems to carry the same meaning.

15. See Jace Weaver's *That the People Might Live: Native American Literatures and Native American Community* and James Ruppert's *Mediation in Contemporary*

Native American Fiction for more nuanced discussions of American Indian writing and audience.

16. Contemporary stomp dancers tend to wear condensed-milk can rattles rather than the traditional turtle shells, to a similar rhythmic effect (Howard and Kurath 1).

17. Patricia Galloway elaborates on the historical evidence of the truly dangerous nature of Hernando de Soto's expedition through the Gulf Coast region: "The Spaniards' only consistent actions, by their own testimony, were demands for obedience to their king, questions about gold and other stones, abuse of hospitality through seizing and chaining bearers and raping women, and capture and imprisonment of chiefs or people they perceived as chiefs" (*Choctaw Genesis* 108).

18. "Mantema" means an official female messenger or someone "to go and carry or deliver something sacred or particular" (Pesantubbee 170; Swanton 121).

19. Sometime in the eighteenth century, pole pulling, which involved placing poles around a grave and then later removing them, replaced bone-picking. More Christian-like ceremonies became dominant near the end of the nineteenth century (Pesantubbee 154).

20. Leslie Marmon Silko's *Ceremony* is the seminal novel in American Indian literature read as ceremonial text.

21. Recent criticism on Howe has emphasized such tribalographic readings of her texts, including Horan and Kim's analysis of *Evidence of Red;* Hollrah's description of Ezol's journal in *Miko Kings* as "a concrete example of tribalography in its compilation of diary entries, letters, drawings, biblical scriptures, and clippings from the *Ada Weekly News*" (44); and Chanette Romero's investigation of cross-cultural connection in *Miko Kings* ("Expanding Tribal Identities" 17).

22. See chapter 1 for a discussion of a literal encounter between one of colonialism's ghosts, Jean-Baptiste Le Moyne, Sieur de Bienville, and the Choctaw protagonist of "The Chaos of Angels."

CHAPTER THREE

1. There is one reference to "Indian Mascot" in *Evidence of Red* as "Indian Sports Mascot" (79); after that, he is called simply "Indian Mascot." The similar character in *The Mascot Opera* is always known as "Indian Sports Mascot," shortened in the stage directions as "ISM."

2. *The Mascot Opera, A Minuet,* was published in *The North American Indian Drama Collection* by Alexander Street Press in 2008. Though I contacted the publisher, I never received a copy of the play; as a result, the citations here are from a manuscript copy provided by LeAnne Howe.

3. I do not think it is an accident that the name of the wooden Indian of Howe's play sounds nearly identical to "Kaw Liga," the namesake of Alabama country-western star Hank Williams's famous tragic song about a wooden Indian who falls

in love but is never able to express himself because he is physically and emotionally frozen by the medium from which he was created.

4. In *The Red Atlantic,* Jace Weaver notes that "non-Natives who practice Native American religious traditions, acting as holy persons for white 'congregations,'" are known by American Indians as "white shamans" (198). Weaver attributes the phrase to Cherokee critic Geary Hobson (306).

5. Since *Big PowWow* is unpublished, my citations come from a manuscript version provided by LeAnne Howe.

6. See chapter 2 for a more extensive discussion of bone-picking as depicted in *Shell Shaker.*

7. DuBois is, of course, referring specifically to African Americans in *The Souls of Black Folk.*

8. See Singh and Schmidt, eds., *Postcolonial Theory and the United States: Race, Ethnicity, and Literature.*

9. A particularly interesting example of this is Jace Weaver's discussion of Mohawk poet and performer E. Pauline Johnson who, he argues, "skillfully manipulated the image of the 'Indian' to carry her message and used every opportunity to 'plead the cause of the Native'" (*The Red Atlantic* 211).

10. See Marcy Norton's excellent study *Sacred Gifts, Profane Pleasures: A History of Tobacco and Chocolate in the Atlantic World* for a detailed examination of the role played by chocolate as a material good of transatlantic exchange.

11. See the introduction and conclusion for more extended discussions of Howe's methodology.

12. Howe uses this quote in an essay, "The Story of America: A Tribalography," to demonstrate the way that biologists' understanding of symbiogenesis is a "Choctawan way of looking at the world" (34).

13. My concluding chapter will discuss Howe's evolving theory of tribalography and its relationship to embodiment.

CHAPTER FOUR

1. Nagar et al. also make claims about the long history of globalization "rooted in colonialism, imperialism, and the discourses and practices of the development industry" (258), citing both Arturo Escobar's *Encountering Development: The Making and Unmaking of the Third World* and Cindi Katz's "On the Grounds of Globalization: A Topography for Feminist Political Engagement."

2. See chapter 1, "Choctaw Homescapes on the Gulf Coast," for a more in-depth discussion of Redford McAlester's historical doppelgänger.

3. In *The Red Atlantic,* Jace Weaver notes the "$170, plus corn and blankets" (26), sent by the Choctaw, and postulates an even more striking connection between Irish and American Indian peoples. Since the potato is an indigenous American food, its

presence in Europe is a direct result of transatlantic exchange. Had such exchange not commenced, it follows that "[there] would have been no potato famine in Ireland and possibly no Irish Diaspora" (26).

4. On March 5, 2015, the University of Georgia's Willson Center for Humanities and Arts held a colloquium entitled "Lo! The Poor Indian No More: The Trans-Atlantic Irish Choctaw Exchange from 1848–1995." Scholar participants included Jace Weaver, Jacki Rand, LeAnne Howe, Padraig Kirwan, and Peter D. O'Neil ("Events"). Howe and Kirwan are coediting a collection of essays, *Transatlantic Reciprocity: Contextualizing Exchanges between the Choctaw and the Irish* (Howe, "Travels and New Paths").

5. The *Nanih Waiya* was returned to the Mississippi Band of Choctaw by the state of Mississippi in 2006, per state Senate Bill 2803. Howe's novel, published five years before this bill's passage, depicts a chief's intentional machinations toward purchasing the mound for the Choctaws. This move aligns with Taylor's claim that "the effort to reclaim cultural sovereignty among southeastern Indians takes both the path and the character of financial recompense in a calculated effort to redeem what has been stolen" (134).

6. Separation of corn from its sacred position in Choctaw culture, which leads to its commodification, is discussed in chapter 2.

7. Horan and Kim describe "Choctalking" as a "five-part autobiographical prose-poem" (34).

8. Chanette Romero points out that an underexamined aspect of tribalography is "expanding [Native] identities" (qtd. in Romero, "Expanding" 13). In her article "Expanding Tribal Identities and Sovereignty through LeAnne Howe's 'Tribalography,'" Romero demonstrates the way Howe's cross-cultural affiliations work toward this goal, especially in *Miko Kings*.

9. I discuss *okchamali* more extensively in chapter 2, "Gender and the Sacred: Healers, Prophets, and Ceremonies."

10. This incident is also detailed in a poem, "The Lie," in *Evidence of Red*.

11. See my discussion of red-tailed hawks in chapter 3, "Interstate Simulations and Postindian Warriors."

12. See chapter 2, "Gender and the Sacred: Healers, Prophets, and Ceremonies," for a more detailed examination of "Grandmother of the Birds."

CONCLUSION

1. "Embodied Tribalography: First Installment" in *Choctalking on Other Realities* (2013), "Embodied Tribalography: Mound Building, Ball Games, and Native Endurance in the Southeast," in *Studies in American Indian Literature* (2014), "The Story of Movement: Natives and Performance Culture" in *The Oxford Handbook of Indigenous American Literature* (2014), and with Jim Wilson, "Life in a 21st Century Mound City" in *The World of Indigenous North America* (2015).

2. Howe discusses this new play in more detail in our interview, "The Native South, Performance, and Globalized Trans-Indigeneity," the appendix to this volume.

3. I have discussed the significance of birds to the Choctaw in chapter 4, "Choctalking Global (Dis)Connections," and red-tailed hawks specifically in chapter 3, "Interstate Simulations and Postindian Warriors."

4. In chapter 2, "Gender and the Sacred: Healers, Prophets, and Ceremonies," I discuss the way that *Miko Kings* describes the pitcher in ancient southeastern ball games as embodying "the center pole that could access the Middle, Upper, and Lower World" (39), that is, the *iti fabassa*.

5. Rader has noted that Howe "seems to have invented new genres" because "[nothing] matches expectations or conventions" (*Engaged Resistance* 137). He describes Howe's texts as examples of "engaged resistance" since they "engage many literary traditions (both Anglo and Native), but resist being controlled or subsumed by any of them" (137).

6. The poem originally appeared in *99 Poems for the 99 Percent: An Anthology of Poetry*, edited by Dean Rader (2013). Howe referred to the piece as a "video poem" in an April 16, 2015, e-mail to the author. The video version of the poem can be accessed at www.youtube.com/watch?v=zZxkKYyeveg&feature=youtu.be.

7. See chapter 3, "Interstate Simulations and Postindian Warriors," for a more detailed discussion of Howe's Noble Savage poems.

8. Jodi Byrd's "'Living My Life Deadly': Red Lake, Ward Churchill, and the Discourses of Competing Genocides" is an excellent resource for both a history of the Dakota Uprising and discussion of racialized violence and colonialism in the United States.

9. Morgan also notes alternate theories on the origin of Faulkner's fictional geography, including Arthur Kinney's study of *Go Down, Moses* (1996) and Faulkner's own assertion that the term meant "water flowing slow through the flatland" (90).

10. I would like to thank Gina Caison for helping to shape my ideas regarding *yakni patafa* as critical praxis. She and I organized the panel "*Yakni Patafa*: Faulkner, Land, and Indigenous Critical Perspectives" for the 2016 Faulkner and Yoknapatawpha Conference, themed "Faulkner and the Native South."

APPENDIX

1. The short story "Choctalking on Other Realities" is set in both Oklahoma and Israel during the twentieth century whereas *Shell Shaker* takes place in the lower Mississippi Valley during the eighteenth century and moves between Oklahoma and Mississippi in the twentieth century.

2. Eric Gary Anderson, author of *American Indian Literature and the Southwest: Contexts and Dispositions*, as well as numerous articles on the intersection of Native American and southern literary studies.

3. Howe is referring to our first interview at the 2008 Society for the Study of Southern Literature biennial conference in Williamsburg, Virginia, where she was an invited speaker.

4. Allison Hedge Coke.

5. What Howe is referring to here is probably best described as "discursive genocide," a term Raheja uses to describe how "Indigenous peoples had been written out of the present and the future of the United States" (15). It is also useful to consider the United Nations' complex definition of genocide. Article 2 of the Convention on the Prevention and Punishment of the Crime of Genocide (1948) defines genocide as "any of the following acts with intent to destroy, in whole or in part, a national, ethnical, racial or religious group, as such: killing members of the group; causing serious bodily or mental harm to members of the group; deliberately inflicting on the group conditions of life calculated to bring about its physical destruction in whole or in part; imposing measures intended to prevent births within the group; [and] forcibly transferring children of the group to another group" (Office of the UN Special Advisor on the Prevention of Genocide [OSAPG]).

6. The controversy surrounding the University of Illinois's decision to remove Chief Illiniwek as mascot in 2007 has continued to have traumatic implications for Native Americans on campus. In her 2012 interview in the *Society for the Study of Southern Literature Newsletter,* Howe describes bomb threats and death threats received by the faculty of the American Indian Studies Program, as recently as 2011. Chief Illiniwek is still the university's unofficial mascot.

7. Hollis E. Roberts.

8. Jacki Thompson Rand, associate professor of history at the University of Iowa.

9. Roxy Gordon, with whom Howe coauthored *Big PowWow* and *Indian Radio Days.*

10. See the introduction and conclusion of this volume for definitions and discussions of tribalography.

11. The conversation now shifts to the use of mixed media in *Miko Kings.*

12. Author of *Trans-Indigenous: Methodologies for Global Native Literary Studies* (2012).

13. Jacki Rand.

14. *Seeing Red: Hollywood's Pixeled Indians* (2013).

15. "Straight Arrow Brand Condoms."

WORKS CITED

Achebe, Chinua. "English and the African Writer." *Transition* 18 (1965): 27–30. *JSTOR*. Web. 1 July 2013.

Alexie, Sherman. "Back Cover." *Evidence of Red: Poems and Stories.* Ed. Janet McAdams. Earthworks Series. Cambridge, UK: Salt, 2005. Print.

Allen, Chadwick. *Trans-Indigenous: Methodologies for Global Native Literary Studies.* Minneapolis: U of Minnesota P, 2012. Print.

———. "A Trans*national* Native American Studies? Why Not Studies That Are Trans-*Indigenous?*" *Journal of Transnational American Studies* 4.1 (2012): 1–22. *eScholarship.* Web. 13 May 2013.

Allen, Paula Gunn. *The Sacred Hoop: Recovering the Feminine in American Indian Traditions.* Boston: Beacon, 1983. Print.

Anderson, Eric Gary. *American Indian Literature and the Southwest: Contexts and Dispositions.* Austin: U of Texas P, 1999. Print.

———. "Earthworks and Contemporary Indigenous American Literature: Foundations and Futures." *Native South* 9 (2016): 1–26. Print.

———. "Literary and Textual Histories of the Native South." Hobson and Ladd, eds. 17–32.

———. "On Native Ground: Indigenous Presences and Countercolonial Strategies in Southern Narratives of Captivity, Removal, and Repossession." *Southern Spaces: An Interdisciplinary Journal about Regions, Places, and Cultures of the American South and Their Global Connections.* 9 August 2007. Web. 2 February 2011.

———. "Reading and Writing Earthworks." Native South Symposium. Mercer University, Macon, GA. 8 April 2014. Keynote Address.

———. "South to a Red Place: Contemporary American Indian Writing and the Problem of Native/Southern Studies." *Mississippi Quarterly: A Journal of Southern Cultures* 60.1: 5–32. Print.

Anderson, Phylis J. "Welcome from the Tribal Chief of the Mississippi Band of Choctaw Indians." *Mississippi Band of Choctaw Indians.* Web. 30 June 2012.

Bauerkemper, Joseph, ed. "Special Issue: Tribalography." *Studies in American Indian Literatures* 26.2 (Summer 2014). Print.

Bergland, Renee. "Diseased States, Public Minds: Native American Ghosts in Early National Literature." *The Gothic Other: Racial and Social Constructions in the Literary Imagination.* Ed. Ruth Bienstock Anolik and Douglas L. Howard. Jefferson, NC: McFarland and Co., Inc., 2004. Print.

Bienvenu, Germain. "The Beginnings of Louisiana Literature." *Louisiana Culture from the Colonial Era to Katrina.* Ed. John Lowe. Baton Rouge: Louisiana State UP, 2008. Print.

Birchfield, Don L. "Choctaw Legacy: How to Lose Your Country Twice in Fourteen Treaties." *Eating Fire, Tasting Blood: Breaking the Great Silence of the American Indian Holocaust.* Ed. MariJo Moore. New York: Thunder's Mouth P, 2006. Print.

Bone, Martyn. *The Postsouthern Sense of Place in Contemporary Fiction.* Baton Rouge: Louisiana State UP, 2005. Print.

Broadwell, George Aaron. *A Choctaw Reference Grammar.* Lincoln: U of Nebraska P, 2006. Print.

Brown, Richmond F. "Introduction." *Coastal Encounters: the Transformation of the Gulf South in the Eighteenth Century.* Ed. Richmond F. Brown. Lincoln: U of Nebraska P, 2008. Print.

Bruyneel, Kevin. *The Third Space of Sovereignty: The Postcolonial Politics of U.S.-Indigenous Relations.* Minneapolis: U of Minnesota P, 2007. Print.

Byington, Cyrus. *A Dictionary of the Choctaw Language.* Ed. John R. Swanton and Henry S. Halbert. Washington: GPO, 1915. Print.

Byrd, Jodi. "'Living My Native Life Deadly:' Red Lake, Ward Churchill, and the Discourses of Competing Genocides." *American Indian Quarterly* 31.2 (Spring 2007): 310–32. *JSTOR.* Web. 1 July 2015.

———. "A Return to the South." *American Quarterly* 66.3 (September 2014): 609–20. *Project Muse.* Web. 29 December 2014.

———. *The Transit of Empire: Indigenous Critiques of Colonialism.* Minneapolis: U of Minnesota P, 2011. Print.

Carson, James Taylor "Dollars Never Fail to Melt Their Hearts: Native Women and the Market Revolution." *Neither Slave Nor Lady: Working Women of the Old South.* Ed. Susanna Delfino and Michele Gillespie. Chapel Hill: U of North Carolina P, 2002. Print.

———. "Greenwood LeFlore: Southern Creole, Choctaw Chief." O'Brien, ed. 221–36.

———. *Searching for the Bright Path: The Mississippi Choctaws from Prehistory to Removal.* Lincoln: U of Nebraska P, 1999. Print.

Cartwright, Keith. *Sacral Grooves, Limbo Gateways: Travels in Deep Southern Time, Circum-Caribbean Space, Afro-creole Authority.* Athens: U of Georgia P, 2013. Print.

Cattelino, Jessica R. "Fungibility: Florida Seminole Casino Dividends and the Fiscal Politics of Indigeneity." *American Anthropologist* 111.2: 190–200. *JSTOR.* Web. 1 June 2011.

Clark, D. Anthony Tyeeme, and Malea Powell. "Resisting Exile in 'The Land of the Free': Indigenous Groundwork at Colonial Intersections." *American Indian Quarterly* 32.1 (Winter 2008): 1–15. *ERIC.* Web. 1 June 2011.

Coke, Allison Adelle Hedge. *Off-Season City Pipe.* Saint Paul: Coffee House Press, 2005. Print.

Cox, James. *Muting White Noise: Native American and European Novel Traditions.* Norman: U of Oklahoma P, 2009. Print.

Cox, James, and Daniel Heath Justice. *The Oxford Handbook of Indigenous American Literature.* Oxford, UK: Oxford UP, 2014. Print.

———. "Introduction: Post-Renaissance Indigenous American Literary Studies." Cox and Justice 1–11.

Cushman, Horatio Bardwell. *History of the Choctaw, Chickasaw, and Natchez Indians.* Ed. Angie Debo. New York: Russell and Russell, 1972. Print.

Darensbourg, Jeffery. Message to the author. 10 May 2016. E-mail.

Deloria, Phillip. "American Indians, American Studies, and the ASA." *American Quarterly* 55.4 (2003): 669–80. *Academic Search Complete.* Web. 10 July 2014.

———. *Playing Indian.* New Haven, CT: Yale UP, 1998. Print.

Deloria, Vine, Jr. *Custer Died for Your Sins: An Indian Manifesto.* New York: Macmillan, 1969. Print.

DeRosier, Arthur H., Jr. *The Removal of the Choctaw Indians.* Knoxville: U of Tennessee P, 1970. Print.

Dimock, Wai Chee. *Through Other Continents: American Literature across Deep Time.* Princeton: Princeton UP, 2006. Print.

Doerfler, Jill. "Making It Work: A Model of Tribalography as Methodology." Bauerkemper 65–74.

Driskill, Qwo-Li, et al. *Queer Indigenous Studies: Critical Interventions in Theory, Politics, and Literature.* Tucson: U of Arizona P, 2011. Print.

———. *Sovereign Erotics: A Collection of Two-Spirit Literature.* Tucson: U of Arizona P, 2011. Print.

DuBois, W. E. B. *The Souls of Black Folk.* Greenwich, CT: Fawcett Publications, 1961. Print.

Ellis, Clyde. "'There's a Dance Every Weekend': Powwow Culture in Southeast North Carolina." *Southern Heritage on Display: Public Ritual and Ethnic*

Diversity within Southern Regionalism. Ed. Celeste Ray. Tuscaloosa: U of Alabama P, 2003. Print.

Escobar, Arturo. *Encountering Development: The Making and Unmaking of the Third World.* Princeton, NJ: Princeton UP, 1995. Print.

"Events." Willson Center for Humanities and Arts, U of Georgia, Athens. Web. 25 May 2016.

Fogelson, Raymond. *Handbook of North American Indians: Southeast.* Washington DC: GPO, 2004. Print.

Foster, Tol. "Of One Blood: An Argument for Relations and Regionality in Native American Studies." Womack, Justice, and Teuton 265–302.

Fryberg, Stephanie, et al. "Warrior Chiefs and Indian Princesses: The Psychological Consequences of American Indian Mascots." *Basic and Applied Social Psychology* 30.3 (208–18). *Academic Search Complete.* Web. 16 June 2014.

Galloway, Patricia. "Choctaw Factionalism and Civil War, 1746–1750." O'Brien, ed. 70–102.

———. *Choctaw Genesis: 1500–1700.* Lincoln: U of Nebraska P, 1995. Print.

———. "The Construction of Faulkner's Indians." *Faulkner Journal* 18.1–2 (Fall 2002–Spring 2003): 9–31. *ProQuest Central.* Web. 7 June 2016.

Geertz, Clifford. *The Interpretation of Cultures: Selected Essays.* New York: Basic Books, 1973. Print.

Gilmore, H. W. "Social Isolation of the French Speaking People of Louisiana." *Social Forces* (U of North Carolina P), vol. 12.1 (October 1933): 78–84. *JSTOR.* Web. 29 December 2010.

Gomez, Rain C. "Hachotakni Zydeco's Round'a Loop Current: Indigenous, African, and Caribbean Mestizaje in Louisiana Literatures." *Southern Literary Journal* 46.2 (Spring 2014): 88–107. Web. 14 April 2016.

Haag, Marcia. "A History of the Choctaw Language." *Choctaw Language and Culture: Chahta Anumpa.* Norman, U of Oklahoma P, 2001. Print.

Hall, Thomas D., and James V. Fenelon. *Indigenous Peoples and Globalization: Resistance and Revitalization.* Boulder, CO: Paradigm, 2009. Print.

Harjo, Joy. "New Orleans." *She Had Some Horses.* New York: Thunder's Mouth Press, 1983. Print.

Harjo, Joy, and Gloria Bird. *Reinventing the Enemy's Language: Contemporary Native Women's Writings of North America.* New York: W. W. Norton and Co., 1998. Print.

Hobson, Fred, and Barbara Ladd. "Introduction." Hobson and Ladd, eds. 1–14.

———. *The Oxford Handbook of the Literature of the U.S. South.* Oxford, UK: Oxford UP, 2016. Print.

Hobson, Geary, Janet McAdams, and Kathryn Walkiewicz. "Introduction: The South Seldom Seen." *The People Who Stayed: Southeastern Indian Writing after Removal.* Ed. Geary Hobson, Janet McAdams, and Kathryn Walkiewicz. Norman: UP of Oklahoma, 2010. Print.

Hoelscher, Steven. "Making Place, Making Race: Performances of Whiteness in the Jim Crow South." *Annals of the Association of American Geographers* 93.3 (September 2003): 657–86. *JSTOR.* Web. 20 May 2011.

Hollenberg, Alexander. "Speaking with the Separatists: Craig Womack and the Relevance of Literary History." *Studies in American Indian Literatures* 20.1 (Spring 2009): 2–17. *ProQuest Research Library.* Web. 21 May 2013.

Hollrah, Patrice. "'The Lord and the Center of the Farthest': Ezol's Journal as Tribalography in LeAnne Howe's *Miko Kings: An Indian Baseball Story.*" Bauerkemper 40–54.

Horan, Elizabeth, and Seonghoon Kim. "'Then One Day We Create Something Unexpected': Tribalography's Decolonizing Strategies in LeAnne Howe's *Evidence of Red.*" *Studies in American Indian Literatures* 25.1 (Spring 2013): 27–52. Print.

Householder, Michael. "Eden's Translations: Women and Temptation in Early America." *Huntington Library Quarterly* 70.1 (2007): 11–36. *ProQuest.* Web. 16 March 2013.

Howard, James H. and Gertrude P. Kurath. "Ponca Dances, Ceremonies, and Music." *Ethnomusicology* 3.1 (January 1959): 1–14. *JSTOR.* Web. 17 September 2007.

Howe, LeAnne. "Acknowledgments." *Evidence of Red.*

———. "Amman, My Life Among the Birds." *On the Prairie Diamond.* Web. 13 October 2010.

———. "'And Here Too Comes an Echo of Our People at Play' in 'Anompa Sipokni,' Old Talking Places." *Journal of the Illinois State Historical Society* 100.3 (Fall 2007): 207–14. *JSTOR.* Web. 1 July 2011.

———. "Author's Note." *Shell Shaker.* San Francisco: Aunt Lute, 2001. Print.

———. "Bird Woman Returns." *Evidence of Red* 96.

———. "Blind Bread and the Business of Theory Making, by Embarrassed Grief." Womack, Justice, and Teuton 325–39.

———. "Carlos Castaneda Lives in Romania." *Choctalking on Other Realities* 125–44.

———. "The Chaos of Angels." *Evidence of Red* 23–33.

———. "Choctalking on Other Realities." *Evidence of Red* 44–57.

———. "Choctalking on Other Realities: A Reading." 20 February 2014. High Point University, High Point, NC. Public Reading.

———. *Choctalking on Other Realities: New and Selected Stories.* San Francisco: Aunt Lute, 2013. Print.

———. "Choctawan Aesthetics, Spirituality, and Gender Relations: An Interview with LeAnne Howe." By Kirstin L. Squint. *MELUS: Multi-Ethnic Literature of the United States* 35.3 (Fall 2010): 211–24. Print.

———. "The Conference of Birds—Take 2." *On the Prairie Diamond.* Web. 4 February 2011.

———. "Danse d'Amour, Danse de Mort." *Earth Song, Sky Spirit: Short Stories of the Contemporary Native American Experience.* Ed. Clifford E. Trafzer. New York: Doubleday, 1993. Print.

———. "Disney's Pocahontas Longs for Noble Savage." *Evidence of Red* 77.

———. "Embodied Tribalography: First Installment." *Choctalking on Other Realities* 173–93.

———. "Embodied Tribalography: Mound Building, Ball Games, and Native Endurance in the Southeast." Bauerkemper 75–93.

———. "Evidence of Red." *Evidence of Red* 5–6.

———. *Evidence of Red: Poems and Stories.* Ed. Janet McAdams. Earthworks Series. Cambridge, UK: Salt, 2005. Print.

———. "Hashi mi Mali." *Evidence of Red* 7–8.

———. "Horse Dreams." *Evidence of Red* 97.

———. "I Fuck Up in Japan." *Choctalking on Other Realities* 95–123.

———. "Indians Never Say Goodbye." *Evidence of Red* 99--101.

———. Interview by Aasif Mandvi. "Trail of Cheers." *The Daily Show.* Comedy Central, New York, 2 May 2007. Television.

———. "Kick Boxing." *Evidence of Red* 98.

———. "The Lie." *Evidence of Red* 93–94.

———. *The Mascot Opera, A Minuet.* 2008. TS.

———. *Miko Kings: An Indian Baseball Story.* San Francisco: Aunt Lute Books, 2007. Print.

———. "My Name Is Noble Savage." *Evidence of Red* 76.

———. "The Native South, Performance, and Globalized Trans-Indigeneity: A Conversation with LeAnne Howe." By Kirstin L. Squint. 23 March 2013.

———. "Noble Savage Learns to Tweet." Message to the author. 16 April 2015. E-mail.

———. "Noble Savage Learns to Tweet." *99 Poems for the 99 Percent: An Anthology of Poetry.* Ed. Dean Rader. Lowell, MA: 99: the Press, 2013. Print.

———. "Noble Savage Learns to Tweet." *YouTube.* 9 April 2015. Web. 30 June 2015.

———. "Noble Savage Sees a Therapist." *Evidence of Red* 78.

———. "Ohoyo Chishba Osh: Woman Who Stretches Way Back." O'Brien, ed. 26–47.

———. "On 'Choctalking.'" *On the Prairie Diamond.* Web. 9 January 2009.

———. *On the Prairie Diamond: the Weblog of LeAnne Howe.* Web.

———. "Post-Mortem." *Evidence of Red* 95.

———. *Playing Pastime: American Indians, Softball, and Survival.* Prod. James M. Fortier. Turtle Island Productions, 2004. MP4 file.

———. "Prologue: My Mothers, My Uncles, Myself." *Choctalking on Other Realities* 1–12.

———. *Shell Shaker.* San Francisco: Aunt Lute Books, 2001. Print.

———. "Still Code Talking." *Evidence of Red* 89.

———. "The Story of America: A Tribalography." *Clearing a Path: Theorizing the Past in Native American Studies.* Ed. Nancy Shoemaker. New York: Routledge, 2002. Print.

———. "The Story of Movement: Natives and Performance Culture." *The Oxford Handbook of Indigenous American Literature.* Ed. James H. Cox and Daniel Heath Justice. Oxford, UK: Oxford UP, 2014. Print.

———. "Travels and New Paths on the Horizon." *On the Prairie Diamond.* Web. 25 May 2016.

———. *The Unknown Women. Evidence of Red* 9–20.

———. "What Happened to Indian Mascot and Noble Savage—After the Shooting?" *Evidence of Red* 85.

———. "Yaa Jordan, Yaa 'Ayouni." *Choctalking on Other Realities* 145–72.

Howe, LeAnne, and Robbie Etheridge. "Interview with LeAnne Howe and Robbie Etheridge." By David Davis. *Society for the Study of Southern Literature Newsletter* 46.2 (November 2012). Web. 16 June 2014.

Howe, LeAnne, and Roxy Gordon. *Big PowWow.* 1987. TS.

———. *Indian Radio Days: An Evolving Bingo Experience. Seventh Generation: An Anthology of Native American Plays.* Ed. Mimi Gisolfi D'Aponte. New York: Theatre Communications Group, 1999. Print.

Howe, LeAnne, Harvey Markowitz, and Denise Cummings. *Seeing Red: Hollywood's Pixeled Skins.* East Lansing: Michigan State University, 2013. Print.

Howe, LeAnne, and Jim Wilson. "Life in a 21st Century Mound City." *The World of Indigenous North America.* Ed. Robert Warrior. New York: Routledge, 2015. Print.

Huhndorf, Shari. *Going Native: Indians in the American Cultural Imagination.* Ithaca, NY: Cornell UP, 2001. Print.

Indian Country Diaries: Spiral of Fire. Native American Public Telecommunications and Adanvdo Vision, 2005. DVD.

"Jena Band of Choctaw Indians Brief Historical Summary." *Jena Band of Choctaw Indians.* Web. 30 June 2012.

Jones, Anne Goodwyn, and Susan V. Donaldson. *Haunted Bodies: Gender and Southern Texts.* Charlottesville: UP of Virginia, 1997. Print.

Jones, Suzanne, and Sharon Monteith. *South to a New Place: Region, Literature, and Culture.* Baton Rouge: Louisiana State UP, 2002. Print.

Justice, Daniel Heath. *Our Fire Survives the Storm: A Cherokee Literary History.* Minneapolis: U of Minnesota P, 2006. Print.

Katz, Cindi. "On the Grounds of Globalization: a Topography for Feminist Political Engagement." *Signs: Journal of Women and Culture in Society* 26: 1213–24. Print.

Keating, AnaLouise. "Speculative Realism, Visionary Pragmatism, and Poet-Shamanic Aesthetics in Gloria Anzaldúa—and Beyond." *Women's Studies Quarterly* 40.3–4 (Fall–Winter 2012): 51–69. *Project Muse.* Web. 26 June 2013.

Kidwell, Clara Sue. *Choctaws and Missionaries in Mississippi, 1818–1918.* Norman: U of Oklahoma P, 1997. Print.

Kilpinen, John T. "The Supreme Court's Role in Choctaw and Chickasaw Dispossession." *Geographical Review* 94.4 (October 2004): 484–501. *JSTOR.* Web. 28 July 2011.

King, C. Richard. "Looking Back to a Future End: Reflections on the Symposium on Racist Stereotypes in American Sport at the National Museum of the American Indian." *American Indian Quarterly* 38.2 (Spring 2014): 135–42. *Academic Search Complete.* Web. 16 June 2014.

King, Thomas. *Green Grass, Running Water.* New York: Bantam, 1993. Print.

Kinney, Arthur F. *Go Down Moses: the Miscegenation of Time.* New York: Twayne Publishers, 1996. Print.

Kirwan, Padraig. *Sovereign Stories: Aesthetics, Autonomy, and Contemporary Native American Writing.* Oxford, UK: Peter Lang, 2013. Print.

Kreyling, Michael. "The Fathers: A Postsouthern Narrative Reading." *Southern Literature and Literary Theory.* Ed. Jefferson Humphries. Athens: U of Georgia P, 1990. Print.

Ladd, Barbara. "Dismantling the Monolith: Southern Places—Past, Present, and Future." Jones and Monteith 44–57.

———. *Resisting History: Gender, Modernity, and Authorship in William Faulkner, Zora Neale Hurston, and Eudora Welty.* Baton Rouge: Louisiana State UP, 2012. Print.

Levine, Victoria Lindsay. "Music Revitalization among the Choctaw." *American Music* 11.4 (Winter 1993): 391–411. *JSTOR.* Web. 6 July 2011.

Lincoln, Kenneth. *Indi'n Humor: Bicultural Play in Native America.* New York: Oxford UP, 1993. Print.

Littlefield, Daniel F., Jr., and James W. Parins. "Muriel Hazel Wright, Choctaw (1889–1975)." Littlefield and Parins, eds. 213–14.

———, eds. *Native American Writing in the Southeast: An Anthology, 1875–1935.* Jackson: UP of Mississippi, 1995. Print.

Markowitz, Harvey, Craig Howe, Dean Rader, and LeAnne Howe. "An Ensemble Performance of Indians in the Act: Native Theater, Past and Present." *Studies in American Indian Literatures* 16.1 (Spring 2004): 32–61. *JSTOR.* Web. 8 July 2014.

Mbembe, J. A. "Necropolitics." *Public Culture* 15.1 (Winter 2003): 11–40. *Project Muse.* Web. 16 May 2013.

McCullough, Ken. "If You See Buddha at the Stomp Dance, Kill Him! The Bicameral World of LeAnne Howe's *Shell Shaker.*" *Studies in American Indian Literatures* 15.2 (Summer 2003): 58–69. Web. *JSTOR.* 19 June 2014.

McGowan, Kay Givens. "Weeping for the Lost Matriarchy." *Daughters of Mother Earth: The Wisdom of Native American Women.* Ed. Barbara Alice Mann. Westport, CT: Praeger, 2006. 59–68. Print.

McLoughlin, William G. *Cherokee Renascence in the New Republic.* Princeton, NJ: Princeton UP, 1986. Print.

McPherson, Tara. *Reconstructing Dixie: Race, Gender, and Nostalgia in the Imagined South.* Durham: Duke UP, 2003. Print.

Meadows, William C. "'They Had a Chance to Talk to One Another . . .': the Role of Incidence in Native American Code Talking." *Ethnohistory* 56.2 (Spring 2009): 269–84. *Academic Search Complete.* Web. 11 June 2013.

Mississippi. Senate. S 2803. Web. 3 July 2014.

Moloney, Mick. "Irish-American Popular Music." *Making the Irish American: History and Heritage of the Irish in the United States.* Ed. J. J. Lee and Marion R. Casey. New York: NYUP, 2006. Print.

Momaday, N. Scott. *House Made of Dawn.* New York: HarperCollins, 1966. 187–93. Print.

———. "The Man Made of Words." *Native American Literature: An Anthology.* Ed. Lawana Trout. Lincolnwood: National Textbook Co., 1999. Print.

———. "A MELUS Interview: N. Scott Momaday. A Slant of Light." By Givens, Bettye. *MELUS* 12.1 (Spring 1985): 79–87. *JSTOR.* Web. 23 September 2007.

Morgan, Phillip Carroll. *Riding Out the Storm: 19th Century Chickasaw Governors, Their Lives, and Intellectual Legacy.* Ada, OK: Chickasaw Press, 2013.

———. "Who Shall Gainsay Our Decision? Choctaw Literary Criticism in 1830." Womack, Justice, and Teuton 126–46.

Murray, David. *Forked Tongues: Speech, Writing, and Representation in North American Indian Texts.* Bloomington: Indiana UP, 1991. Print.

Nagar, Richa, et al. "Locating Globalization: Feminist (Re)readings of the Subjects and Spaces of Globalization." *Economic Geography* 78.3 (July 2002): 257–84. *JSTOR.* Web. 1 June 2011.

Newton, Melanie J. "Returns to a Native Land: Indigeneity and Decolonization in the Anglophone Caribbean." *Small Axe: A Caribbean Journal of Criticism* 17.2 (July 2013): 108–22. Print.

Norton, Marcy. *Sacred Gifts, Profane Pleasures: A History of Tobacco and Chocolate in the Atlantic World.* Ithaca, NY: Cornell UP, 2008. Print.

O'Brien, Greg. "The Conqueror Meets the Unconquered: Negotiating Cultural Boundaries on the Post-Revolutionary Southern Frontier." O'Brien, ed. 148–82.

———. "Protecting Trade through War: Choctaw Elites and British Occupation of the Floridas." O'Brien, ed. 103–22.

O'Brien, Greg, ed. *Pre-removal Choctaw History: Exploring New Paths.* Norman: U of Oklahoma P, 2008. Print.

O'Donnell, Edward T. "154 Years Ago: The Choctaw Send Aid." *The Irish Echo.* 21 March 2001. *Edward T. O'Donnell.* Web. 29 June 2011.

Office of the UN Special Advisor on the Prevention of Genocide (OSAPG). "Analysis Framework." *United Nations.* Web. 22 July 2015.

Ortiz, Simon. "Appendix: Towards a National Indian Literature: Cultural Authenticity in Nationalism." Weaver, Warrior, and Womack 253–60.

———. "Travels in the South." *Woven Stone.* Tucson: UP of Arizona, 1992.

Parins, James. *Literacy and Intellectual Life in the Cherokee Nation, 1820–1906.* Norman: U of Oklahoma P, 2013. Print.

Parker, Robert Dale. "Red Slippers and Cottonmouth Moccasins: White Anxieties in Faulkner's Indian Stories." *Faulkner Journal* 18.1–2 (Fall 2002–Spring 2003): 81–100. *ProQuest Central.* Web. 7 June 2016.

Parkman, Francis. *Parkman: The Oregon Trail, the Conspiracy of Pontiac.* New York: Library of America, 1991. Print.

Peacock, James L. *Grounded Globalism: How the U.S. South Embraces the World.* Athens: U of Georgia P, 2007. Print.

Perdue, Theda. *Cherokee Women: Gender and Culture Change, 1700–1835.* Lincoln: U of Nebraska P, 1998. Print.

———. "The Legacy of Indian Removal." *Journal of Southern History* 78.1 (February 2012): 3–36. *ProQuest Central.* Web. 21 April 2016.

Pesantubbee, Michelene. *Choctaw Women in a Chaotic World: The Clash of Cultures in the Colonial Southeast.* Albuquerque: U of New Mexico P, 2005. Print.

Peterson, Nancy J. "History, Postmodernism, and Louise Erdrich's *Tracks*." *PMLA* 109.5 (1994): 982–94. *JSTOR*. Web. 7 July 2006.

Price, Richard. "From *The Teachings of Don Juan* to *Travels with Tooey:* One Anthropologist's Trip." *Anthropology of Consciousness* 22.2: 136–58. *Academic Search Complete*. Web. 18 June 2014.

Rader, Dean. *Engaged Resistance: American Indian Art, Literature, and Film from Alcatraz to the NMAI*. Austin: U of Texas P, 2011. Print.

———. "Foreword." *Choctalking on Other Realities* i-vii.

Raheja, Michelle. *Reservation Reelism: Redfacing, Visual Sovereignty, and Representations of Native Americans in Film*. Lincoln: U of Nebraska P, 2010. Print.

Rainwater, Catherine. "'Maybe Einstein Was Part Yaqui': Deposing Thought in Works by Endrezze and Silko." *Studies in American Indian Literatures* 26.1 (Spring 2014): 1–28. Print.

Reagan, Ronald. "Proclamation 4954—National Navaho Code Talkers Day." July 28, 1982. Online by Gerhard Peters and John T. Woolley. *American Presidency Project*. Web. 12 June 2013.

"Rest Area Locations." *Illinois Department of Transportation*. Web. 23 May 2013.

Rifkin, Mark. *The Erotics of Sovereignty: Queer Native Writing in the Era of Self-Determination*. Minneapolis: U of Minnesota P, 2012. Print.

Riley, Angela R. "Good (Native) Governance. *Columbia Law Review* 107.5 (June 2007): 1049–1125. *JSTOR*. Web. 1 June 2011.

Romero, Chanette. *Activism in the American Novel: Religion and Resistance in Fiction by Women of Color*. Charlottesville: U of Virginia P, 2012. Print.

———. "Expanding Tribal Identities and Sovereignty through LeAnne Howe's 'Tribalography.'" Bauerkemper 13–25.

Romine, Scott. *The Real South: Southern Narrative in the Age of Cultural Reproduction*. Baton Rouge: Louisiana State UP, 2008. Print.

———. "Where Is Southern Literature?" Jones and Monteith 23–43.

Ruppert, James. *Mediation in Contemporary Native American Fiction*. Norman: U of Oklahoma P, 1995. Print.

"S. 2681 (110th): Code Talkers Recognition Act of 2008." GovTrack.us. 12 June 2013. Web.

Siebert, Monika Barbara. *Indians Playing Indian: Multiculturalism and Contemporary Indigenous Art in North America*. Tuscaloosa: U of Alabama P, 2015. Print.

———. "Repugnant Aboriginality: LeAnne Howe's *Shell Shaker* and Indigenous Representation in the Age of Multiculturalism." *American Literature* 83.1 (March 2011): 93–119. *MLA Bibliography*. Web. 7 April 2011.

Silko, Leslie Marmon. *Ceremony.* New York: Penguin. 1977. Print.

Simpson, LeAnne Betasamosake. "Land as Pedagogy: Nishnaabeg Intelligence and Rebellious Transformation." *Decolonization: Indigeneity, Education, and Society* 3.3 (2014). Web. 29 July 2015.

Singh, Amritjit, and Peter Schmidt, eds. *Postcolonial Theory and the United States: Race, Ethnicity, and Literature.* Jackson: UP of Mississippi, 2000. Print.

Stanlake, Christy. *Native American Drama: A Critical Perspective.* Cambridge, UK: Cambridge UP, 2009. Print.

Star Trek: Generations. Dir. David Carson. Patrick Stewart, William Shatner, Malcolm McDowell. Paramount, 1998. DVD.

Swanton, John R. *Source Material for the Social and Ceremonial Life of the Choctaw Indians.* Washington, DC: GPO, 1931. Print.

Taylor, Melanie Benson. *Reconstructing the Native South: American Indian Literature and the Lost Cause.* Athens: U of Georgia P, 2012. Print.

"Trail of Tears National Historic Trail." National Park Service. Web. 15 July 2015.

Trefzer, Annette. *Disturbing Indians: The Archaeology of Southern Fiction.* Tuscaloosa: U Alabama P, 2007. Print.

Vernon, Irene S. "'A Happiness That Sleeps with Sadness': An Examination of 'White Scabs' in *Fools Crow.*" *American Indian Quarterly* 29.1–2 (Winter and Spring 2005): 178. *Academic Search Complete.* Web. 13 September 2007.

Vizenor, Gerald. *Manifest Manners: Postindian Warriors of Survivance.* Hanover, NH: UP of New England, 1994. Print.

Warrior, Robert. "A Room of One's Own at the ASA: An Indigenous Provocation." *American Quarterly* 55.4 (2003): 681–87. *Project Muse.* Web. 10 July 2014.

———. *Tribal Secrets: Recovering American Indian Intellectual Traditions.* Minneapolis: U of Minnesota P, 1994.

Weaver, Jace. E-mail interview. 10 May 2015.

———. *The Red Atlantic: American Indigenes and the Making of the Modern World, 1000–1927.* Chapel Hill: U of North Carolina P, 2014. Print.

———. "The Red Atlantic: Transoceanic Cultural Exchanges." *American Indian Quarterly* 35.3 (Summer 2011): 419–63. *MLA International Bibliography.* 17 July 2012. Web.

———. "Splitting the Earth: First Utterances and Pluralist Separatism." Weaver, Womack, and Warrior 1–89.

———. *That the People Might Live: Native American Literatures and Native American Community.* New York: Oxford UP, 1997. *eBook Collection (EBSCOhost).* Web. 27 May 2013.

Weaver, Jace, Robert Warrior, and Craig Womack. *American Indian Literary Nationalism.* Albuquerque: U of New Mexico P, 2006. Print.

Wolfe, Patrick. "Settler Colonialism and the Elimination of the Native." *Journal of Genocide Research* 8.4 (2006): 387–409. Print.

Womack, Craig. *Red on Red: Native American Literary Separatism.* Minneapolis: U of Minnesota P, 1999. Print.

———. "Review of *Anti-Indianism in Modern America: A Voice from Tatekeya's Earth.*" *American Indian Quarterly* 28.1–2 (Winter–Spring 2004): 130–41. *JSTOR.* Web. 1 July 2011.

———. "Review of *Evidence of Red: Poems and Prose.*" *Studies in American Indian Literatures* 17.4 (Winter 2005): 157–61. *Proquest Research Library.* Web. 21 May 2013.

———. "A Single Decade: Book-Length Native Literary Criticism between 1986 and 1997." Womack, Justice, and Teuton 3–104.

———. "Theorizing American Indian Experience." Womack, Justice, and Teuton 353–410.

Womack, Craig, Daniel Heath Justice, and Christopher B. Teuton, eds. *Reasoning Together: The Native Critics Collective.* Norman: U of Oklahoma P, 2008. Print.

Wright, Muriel Hazel. "Legend of Nanih Waya." Littlefield and Parins, eds. 214–20.

INDEX